The Economics
of Contracts

The Economics of Contracts

A Primer

second edition

Bernard Salanié

The MIT Press
Cambridge, Massachusetts
London, England

This book was set in Palatino by Omegatype, Inc.

Library of Congress Cataloging-in-Publication Data

Salanié, Bernard.
[Theorie des contrats. English]
The economics of contracts : primer / Bernard Salanié.—2nd ed.
  p. cm.
Includes bibliographical references and index.
ISBN 978-0-262-19525-6 (hc: alk. paper), 978-0-262-53422-2 (pb.)
1. Contracts—Economic aspects. I. Title.
K840.S25 2005
346.02—dc22

                              2004061055
                              CIP

Contents

Foreword to the Second Edition   ix

Foreword to the First Edition   xi

1 Introduction   1
 1.1 The Great Families of Models   3
 1.2 The Principal–Agent Model   5
 1.3 Overview of the Book   6
 References   8

2 Adverse Selection: General Theory   11
 *2.1 Mechanism Design   13
 2.1.1 General Mechanisms   15
 2.1.2 Application to Adverse Selection Models   16
 2.2 A Discrete Model of Price Discrimination   18
 2.2.1 The Consumer   19
 2.2.2 The Seller   19
 2.2.3 The First-Best: Perfect Discrimination   20
 2.2.4 Imperfect Information   21
 2.3 The Standard Model   27
 2.3.1 Analysis of the Incentive Constraints   29
 2.3.2 Solving the Model   33
 Exercises   40
 References   42

3 Adverse Selection: Examples and Extensions   43
 3.1 Examples of Applications   43
 3.1.1 Regulating a Firm   43
 3.1.2 Optimal Taxation   47

3.1.3 *The Insurer as a Monopolist* 51
3.2 Extensions 57
3.2.1 *Perfect Competition in Contracts* 57
*3.2.2 *Multiple Principals* 61
3.2.3 *The Theory of Auctions* 65
3.2.4 *Collusion* 73
3.2.5 *Risk-Averse Agents* 76
*3.2.6 *Multidimensional Characteristics* 78
3.2.7 *Bilateral Private Information* 82
3.2.8 *Type-Dependent Reservation Utilities* 88
3.2.9 *Auditing the Agent* 89
Exercises 91
References 93

4 Signaling Models 97
4.1 The Market for Secondhand Cars 98
4.2 Costly Signals 99
4.2.1 *Separating Equilibria* 102
4.2.2 *Pooling Equilibria* 103
4.2.3 *The Selection of an Equilibrium* 103
4.3 Costless Signals 107
4.3.1 *A Simple Example* 108
4.3.2 *The General Model* 109
4.4 Other Examples 114
4.5 The Informed Principal 116
Exercises 117
References 118

5 Moral Hazard 119
5.1 A Simple Example 122
5.2 The Standard Model 124
5.2.1 *The Agent's Program* 125
5.2.2 *The Principal's Program* 126
5.2.3 *Properties of the Optimal Contract* 129
5.3 Extensions 134
5.3.1 *Informativeness and Second-Best Loss* 134
5.3.2 *A Continuum of Actions* 135
5.3.3 *The Limited Liability Model* 136

*5.3.4 *An Infinity of Outcomes*   138
5.3.5 *The Multisignal Case*   139
5.3.6 *Imperfect Performance Measurement*   140
5.3.7 *Models with Several Agents*   140
5.3.8 *Models with Several Principals*   142
*5.3.9 *The Robustness of Contracts*   144
5.3.10 *The Multitask Model*   146
5.4 Examples of Applications   149
5.4.1 *Insurance*   149
5.4.2 *Wage Determination*   151
Exercises   156
References   159

6 **The Dynamics of Complete Contracts**   161
6.1 Commitment and Renegotiation   162
6.2 Strategic Commitment   164
6.3 Adverse Selection   168
6.3.1 *Full Commitment*   170
6.3.2 *Long-Term Commitment*   172
6.3.3 *No Commitment*   176
6.3.4 *Short-Term Commitment*   177
6.3.5 *Conclusion*   178
6.4 Moral Hazard   179
6.4.1 *Renegotiation after Effort*   179
*6.4.2 *Convergence to the First-Best*   181
6.4.3 *Finitely Repeated Moral Hazard*   183
References   190

7 **Incomplete Contracts**   193
7.1 Property Rights, Holdup, and Underinvestment   195
7.1.1 *The Buyer–Seller Model*   196
7.1.2 *The Complete Contract*   197
7.1.3 *Incomplete Contracts and Property Rights*   198
7.2 The Irrelevance Theorems   200
7.2.1 *Restoring Efficient Investment Incentives*   200
7.2.2 *Using Mechanism Design*   204
7.3 Concluding Remarks   205
References   209

8 Some Empirical Work   211
8.1 Dealing with Unobserved Heterogeneity   212
8.2 Auctions   216
8.3 Tests of Asymmetric Information
     in Insurance Markets   218
References   221

Appendix: Some Noncooperative Game Theory   223
A.1 Games of Perfect Information   224
A.1.1 Nash Equilibrium   224
A.1.2 Subgame-Perfect Equilibrium   224
A.2 Games of Incomplete Information   226
A.2.1 Bayesian Equilibrium   226
A.2.2 Perfect Bayesian Equilibrium   227
A.2.3 Refinements of Perfect Bayesian Equilibrium   229
References   232

Name Index   233

Subject Index   235

Foreword to the
Second Edition

Feedback from my readers indicates that one reason why the first edition of this book met with some approval is that it was concise. I have tried to preserve this quality in this new edition. Nevertheless, despite the self-imposed constraint to keep the book short, readers of the first edition will find that I completely rewrote chapters 7 (on incomplete contracts) and chapters 8 (on empirical work). I have also made important changes to chapters 3 and 5. Chapter 3 now covers multiprincipals, collusion, and multidimensional adverse selection much more thoroughly. I added the limited liability model, career concerns, and common agency to the topics of chapter 5. Finally, I have made many smaller changes throughout the text.

I am very grateful to Bernard Caillaud, Oliver Hart, Radoslova Nikolova, Jérôme Pouyet, Patrick Rey, François Salanié, and Jean Tirole for helping me decide on the changes to the first edition. I thank students at Columbia and Yale for pointing out errors in earlier printings. As always, I am solely responsible for any errors or imperfections that may remain in the book.

Foreword to the
First Edition

This book aims at introducing Ph.D. students and professional economists to the theory of contracts. It originated in graduate-level courses I gave at Stanford University and at ENSAE (Ecole Nationale de la Statistique et de l'Administration Economique) to third-year students. This book has benefited from discussions with these students.

The course notes were published as *Théorie des contrats* in France by Economica. The present book is a fully revised, somewhat expanded, and hopefully improved translation of that book.

I am grateful to Jérôme Accardo, Jérôme Philippe, Patrick Rey, and two anonymous reviewers, who read a first draft of the French version and provided very useful comments. I also thank Bruno Jullien, Jean-Jacques Laffont, Tom Palfrey, François Salanié, Jean Tirole, and three anonymous reviewers who read all or part of the English version and greatly helped me improve it. My intellectual debt extends to my coauthors in this field, Pierre-André Chiappori and Patrick Rey, and to Guy Laroque, who was a very effective and critical tutor when I started doing research in economics.

Finally, I thank Terry Vaughn and The MIT Press for their encouragement and support in this project. Needless to say, I am solely responsible for any errors or imperfections that may remain in the book.

1   Introduction

The theory of general equilibrium is one of the most impressive achievements in the history of economic thought. In the 1950s and 1960s the proof of the existence of equilibrium and of the close correspondences among equilibria, Pareto optima, and the core seemed to open the way for a reconstruction of the whole of economic theory around these concepts. However, it quickly appeared that the general equilibrium model was not a fully satisfactory descriptive tool. Strategic interactions between agents are heavily constrained in that model. This is because agents only interact through the price system, which the pure competition assumption says they cannot influence. In the logical limit one gets the models of the Aumann-Hildenbrand school in which there is a continuum of nonatomic agents, none of which can influence equilibrium prices and allocations. Similarly the organization of the many institutions that govern economic relationships is entirely absent from these models. This is particularly striking in the case of firms, which are modeled as a production set. This makes the very existence of firms difficult to justify in the context of general equilibrium models, since all interactions are expected to take place through the price system in these models. As Coase said long ago in one of his most influential papers (Coase 1937), "The distinguishing mark of the firm is the supersession of the price mechanism."

Creating general equilibrium models that could account for informational asymmetries presented another challenge. Arrow and Debreu had shown that it is fairly straightforward to extend the

general equilibrium model to cover uncertainty as long as information is kept symmetric. Unfortunately, asymmetries of information
are pervasive in economic relationships. That is to say, customers
know more about their tastes than firms, firms know more about
their costs than the government, and all agents take actions that are
at least partly unobservable. So rational expectations equilibria were
conceived, at least in part, to encompass asymmetric information.
However, while they offered interesting insights on the revelation of
information by prices, their treatment of asymmetric information
did not prove satisfactory. A *homo œconomicus* who possesses private
information can be expected to try to manipulate that information,
since he has in effect a monopoly over his own piece of private information. If we want to take this into account, we must forsake general
equilibrium models. We then need to resort to other tools and, in
particular, to game-theoretic tools.

The theory of contracts thus evolved from the failures of general
equilibrium theory. In the 1970s several economists settled on a new
way to study economic relationships. The idea was to turn away
temporarily from general equilibrium models, whose description of
the economy is consistent but not realistic enough, and to focus on
necessarily partial models that take into account the full complexity
of strategic interactions between privately informed agents in well-
defined institutional settings. It was hoped then that lessons drawn
from these studies could later be integrated inside a better theory of
general equilibrium.

The theory of contracts, and more generally what was called the
"economics of information," were the tools used to explore this new
domain. Because they are just that—tools—it is somewhat difficult
to define their goals other than by contrasting their shared characteristics with previous approaches:

• For the most part, the models are partial equilibrium models. They
isolate the markets for one good (sometimes two goods) from the
rest of the economy.

• The models describe the interactions of a small number of agents (often just two, one of whom possesses some private information and is call the "informed party").

• The models sum up the constraints imposed by the prevailing institutional setting through a *contract*. The contract may be explicit and in the form of a written agreement, or may be implicit and depend on a system of behavioral norms. An explicit contract will be guaranteed by a "third party" (e.g., a court or a mediator) or by the desire agents to maintain a reputation for fair trading. An implicit contract is sustained by an equilibrium tacitly observed in the interactions between the agreeing parties.

• The models make an intensive use of noncooperative game theory with asymmetric information, although their description of the bargaining process generally calls for a simplistic device known as the Principal-Agent model (on which more is provided later in this introduction). They are embedded in a Bayesian universe in which parties have an a priori belief on the information they do not possess, and they revise this belief as the interaction unfolds. The equilibrium concept they use in fact belongs to the family of perfect Bayesian equilibria.

The theory of contracts obviously covers a lot of ground and many varied situations. As a consequence early empirical studies were mostly case studies. Only recently has a body of literature emerged that tries to test the main conclusions of the theory of contracts using standard econometric techniques, as is discussed in chapter 8.

1.1 The Great Families of Models

The models of the theory of contracts can be distinguished along several axes, depending on whether they are static or dynamic, whether they involve complete or incomplete contracts, whether they describe a bilateral or multilateral relationship, and so on. A large class of models, which can easily be divided into three families, is that where an informed party meets an uninformed party. I have chosen, somewhat arbitrarily of course, to classify these models according to two criteria. First is to distiguish whether the private information bears on

- what the agent *does*, the decisions he takes ("hidden action"),
- who the agent *is*, what his characteristics are ("hidden information").

Second, as in the form of the strategic game, is to distinguish the models in which the initiative belongs to the uninformed party from those in which it belongs to the informed party.

This classification yields three important families[1]:

- *Adverse selection* models. The uninformed party is imperfectly informed of the characteristics of the informed party; the uninformed party moves first.

- *Signaling* models. The informational situation is the same but the informed party moves first.

- *Moral hazard* models. The uninformed party moves first and is imperfectly informed of the actions of the informed party.

In chapters 2 to 5, I will study the basic structure of each of the three families. I should mention here, however, that one important class of models does not fit this system: models of incomplete contracting. This is because these models have so far only been developed in situations of symmetric information. They are studied in chapter 7.

---

1. The fourth case is that where the uninformed party does not observe the actions of the informed party. The informed party then takes the initiative of the contract. It is difficult to imagine a real-world application of such a model, and I do not know of any paper that uses it.

1.2   The Principal–Agent Model

Most of this book will use the Principal–Agent paradigm. There are two economic agents in this model: the informed party, whose information is relevant for the common welfare, and the uninformed party. Since this is a bilateral monopoly situation, we cannot go very far unless we specify how the parties are going to bargain over the terms of exchange. Unfortunately, the study of bargaining under asymmetric information is very complex.[2] The Principal–Agent model is a simplifying device that avoids these difficulties by allocating all bargaining power to one of the parties. This party will propose a "take it or leave it" contract and therefore request a "yes or no" answer; the other party is not free to propose another contract.

The Principal–Agent game is therefore a Stackelberg game in which the *leader* (who proposes the contract) is called the Principal and the *follower* (the party who just has to accept or reject the contract) is called the Agent.[3] While this modeling choice makes things much simpler, the reader should keep in mind that actual bargaining procedures are likely to be much more complex. For instance, if the Agent rejects the contract, the interaction would stop in the Principal–Agent model, whereas in the real world it would be expected to continue.

Because much of the book's discussion is informed by the Principal–Agent model, let us explore it a bit. One way to justify the Principal–Agent paradigm is to observe that the set of (constrained) Pareto optima can always be obtained by maximizing the utility of one

---

2. The main difficulty is that the natural equilibrium concept, perfect Bayesian equilibrium, leads to a large multiplicity of equilibria. See Ausubel-Cramton-Deneckere (2002) for a recent survey of bargaining models with asymmetric information.
3. I have tried to use consistent notation throughout the book: thus the "Agent" will always be the follower in a Principal–Agent game, while an "agent" is simply an economic agent, so that the Principal is also an agent. I hope this will create no confusion.

agent while the other is held to a given utility level. This is precisely what the Principal–Agent model does; so if we are only interested in common properties of the optima and not in one particular optimum, this approach brings no loss of generality. On the other hand, it may be that reasons outside the model should make us fix the Agent's reservation utility at some given level; if, for instance, the Principal is an employer and the Agent a prospective employee, the level of unemployment benefits and/or the market wage determine his reservation utility. In that case the peculiar properties of the Principal–Agent bargaining solution—it gives all surplus to the Principal—may make it less attractive as it picks a single point on the utility possibility frontier.

Finally, the choice of the words "Principal" and "Agent" should not be taken to imply that one of the parties works for the other or that the modeler is more interested in one than in the other. Each model has its own logic and should be interpreted accordingly. I should also point out that this terminology is taken by several authors, starting with the pioneering paper by Ross (1973), to refer to what they call the problem of agency, which is a moral hazard problem. My use of the Principal–Agent paradigm is both wider and more abstract; to me, it basically means that a Stackelberg game is being played.

1.3   Overview of the Book

An exhaustive look at the theory of contracts and its applications would make a very thick book. Such is not my ambition here. I merely want to present the main models of the theory of contracts, and particularly the basic models of the three great families described in section 1.1. It is not always easy to determine what belongs to the theory of contracts and what belongs to the wider field of the economics of information. I have chosen to include a brief description of auction models because their study relies on the same tools as the theory of contracts. On the other hand, I have preferred not to give a central role to models of insurance markets, even though their historical importance in shaping the field is well-established. As I will argue in section 3.1.3, these models have some peculiar features, and they deserve a fuller treatment than I can give them in a short book.

I have deliberately chosen to emphasize the methods used to analyze the models of the theory of contracts rather than the many applications that it has generated in various fields of economics. I have included brief introductions to these applications, but without any claim to completeness; most of the applications are not elaborated in the text. The reader interested in a particular application is urged to peruse the lists of references and to read the original papers. My goal in writing this book was to give the basic tools that allow the reader to understand the basic models and to come up with his own. I have tried to include recent developments, except where this could have led to overtechnical analyses. In most cases the lists of references will be sufficiently rich to allow the reader to find his way through this burgeoning literature.

Chapter 2 presents the general theory of adverse selection models. It starts with a brief summary of mechanism design, and proceeds to solve a basic model of second-degree price discrimination of two types. It then presents the solution in a more general continuous-type model. Several examples of applications and some more recent extensions are studied in chapter 3.

Chapter 4 turns to signaling models, and considers both signals that are costly and that are free. The basic moral hazard model, and some of its extensions and its application to insurance and wage contracts, are studied in chapter 5.

Chapter 6 is dedicated to the dynamic aspects of the theory of complete contracts. It introduces concepts like commitment and renegotiation that have been at the forefront of recent research. Because this field is very technical, I have not tried to provide complete proofs of the results in this chapter. This is a clear case where interested readers should refer to the original papers. Chapter 7 introduces the theory of incomplete contracts. The emphasis is more on the foundation of theory than on applications.

The book concludes with chapter 8, which examines the empirical and econometric literature based on the theory of contracts.

The reader might rightly judge by the number of equations that this is a fairly formal book. However, mathematical requirements for reading this book are low. Elementary concepts of calculus are sufficient. The only exceptions occur in chapters 4 and 6, which use somewhat more advanced concepts of noncooperative game theory. An appendix presents some background information for the readers who might need this. Throughout the book the sections that are more advanced are starred and can be skipped if necessary.

My original plan did not call for exercises. However, I found that in writing chapters 2 through 5 several came to mind. For this reason these chapters end with exercises.

References

Works Cited

Ausubel, L., P. Cramton, and R. Deneckere. 2002 Bargaining with incomplete information. In *Handbook of Game Theory*, vol. 3, R. Aumann and S. Hart, eds. Dordrecht: North-Holland.

Coase, R. 1937. The nature of the firm. *Economica* 4:386–405.

Ross, S. 1973. The economic theory of agency: The principal's problem. *American Economic Review* 63:134–39.

General References

At least two, and one forthcoming, textbooks take the theory of contracts as their subject:

Bolton, P., and M. Dewatripont. 2005. *Contract Theory.* Cambridge: MIT Press Forthcoming.

This is a comprehensive textbook. It differs from mine in that is emphasizes applications rather than general theorems; it is also a much thicker book.

Laffont, J.-J., and D. Martimort. 2001. *The Theory of Incentives.* Princeton: Princeton University Press.

This book studies the basic models in more depth than I do here.

Macho-Stadler, I., and D. Perez-Castrillo, 2001. *An Introduction to the Economics of Information: Incentives and Contracts;* 2d ed. Oxford: Oxford University Press.

This is a shorter book, and comparable to mine in its aims. It does not take into account recent developments.

Several more general books dedicate some space to the theory. Their approaches should be viewed as complementary to mine.

Diamond, P., and M. Rothschild. 1989. *Uncertainty in Economics.* San Diego: Academic Press.

A book of readings that collects and puts into perspective many important papers.

Fudenberg, D., and J. Tirole. 1991. *Game Theory.* Cambridge: MIT Press.

A rather formal textbook that contains results relevant to the theory of contracts, especially in chapter 7.

Hirshleifer, J., and J. Riley. 1992. *The Analytics of Uncertainty and Information.* Cambridge: Cambridge University Press.

Useful for chapters 8 and 11.

Kreps, D. 1990. *A Course in Microeconomic Theory.* Princeton: Princeton University Press.

A very accessible text; readers of this book should mainly be concerned with chapters 16 to 18.

Laffont, J.-J. 1989. *The Economics of Uncertainty and Information.* Cambridge: MIT Press.

A book that is more analytical and much more concise than Kreps's; see chapters 8, 10, and 11 and also the problems at the end of the book.

Laffont, J.-J., and J. Tirole. 1993. *A Theory of Incentives in Procurement and Regulation.* Cambridge: MIT Press.

A very complete book on procurement and the regulation of firms that contains many chapters of more general interest, especially on the dynamics of complete contracts.

Mas-Colell, A., M. Whinston, and J. Green. 1995. *Microeconomic Theory*. Oxford: Oxford University Press.

An excellent graduate textbook that devotes its chapters 13 and 14 to theory of contracts models.

Milgrom, P., and J. Roberts. 1992. *Economics, Organization and Management*. Englewood Cliffs, NJ: Prentice Hall.

Not really a theory book, but it presents in detail several key applications of the theory of contracts in the context of firms; it is highly readable.

Rasmusen, E. 1989. *Games and Information*. Oxford: Basil Blackwell.

A game-theoretic study of theory of contracts models can be found in part II of this book.

Tirole, J. 1988. *Industrial Organization*. Cambridge: MIT Press.

For many examples of applications of the theory of contracts and also for chapter 11, the best introduction I know to perfect Bayesian equilibria.

2   Adverse Selection: General Theory

We use the term "adverse selection" when a characteristic of the Agent is imperfectly observed by the Principal.[1] This term comes from a phenomenon well known to insurers: If a company offers a rate tailored only to the average-risk population, this rate will attract only the high risk population, and the company will therefore lose money. This effect may even induce the insurer to deny insurance to some risk groups. Other terms sometimes used are "self-selection" and "screening." The general idea of adverse selection can be grasped from the following example, which will be analyzed fully in section 2.2.

Suppose that the Principal is a wine seller and the Agent a buyer. The Agent may have cultivated tastes for good wines or have more modest tastes. We will say there are two "types": the sophisticated Agent who is ready to pay a high price for good vintage and the frugal Agent whose tastes—or means—may be less developed.

We can assume that the Principal cannot observe the type of any given Agent, or at least that the law (as is often the case) forbids him to use nonanonymous prices that discriminate between the two types.[2]

The key to the solution of the adverse selection problem is the following observation: if the sophisticated Agent is willing to pay more

---

1. This chapter and the next chapter develop the Principal–Agent paradigm introduced in section 1.2.
2. In Pigou's terms, first-degree price discrimination is infeasible besides being illegal.

than the frugal Agent for a given increase in the quality of the wine, then the Principal can segment the market by offering two different wine bottles:

$$\left\{\begin{array}{l} \text{a wine of high quality for a high price} \\ \text{a wine of lower quality for a lower price} \end{array}\right.$$

We will see in section 2.2 how these qualities and prices can be chosen optimally.

If all goes according to plan, the sophisticated type will choose the top high-priced wine, while the frugal type will pick a lower quality bottle. Thus the two types of Agent "reveal themselves" through their choices of wine. As we will see, this implies that the frugal type buys a lower quality than might be socially optimal. The whole point of adverse selection problems is to make the Agents reveal their type without incurring too high a social distortion.

Let us briefly consider a few other relevant examples of adverse selection.

• In life insurance, the insured's state of health (and therefore risk of dying soon) is not known to the insurer, even if the insured has had a medical checkup. As a result the insurer is better off offering several insurance packages, each tailored to a specific risk class. (This situation will be studied in section 3.1.3.)

• In banking, the borrowers' default risk can be only imperfectly assessed, in particular, where entrepreneurs request financing for risky projects. A natural idea is to use interest rates to discriminate among entrepreneurs. However, this may induce credit rationing, unless banks also vary collateral levels.[3]

• In labor markets, potential workers have an informational advantage over employers in that they know their innate abilities better.

---

3. This is an admittedly very brief summary of a body of literature that started with Stiglitz-Weiss (1981).

Because of this firms must screen workers to select the promising candidate and reject all others.

• In government-regulated firms (state-owned or not), the regulated firm has better information on its costs or productivity than the regulator. The obvious implication is that it can manipulate the way it discloses information to the regulator to maximize its profits (see section 3.1.1).

*2.1   Mechanism Design

Mechanism design is at the root of the study of adverse selection. Mechanism design is so important to adverse selection models that some authors also call these models mechanism design problems. I will not attempt here to give a self-contained presentation of mechanism design. I will assume that the reader has already been exposed to this theory. My sole aim will be to remind the reader of the general formalistic properties and the results that will be needed later in the book.[4] The reader who finds this section too abstract can skip it without losing the thread of the chapter.

The object of mechanism design theory is to explore the means of implementing a given allocation of available resources when the relevant information is dispersed in the economy. Take, for instance, a social choice problem where each agent $i = 1, ..., n$ has some relevant private information θ_i. Assume that despite all the reservations exemplified by Arrow's theorem, society has decided that the optimal allocation is

$$y(\theta) = (y_1(\theta_1, ..., \theta_n), ..., y_n(\theta_1, ..., \theta_n))$$

Presumably it is be easy to implement the allocation if the government knows all the θ_i's. However, if only i knows his θ_i and, say, his

---

4. See Laffont (1989) or Moore (1992) for a more complete exposition.

optimal allocation $y_i(\theta)$ increases with θ_i, he is likely to overstate his θ_i so as to obtain a larger allocation. This can make it very difficult for the government to implement $y(\theta)$.

The provision of public goods is another example. Everyone benefits from a bridge, but no one particularly cares to contribute to its building costs. The optimal financing scheme presumably depends on each agent's potential use of the bridge: for example, commuters heavily using the bridge might be asked to pay more than infrequent commuter types. In the absence of a reliable way to differentiate between these individuals, the government will have to rely on voluntary declarations. Naturally, to avoid bearing a large portion of the cost, the heavy user type of Agent will understate the utility he derives from the bridge. As a result the bridge may not be built, as its cost may exceed the reported benefits.

As a final example, consider the implementation of a Walrasian equilibrium in an exchange economy. We all know that this has good properties under the usual assumptions. However, it is not clear how the economy can move to a Walrasian equilibrium. If information were publicly available, the government could just compute the equilibrium and give all consumers their equilibrium allocations.[5] In practice, the agents' utility functions (or their true demand functions) are their private information, and they can be expected to lie so as to maximize their utility. As information is dispersed throughout the economy, implementable allocations are subject to a large number of incentive constraints.

In all these examples, two related questions arise:

Can $y(\theta)$ be implemented? In other words, is it incentive compatible (some authors say "feasible")? What is the optimal choice among incentive compatible allocations?

In more abstract terms we consider a situation where

---

5. This was the original vision of the proponents of market socialism.

- there are n agents $i = 1, ..., n$ characterized by parameters $\theta_i \in \Theta_i$, which are their private information and are often called their "types";

- agents are facing a "Center" whose aim is to implement a given allocation of resources, and generally (which is the more interesting case) this allocation will depend on the agents' private characteristics θ_i.

Think of the Center as government, or as some economic agent who has been given the responsibility of implementing an allocation, or even as an abstract entity such as the Walrasian auctioneer. The Center needn't be a benevolent dictator; he may be, for instance, the seller of a good who wants to extract as much surplus as possible from agents whose valuations for the good he cannot observe.

2.1.1   General Mechanisms

The problem facing the Center is an incentive problem. The Center must try to extract information from the Agents so that he can implement the right allocation. To do this, he may resort to very complicated procedures, using bribes to urge the Agents to reveal some of their private information. This process, however complicated, can be summed up by a *mechanism* $(y(.), M_1, ..., M_n)$. This consists of a message space M_i for each Agent i and a function $y(.)$ from $M_1 \times ... \times M_n$ to the set of feasible allocations. The allocation rule $y(.) = (y_1(.), ..., y_n(.))$ determines the allocations of all n Agents as a function of the messages they send to the Center.[6] Note that generally these allocations are vectors.

Given an allocation rule $y(.)$, the Agents play a message game in which the message spaces M_i are their strategy sets and the allocation rule $y(.)$ determines their allocations and therefore their utility

---

6. In general, the mechanism involves stochastic allocation rules. Here we will assume that they are deterministic.

levels. Agent i then chooses a message m_i in M and sends it to the Center, who imposes the allocation $y(m_1, \ldots, m_n)$.

Note that in general, the message chosen by Agent i will depend on his information I_i, which contains his characteristic θ_i. The Agent's information may in fact be richer, as is the case where each Agent knows the characteristic of some of his neighbors. Equilibrium messages thus will be functions $m_i^*(I_i)$ and the implemented allocation will be

$$y^*(I_1, \ldots, I_n) = y\big(m_1^*(I_1), \ldots, m_n^*(I_n)\big)$$

Assume, for instance, that the Center is the proverbial Walrasian auctioneer and tries to implement a Walrasian equilibrium in a context where he does not know the Agents' preferences. Then one way for him to proceed is to ask the agents for their demand functions, to compute the corresponding equilibrium, and to give each agent his equilibrium allocation. If he is the builder of a bridge, he might announce a rule stating under which conditions he will decide to build the bridge and how it will be financed; then he would ask each Agent for his willingness to pay.

2.1.2   Application to Adverse Selection Models

The models we are concerned with in this chapter are very special and simple instances of mechanism design. The Principal here is the Center, and only one Agent is involved. Thus $n = 1$, and the information I of the Agent boils down to his type θ. Given a mechanism $(y(.), M)$, the Agent chooses the message he sends so as to maximize his utility $u(y, \theta)$:

$$m^*(\theta) \in \arg\max_{m \in M} u(y(m), \theta)$$

and he obtains the corresponding allocation

$$y^*(\theta) = y(m^*(\theta))$$

The revelation principle below[7] implies that one can confine attention to mechanisms that are both *direct* (where the Agent reports his information) and *truthful* (so that the Agent finds it optimal to announce the true value of his information).

Revelation Principle.
If the allocation $y^*(\theta)$ can be implemented through some mechanism, then it can also be implemented through a direct truthful mechanism where the Agent reveals his information θ.

The proof of this result is elementary. Let $(y(.), M)$ be a mechanism that implements the allocation y^*, and let $m^*(\theta)$ be the equilibrium message, so that $y^* = y \circ m^*$. Now consider the direct mechanism $(y^*(.), \Theta)$. If it were not truthful, then an Agent would prefer to announce some θ' rather than his true type θ. So we would have

$$u(y^*(\theta), \theta) < u(y^*(\theta'), \theta)$$

But, by the definition of y^*, this would imply that

$$u(y(m^*(\theta)), \theta) < u(y(m^*(\theta')), \theta)$$

Consequently m^* cannot be an equilibrium in a game generated by the mechanism $(y(.), M)$, since the Agent of type θ prefers to announce $m^*(\theta')$ rather than $m^*(\theta)$. Thus the direct mechanism (y^*, Θ) must be truthful, and by construction, it implements the allocation y^*.

Note that in a direct mechanism the message space of the Agent coincides with his type space. Thus in the example of the bridge, the Agent needs only to announce his willingness to pay.

Assume that as is often the case, the allocation y consists of an allocation q and a monetary transfer p. The revelation principle states that to implement the quantity allocation $q(\theta)$ using transfers

---

7. I only state this principle for the case where $n = 1$. It is valid more generally, but the shape it takes depends on the equilibrium concept used for the message-sending game among the n agents. These complications do not concern us here.

$p(\theta)$, it is enough to offer the Agent a menu of contracts. If the Agent announces that his type is θ, he will receive the allocation $q(\theta)$ and will pay the transfer $p(\theta)$.

Direct truthful mechanisms are very simple but rely on messages that are not explicit. In the example of the wine seller, one can hardly expect the buyer to come into the shop and declare "I am sophisticated" or "I am frugal." A second result sometimes called the *taxation principle* comes to our aid in showing that these mechanisms are equivalent to a nonlinear tariff $\tau(.)$ that lets the Agent choose an allocation q and pay a corresponding transfer $p = \tau(q)$. The proof of this principle again is simple. Let there be two types θ and θ' such that $q(\theta) = q(\theta')$; if $p(\theta)$ is larger than $p(\theta')$, then the Agent of type θ can pretend to be of type θ', and the mechanism will not be truthful. Therefore we must have $p(\theta) = p(\theta')$, and the function $\tau(.)$ is defined unambiguously by

if $q = q(\theta)$,   then $\tau(q) = p(\theta)$

In our earlier example the wine seller only needs to offer the buyer two wine bottles that are differentiated by their quality and price. This is, of course, more realistic; although most retailers do not post a nonlinear tariff on their doors, they often use a system of rebates that approximates a nonlinear tariff.

2.2   A Discrete Model of Price Discrimination

In section 2.3, we will obtain the general solution for the standard adverse selection model with a continuous set of types. Here we learn first to derive the optimum in a simple two-type model by way of heavily graphical techniques and very simple arguments.

To simplify things, we will reuse the example of a wine seller who offers wines of different qualities (and at different prices) in order to segment a market in which consumers' tastes differ. This is therefore a model that exhibits both vertical differentiation and second-degree price discrimination.[8]

2.2.1   The Consumer

Let the Agent be a moderate drinker who plans to buy at most one bottle of wine within the period we study. His utility is $U = \theta q - t$, where q is the quality he buys and θ is a positive parameter that indexes his taste for quality. If he decides not to buy any wine, his utility is just 0.

Note that with this specification,

$$\forall \theta' > \theta, \quad u(q, \theta') - u(q, \theta) \quad \text{increases in } q$$

This is the discrete form of what I call the Spence-Mirrlees condition in section 2.3. For now, just note its economic significance: At any given quality level, the more sophisticated consumers are willing to pay more than the frugal consumers for the same increase in quality. This is what gives us the hope that we will be able to segment the market on quality.

There are two possible values for θ: $\theta_1 < \theta_2$; the prior probability that the Agent is of type 1 (or the proportion of types 1 in the population) is π. In the following, I will call "sophisticated" the consumers of type 2 and "frugal" the consumers of type 1.

2.2.2   The Seller

The Principal is a local monopolist in the wine market. He can produce wine of any quality $q \in (0, \infty)$; the production of a bottle of good quality q costs him $C(q)$. I will assume that C is twice differentiable and strictly convex, that $C'(0) = 0$ and $C'(\infty) = \infty$.

---

8. The classic reference for this model is Mussa-Rosen (1978), who use a continuous set of types.

The utility of the Principal is just the difference between his receipts and his costs, or $t - C(q)$.

2.2.3 The First-Best: Perfect Discrimination

If the producer can observe the type θ_i of the consumer, he will solve the following program:

$$\max_{q_i, t_i} (t_i - C(q_i))$$

$$\theta_i q_i - t_i \geq 0$$

The producer will therefore offer $q_i = q_i^*$ such that $C'(q_i^*) = \theta_i$ and $t_i^* = \theta_i q_i^*$ to the consumer of type θ_i, thus extracting all his surplus; the consumer will be left with zero utility.

Figure 2.1 represents the two first-best contracts in the plane (q, t). The two lines shown are the indifference lines corresponding to zero utility for the two types of Agent. The curves tangent to them are iso-profit curves, with equation $t = C(q) + K$. Their convexity is a consequence of our assumptions on the function C. Note that the utility of the Agent increases when going southeast, while the profit of the Principal increases when going northwest.

Both q_1^* and q_2^* are the "efficient qualities." Since $\theta_1 < \theta_2$ and C' is increasing, we get $q_2^* > q_1^*$, and the sophisticated consumer buys a higher quality wine than the frugal consumer. This type of discrimination, called first-degree price discrimination, is generally forbidden by the law, according to which the sale should be anonymous: You cannot refuse a consumer the same deal you prepared for another consumer.[9] However, we are interested in the case

---

9. As we will see shortly, the sophisticated consumer envies the frugal consumer's deal.

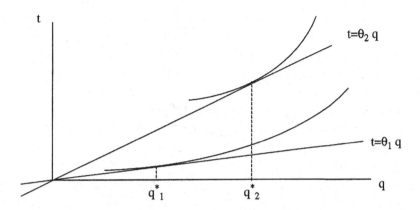

Figure 2.1
The first-best contracts

where the seller cannot observe directly the consumer's type. In this case perfect discrimination is infeasible no matter what is its legal status.

2.2.4   Imperfect Information

Now in the second-best situation information is asymmetric. The producer now only knows that the proportion of frugal consumers is π. If he proposes the first-best contracts (q_1^*, t_1^*), (q_2^*, t_2^*), the sophisticated consumers will not choose (q_2^*, t_2^*) but (q_1^*, t_1^*), since

$$\theta_2 q_1^* - t_1^* = (\theta_2 - \theta_1)q_1^* > 0 = \theta_2 q_2^* - t_2^*$$

The two types cannot be treated separately any more. Both will choose the low quality deal (q_1^*, t_1^*).

Of course, the producer can get higher profits by proposing (q_1^*, t_1^*) the point designated A in figure 2.2, since A will be chosen only by the sophisticates and only by them. Note that A is located on a higher isoprofit curve than (q_1^*, t_1^*), and therefore it gives a higher profit to the seller.

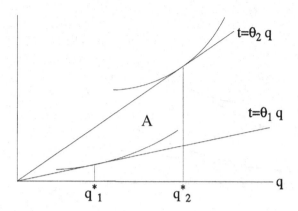

Figure 2.2
A potentially improving contract

A number of other contracts are better than A. Our interest is in the best pair of contracts (the second-best optimum). This is obtained by solving the following program:

$$\max_{t_1, q_1, t_2, q_2} \{\pi[t_1 - C(q_1)] + (1 - \pi)[t_2 - C(q_2)]\}$$

subject to

$$\begin{cases} \theta_1 q_1 - t_1 \geq \theta_1 q_2 - t_2 & (IC_1) \\ \theta_2 q_2 - t_2 \geq \theta_2 q_1 - t_1 & (IC_2) \\ \theta_1 q_1 - t_1 \geq 0 & (IR_1) \\ \theta_2 q_2 - t_2 \geq 0 & (IR_2) \end{cases}$$

The constraints in this program are identified as follows:

• The two (IC) constraints are the *incentive compatibility* constraints; they state that each consumer prefers the contract that was designed for him.

• The two (IR) constraints are the *individual rationality,* or *participation* constraints; they guarantee that each type of consumer accepts his designated contract.

We will prove that at the optimum:

1. (IR_1) is active, so $t_1 = \theta_1 q_1$.
2. (IC_2) is active, whence

$$t_2 - t_1 = \theta_2(q_2 - q_1).$$

3. $q_2 \geq q_1$.
4. (IC_1) and (IR_2) can be neglected.
5. Sophisticated consumers buy the efficient quality

$$q_2 = q_2^*.$$

Proofs We use (IC_2) to prove property 1:

$$\theta_2 q_2 - t_2 \geq \theta_2 q_1 - t_1 \geq \theta_1 q_1 - t_1$$

since $q_1 \geq 0$ and $\theta_2 > \theta_1$. If (IR_1) was inactive, so would be (IR_2), and we could increase t_1 and t_2 by the same amount. This would increase the Principal's profit without any effect on incentive compatibility.

Property 2 is proved by assuming that (IC_2) is inactive. Then

$$\theta_2 q_2 - t_2 > \theta_2 q_1 - t_1 \geq \theta_1 q_1 - t_1 = 0$$

We can therefore augment t_2 without breaking incentive compatibility or the individual rationality constraint (IR_2). This obviously increases the Principal's profit, and therefore the original mechanism cannot be optimal.

To prove property 3, let us add (IC_1) and (IC_2). The transfers t_i cancel out, and we get

$$\theta_2(q_2 - q_1) \geq \theta_1(q_2 - q_1)$$

and

$$q_2 - q_1 \geq 0$$

since $\theta_2 > \theta_1$.

By property 4, the (IC_1) can be neglected, since (IC_2) is active. By property 3,

$$t_2 - t_1 = \theta_2(q_2 - q_1) \geq \theta_1(q_2 - q_1)$$

The proof of assertion 1 shows that (IR_2) can be neglected.

Finally, by property 5, we can prove that $C'(q_2) = \theta_2$. If $C'(q_2) < \theta_2$, for instance, let ε be a small positive number, and consider the new mechanism (q_1, t_1), $(q'_2 = q_2 + \varepsilon, t'_2 = t_2 + \varepsilon\theta_2)$. It is easily seen that

$$\theta_2 q'_2 - t'_2 = \theta_2 q_2 - t_2 \text{ and } \theta_1 q'_2 - t'_2 = \theta_1 q_2 - t_2 - \varepsilon(\theta_2 - \theta_1)$$

so the new mechanism satisfies all four constraints. Moreover

$$t'_2 - C(q'_2) \simeq t_2 - C(q_2) + \varepsilon(\theta_2 - C'(q_2))$$

This tells us that the new mechanism yields higher profits than the original one, which is absurd. We can prove in the same way that $C'(q_2) > \theta_2$ is impossible (just change the sign of ε).

It is an easy and useful exercise to obtain graphical proofs of these five points. The optimal pair of contracts appears to be located as shown in figure 2.3. (q_1, t_1) is on the zero utility indifference line of the Agent of type 1, and (q_2, t_2) is the tangency point between an iso-

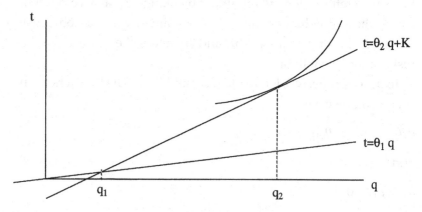

Figure 2.3
The second-best optimum

profit curve of the seller and the indifference line of the Agent of type 2 that goes through (q_1, t_1).

To fully characterize the optimal pair of contracts, we just have to let (q_1, t_1) in figure 2.3 slide on the line $t_1 = \theta_1 q_1$. Formally the optimum is obtained by replacing q_2 with q_2^* and expressing the values of t_1 and t_2 as functions of q_1, using

$$\begin{cases} t_1 = \theta_1 q_1 \\ t_2 - t_1 = \theta_2(q_2 - q_1) \end{cases}$$

This gives

$$\begin{cases} q_2 = q_2^* \\ t_1 = \theta_1 q_1 \\ t_2 = \theta_1 q_1 + \theta_2(q_2^* - q_1) \end{cases}$$

We can substitute these values in the expression of the Principal's profit and solve

$$\max_{q_1} \left(\pi(\theta_1 q_1 - C(q_1)) - (1 - \pi)(\theta_2 - \theta_1)q_1 \right)$$

Note that the objective of this program consists of two terms. The first term is proportional to the social surplus[10] on type 1 and the second represents the effect on incentive constraints on the seller's objective. Dividing by π, we see that the Principal should maximize

$$(\theta_1 q_1 - C(q_1)) - \frac{1 - \pi}{\pi}(\theta_2 - \theta_1)q_1$$

which we can call the *virtual surplus*. We will see a similar formula in section 2.3. The difference between the social surplus and the virtual surplus comes from the fact that when the Principal increases q_1, he makes the type 1 package more alluring to type 2. To prevent type 2

---

10. The social surplus is the sum of the objectives of the Principal and the type 1 Agent. We do not have to worry about the social surplus derived from selling to Agent 2, since we know that we implement the first-best $q_2 = q_2^*$.

from choosing the contract designated for type 1, he must therefore reduce t_2, which decreases his own profits.

We finally get

$$C'(q_1) = \theta_1 - \frac{1 - \pi}{\pi}(\theta_2 - \theta_1) < \theta_1$$

so that $q_1 < q_1^*$: the quality sold to the frugal consumers is sub-efficient.[11]

The optimal mechanism has five properties that are common to all discrete-type models and can usually be taken for granted, thus making the resolution of the model much easier:

• The highest type gets an efficient allocation.

• Each type but the lowest is indifferent between his contract and that of the immediately lower type.

• All types but the lowest type get a positive surplus: their *informational rent*, which increases with their type.

• All types but the highest type get a subefficient allocation.

• The lowest type gets zero surplus.

Informational rent is a central concept in adverse selection models. The Agent of type 2 gets it because he can always pretend his type is 1, consume quality q_1, pay the price t_1, and thus get utility

$$\theta_2 q_1 - t_1$$

which is positive. However, type 1 cannot gain anything by pretending to be type 2, since this nets him utility

$$\theta_1 q_2 - t_2$$

---

11. If the number of frugal consumers π is low, the formula will give a negative $C'(q_1)$. Then it is optimal for the seller to propose a single contract designed for the sophisticated consumers. A more general treatment should take this possibility into account from the start. Here this *exclusion* phenomenon can be prevented by assuming that π is high enough. We will see in section 3.2.6 that this is not possible when the Agent's characteristic is multidimensional.

which is negative. For n types of consumers $\theta_1 < \ldots < \theta_n$, each type $\theta_2, \ldots, \theta_n$ can get informational rent, and this rent will increase from θ_2 to θ_n. Only the lowest type, θ_1, will receive no rent.

Remark   By the taxation principle, there is a nonlinear tariff that is equivalent to the optimal mechanism. It is simply

$$\begin{cases} t = t_1 & \text{if } q = q_1 \\ t = t_2 & \text{if } q = q_2 \\ t = \infty & \text{otherwise} \end{cases}$$

So the seller needs only to propose the two qualities that will segment the market.[12]

2.3   The Standard Model

The model we study in this section sums up reasonably well the general features of standard adverse selection models. It introduces a Principal and an Agent who exchange a vector of goods q and a monetary transfer p. The Agent has a characteristic θ that constitutes his private information. The utilities of both parties are given by

$$\begin{cases} W(q, t) & \text{for the Principal} \\ U(q, t, \theta) & \text{for the Agent of type } \theta \end{cases}$$

Note that we do not make the Principal's utility function depend on the type θ of the Agent. This is because the model involves "private values" as opposed to "common values." This distinction will be used again in chapter 3. When the contract is signed, the Agent knows his

---

12. Such an extremely nonlinear tariff is less reasonable when the variable q is a quantity index, as it is in the price discrimination problem studied by Maskin-Riley (1984). Then it is sometimes possible to implement the optimum mechanism by using a menu of linear tariffs. Rogerson (1987) proves that a necessary and sufficient condition is that the optimal nonlinear schedule $t = T(q)$ be convex.

type θ.[13] The Principal entertains an a priori belief about the Agent's type. This belief is embodied in a probability distribution f with cumulative distribution function F on Θ, which we will call the Principal's *prior*. Because the Agent has a continuous set of possible types to choose from, the graphical analysis we used in section 2.2 no longer meets our needs, so we must use differential techniques.

From the revelation principle we already know that the Principal just has to offer the Agent a menu of contracts $(q(.), t(.))$ indexed by an announcement of the Agent's type θ that must be truthful at the equilibrium. We need to characterize the menus of contracts such that

(IC) Agent θ chooses the $(q(\theta), t(\theta))$ that the Principal designed for him,

(IR) Agent θ thus obtains a utility level at least as large as his reservation utility, meaning the utility he could obtain by trading elsewhere (his second-best opportunity).

The menu of contracts $(q(.), t(.))$ maximizes the expected utility of the Principal among all menus that satisfy (IR) and (IC).

Remarks

• As in section 2.2, the acronyms (IR) and (IC) come from the terms *individual rationality* and *incentive compatibility*.

• As in section 2.2.4, it may be optimal for the Principal to exclude some types θ from the exchange by denying them a contract (or at least falling back on a prior "no trade" contract). We, however, neglect this possibility in the following analysis.

• We can neglect the possibility that the optimal mechanism is random; exercise 2.5 gives a sufficient condition for the optimal mechanism to be deterministic.

---

13. It may be more reasonable to expect the Agent to learn his type only at some point after the contract has been signed but before its provisions are executed. I discuss this variant of the standard model in section 3.2.5.

• We can assume that the Principal faces a population of Agents whose types are drawn from the cumulative distribution function F. This case is isomorphic to that we study here, with a single Agent whose type is random in the Principal's view. Many papers vacillate between the two interpretations, and so will I here.

2.3.1   Analysis of the Incentive Constraints

Let $V(\theta, \hat{\theta})$ be the utility achieved by an Agent of type θ who announces his type as $\hat{\theta}$ and therefore receives utility

$$V(\theta, \hat{\theta}) = U(q(\hat{\theta}), t(\hat{\theta}), \theta)$$

The mechanism (q, t) satisfies the incentive constraints if, and only if, being truthful brings every type of Agent at least as much utility as any kind of lie:

$$\forall (\theta, \hat{\theta}) \in \Theta^2, \quad V(\theta, \theta) \geq V(\theta, \hat{\theta}) \qquad (IC)$$

To simplify notation, we can assume that q is one-dimensional. More important, we can take Θ to be a real interval[14] $[\underline{\theta}, \overline{\theta}]$ and let the Agent's utility function take the following form:

$$U(q, t, \theta) = u(q, \theta) - t$$

This presumes a quasi-linearity that implies that the Agent's marginal utility for money is constant; it simplifies some technical points but primarily allows us to use surplus analysis.

We can further assume that the mechanism (q, t) is differentiable enough. It is sometimes possible to justify this assumption rigorously by proving that the optimal mechanism indeed is at least piecewise differentiable.

---

14. The problem becomes more complicated, and the solution takes a very different form when θ is multidimensional; see section 3.2.6.

For (q, t) to be incentive compatible, it must be that the following first- and second-order necessary conditions hold:[15]

$$\forall \theta \in \Theta, \quad \begin{cases} \dfrac{\partial V}{\partial \hat{\theta}}(\theta, \theta) = 0 \\[2mm] \dfrac{\partial^2 V}{\partial \hat{\theta}^2}(\theta, \theta) \le 0 \end{cases}$$

The first-order condition boils down to

$$\frac{dt}{d\theta}(\theta) = \frac{\partial u}{\partial q}(q(\theta), \theta)\frac{dq}{d\theta}(\theta) \qquad (IC_1)$$

As to the second-order condition, that is,

$$\frac{d^2 t}{d\theta^2}(\theta) \ge \frac{\partial^2 u}{\partial q^2}(q(\theta), \theta)\left(\frac{dq}{d\theta}(\theta)\right)^2 + \frac{\partial u}{\partial q}(q(\theta), \theta)\frac{d^2 q}{d\theta^2}(\theta) \qquad (IC_2)$$

it can be simplified by differentiating (IC_1), which gives

$$\frac{d^2 t}{d\theta^2}(\theta) = \frac{\partial^2 u}{\partial q^2}(q(\theta), \theta)\left(\frac{dq}{d\theta}(\theta)\right)^2 + \frac{\partial u}{\partial q \partial \theta}(q(\theta), \theta)\frac{dq}{d\theta}(\theta)$$

$$+ \frac{\partial u}{\partial q}(q(\theta), \theta)\frac{d^2 q}{d\theta^2}(\theta)$$

whence by substituting into (IC_2),

$$\frac{\partial^2 u}{\partial q \partial \theta}(q(\theta), \theta)\frac{dq}{d\theta}(\theta) \ge 0$$

The first- and second-order necessary incentive conditions thus can be written as

---

15. These conditions are clearly not sufficient in general; however, we will soon see that they are sufficient in some circumstances.

$$\forall \theta \in \Theta, \quad \begin{cases} \dfrac{dt}{d\theta}(\theta) = \dfrac{\partial u}{\partial q}(q(\theta), \theta)\dfrac{dq}{d\theta}(\theta) & (IC_1) \\[3mm] \dfrac{\partial^2 u}{\partial q \partial \theta}(q(\theta), \theta)\dfrac{dq}{d\theta}(\theta) \geq 0 & (IC_2) \end{cases}$$

Most models used in the literature simplify the analysis by assuming that the cross-derivative $\partial^2 u/\partial q\partial\theta$ has a constant sign. This is called the Spence-Mirrlees condition. I will assume that this derivative is positive:

$$\forall \theta, \forall q, \quad \frac{\partial^2 u}{\partial q \partial \theta}(q, \theta) > 0$$

This condition is also called the *single-crossing condition*; it indeed implies that the indifference curves of two different types can only cross once,[16] as is shown in figure 2.4 (where, for the sake of concreteness, I take u to be increasing and concave in q).

The Spence-Mirrlees condition has an economic content; it means that higher types (those Agents with a higher θ) are willing to pay more for a given increase in q than lower types. We may thus hope that we will be able to separate the different types of Agents by offering larger allocations q to higher types and making them pay for the privilege. This explains why the Spence-Mirrlees condition is also called the *sorting condition*, as it allows us to sort through the different types of Agent.

Let us now prove that if q belongs to a direct truthful mechanism (q, t) if, and only if, q is nondecreasing.[17] To see this, consider

$$\frac{\partial V}{\partial \hat\theta}(\theta, \hat\theta) = \frac{\partial u}{\partial q}(q(\hat\theta), \theta)\frac{dq}{d\theta}(\hat\theta) - \frac{dt}{d\theta}(\hat\theta)$$

16. The simplest way to see this is to note that for a given q where they cross, the indifference curves of different types are ordered. Higher types have steeper indifference curves because the slopes $\partial u/\partial q$ increase with θ.
17. If we had assumed the Spence-Mirrlees condition with $\partial^2 u/\partial q\partial\theta < 0$, then q would be nonincreasing.

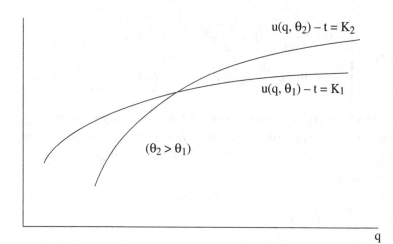

Figure 2.4
The Spence-Mirrlees condition

By writing (IC_1) in $\hat{\theta}$, we get

$$\frac{\partial u}{\partial q}(q(\hat{\theta}), \hat{\theta})\frac{dq}{d\theta}(\hat{\theta}) = \frac{dt}{d\theta}(\hat{\theta})$$

whence

$$\frac{\partial V}{\partial \hat{\theta}}(\theta, \hat{\theta}) = \left(\frac{\partial u}{\partial q}(q(\hat{\theta}), \theta) - \frac{\partial u}{\partial q}(q(\hat{\theta}), \hat{\theta})\right)\frac{dq}{d\theta}(\hat{\theta})$$

But the sign of the right-hand side is that of

$$\frac{\partial^2 u}{\partial q \partial \theta}(q(\hat{\theta}), \theta^*)\,(\theta - \hat{\theta})\frac{dq}{d\theta}(\hat{\theta})$$

for some θ^* that lies between θ and $\hat{\theta}$. Given the Spence-Mirrlees condition, this term has the same sign as $\theta - \hat{\theta}$ if q is nondecreasing. That is, the function $\hat{\theta} \to V(\theta, \hat{\theta})$ increases until $\hat{\theta} = \theta$ and then decreases. Therefore $\hat{\theta} = \theta$ is the global maximizer of $V(\theta, \hat{\theta})$.

This is a remarkable result. We started with the doubly infinite (in number) global incentive constraints (IC) and the Spence-Mirrlees condition allowed us to transform the constraints into the much simpler local conditions, (IC_1) and (IC_2), without any loss of generality. Note how the problem separates nicely: (IC_2) requires that q be nondecreasing and (IC_1) gives us the associated t. This will be very useful in solving the model. If the Spence-Mirrlees condition did not hold, the study of the incentive problem would be global and therefore much more complex.[18]

2.3.2   Solving the Model

Let us go on analyzing this model with a continuous set of types. We will neglect technicalities in the following. In particular, we assume that all differential equations can safely be integrated.[19] We also assume that the Principal's utility function is quasi-separable and is

$$t - C(q)$$

We further assume that

$$\forall q, \forall \theta, \quad \frac{\partial u}{\partial \theta}(q, \theta) > 0$$

meaning that a given allocation gives the higher types a higher utility level. Finally, we assume that the Spence-Mirrlees condition holds:

$$\forall \theta, \forall q, \quad \frac{\partial^2 u}{\partial q \partial \theta}(q, \theta) > 0$$

---

18. In the few papers (e.g., Moore 1988) that adopt a "nonlocal" approach that does not rely on the Spence-Mirrlees condition, typically assumes that only the downward incentive constraints are assumed to bind. Milgrom-Shannon (1994) establish a connection between the Spence-Mirrlees condition and the theory of supermodular functions.

19. Readers interested in a more full and rigorous analysis should turn to Guesnerie-Laffont (1984).

Let $v(\theta)$ denote the utility the Agent of type θ gets at the optimum of his program. As the optimal mechanism is truthful, we get

$$v(\theta) = V(\theta, \theta) = u(q(\theta), \theta) - t(\theta)$$

and IC_1 implies that

$$\frac{dv}{d\theta}(\theta) = \frac{\partial u}{\partial \theta}(q(\theta), \theta)$$

which we have assumed is positive. The utility $v(\theta)$ represents the *informational rent* of the Agent; the equation above shows that this rent is an increasing function of his type. Higher types thus benefit more from their private information. That is, if type θ can always pretend his type is $\hat{\theta} < \theta$, he will obtain a utility

$$u(q(\hat{\theta}), \theta) - t(\hat{\theta}) = v(\hat{\theta}) + u(q(\hat{\theta}), \theta) - u(q(\hat{\theta}), \hat{\theta})$$

which is larger than $v(\hat{\theta})$ since u increases in θ. The ability of higher types to "hide behind" lower types is responsible for their informational rent.[20] This rent is the price that the Principal has to pay for higher types to reveal their information.

In most applications the individual rationality constraint is taken to be independent of the Agent's type.[21] This amounts to assuming that the Agent's private information is only relevant in his relationship with the Principal. Under this assumption, which is not innocuous,[22] we can normalize the Agent's reservation utility to 0 and write his individual rationality constraint as

$$\forall \theta, \quad v(\theta) \geq 0 \qquad (IR)$$

Given that v is increasing, the individual rationality constraint (IR) boils down to

---

20. Note, however, that lower types have no incentive to hide behind higher types.
21. We will make an important exception in section 3.1.3.
22. See section 3.2.8 for a general analysis of the adverse selection problem in which reservation utilities are allowed to depend on types in a nonrestricted way.

$$v(\underline{\theta}) \geq 0$$

which must actually be an equality, since transfers are costly for the Principal.

These preliminary computations allow us to eliminate the transfers $t(\theta)$ from the problem; so we have

$$v(\theta) = \int_{\underline{\theta}}^{\theta} \frac{\partial u}{\partial \theta}(q(\tau), \tau)d\tau$$

whence

$$t(\theta) = u(q(\theta), \theta) - v(\theta)$$
$$= u(q(\theta), \theta) - \int_{\underline{\theta}}^{\theta} \frac{\partial u}{\partial \theta}(q(\tau), \tau)d\tau$$

Let us now return to the Principal's objective[23]

$$\int_{\underline{\theta}}^{\bar{\theta}} \Big(t(\theta) - C(q(\theta))\Big)f(\theta)d\theta$$

Substituting for t, it can be rewritten as

$$\int_{\underline{\theta}}^{\bar{\theta}} \left(u(q(\theta), \theta) - \int_{\underline{\theta}}^{\theta} \frac{\partial u}{\partial \theta}(q(\tau), \tau)d\tau - C(q(\theta)) \right)f(\theta)d\theta$$

Let us define the *hazard rate*

$$h(\theta) = \frac{f(\theta)}{1 - F(\theta)}$$

This definition is borrowed from the statistical literature on duration data:[24] if $F(\theta)$ is the probability of dying before age θ, then $h(\theta)$ represents the instantaneous probability of dying at age θ provided that one has survived until then.

---

23. Recall that f is the probability distribution function and F the cumulative distribution function of the Principal's prior on Θ.
24. Some economists improperly define the hazard rate as $1/h(\theta)$.

Now applying Fubini's theorem[25] or simply integrating by parts, the Principal's objective becomes

$$I = \int_{\underline{\theta}}^{\overline{\theta}} H(q(\theta), \theta) f(\theta) d\theta$$

where

$$H(q, \theta) = u(q, \theta) - C(q) - \frac{\partial u}{\partial \theta}(q, \theta)\frac{1}{h(\theta)}$$

The function $H(q(\theta), \theta)$ is the *virtual surplus*. It consists of two terms. The first term,

$$u(q(\theta), \theta) - C(q(\theta))$$

is the first-best social surplus,[26] namely the sum of the utilities of the Principal and the type θ Agent. The second term, $-v'(\theta)/h(\theta)$, therefore measures the impact of the incentive problem on the social surplus. This term originates in the necessity of keeping the informational rent $v(\theta)$ increasing. That is, type θ's allocation is increased, then so is his informational rent, and to maintain incentive compatibility, the Principal must also increase the rents of all types $\theta' > \theta$ who are in proportion $1 - F(\theta)$.

We still need to take into account the second-order incentive constraint

$$\frac{dq}{d\theta}(\theta) \geq 0$$

The simplest way to proceed is to neglect this constraint in a first attempt. The (presumed) solution then is obtained by maximizing the integrand of I in every point, whence

---

25. Fubini's theorem states that if f is integrable on $[a, b] \times [c, d]$, then

$$\int_a^b \int_c^d f(x, y) dx dy = \int_a^b \left(\int_c^d f(x, y) dy \right) dx = \int_c^d \left(\int_a^b f(x, y) dx \right) dy$$

26. It is appropriate to speak of surplus here because the transfers have a constant marginal utility equal to one for both Principal and Agent.

$$\frac{\partial H}{\partial q}(q^*(\theta), \theta) = 0$$

Writing this equation in full, we have

$$\frac{\partial u}{\partial q}(q^*(\theta), \theta) = C'(q^*(\theta)) + \frac{\partial^2 u}{\partial q \partial \theta}(q^*(\theta), \theta)\frac{1}{h(\theta)}$$

Note that the left-hand side of this equation has the dimension of a price; it is in fact just the inverse demand function of Agent θ. Since we have assumed that the cross-derivative is positive, this equation tells us that price is greater than marginal cost. The difference between them is the source of the informational rent, and this difference represents the deviation from the first-best.

The Separating Optimum.
If the function q^* is nondecreasing, it is an optimum. We can say that types are separated and that revelation is then perfect, as shown in figure 2.5.

Higher types θ have a larger allocation q, and they pay more for it. Note that it is often possible to make assumptions that guarantee the separation result. If, for instance, $u(q, \theta) = \theta q$ and C is convex, then it is easily varified that assuming the hazard rate h to be nondecreasing is sufficient to imply that q^* is increasing. The literature often resorts to such an assumption because it is satisfied by many classic probability distributions.

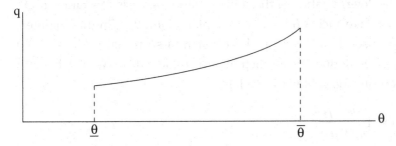

Figure 2.5
A separating optimum

It is hard to say much about the shape of the tariff $t(q)$ in general. The reader is referred to exercise 2.4 to prove that $t(q)$ is convex if $u(q, \theta)$ is linear. As Rogerson (1987) has shown, such a convex $t(q)$ can be approximated by a menu of linear tariffs.

The Bunching Optimum.

If the function q^* happens to be decreasing on a subinterval, it cannot be the solution. It is then necessary to take into account the constraint that q should be nondecreasing, which means resorting to optimal control theory. Since I do not expect optimal control theory to be a prerequisite to understanding the discussions in this book, I give a self-contained analysis below, using only elementary concepts. Readers who prefer a more direct treatment should consult Laffont (1989, 10) and Kamien-Schwartz (1981), for example, for the basics of optimal control theory.

First, note that the solution will consist of subintervals in which q is increasing and subintervals in which it is constant. Take a subinterval $[\theta_1, \theta_2]$ in which q is increasing and $\partial H / \partial q$ is positive. We then add a positive infinitesimal function $dq(\theta)$ to $q(\theta)$ in that subinterval so that $dq(\theta_1) = dq(\theta_2) = 0$ and $q + dq$ stays increasing. This clearly increases H on $[\theta_1, \theta_2]$ and so improves the objective of the Principal. A similar argument applies when $\partial H / \partial q$ is negative on a subinterval where q is increasing. Thus, whenever q is increasing, the solution must satisfy $\partial H / \partial q = 0$, which is just to say that it must coincide with q^*.

The determination of the subintervals where q is constant is trickier. We take such a (maximal) subinterval $[\theta_1, \theta_2]$. On this subinterval the solution must equal a constant $\tilde{q}$ such that $q^*(\theta_1) = q^*(\theta_2) = \tilde{q}$. This defines two functions $\theta_1(\tilde{q})$ and $\theta_2(\tilde{q})$. We just have to determine the value of $\tilde{q}$. We let

$$F(q) = \int_{\theta_1(q)}^{\theta_2(q)} \frac{\partial H}{\partial q}(q, \theta) d\theta$$

and assume that $F(\tilde{q}) > 0$. Then we add to the solution an infinitesimal positive constant on $[\theta_1, \theta_2]$ (and afterward, a smaller, decreasing amount on $[\theta_2, \theta_2 + \varepsilon]$, where $q^*(\theta_2 + \varepsilon) = \tilde{q} + dq$). The Principal's objective will be unchanged on $[\theta_2, \theta_2 + \varepsilon]$, since $\partial H/\partial q = 0$ there by assumption. However, the objective will increase by $F(\tilde{q})dq$ on $[\theta_1, \theta_2]$. This, and a similar reasoning when $F(\tilde{q}) < 0$, prove that we must have $F(\tilde{q}) = 0$. Because $\partial H/\partial q = 0$ in θ_1 and θ_2, we can easily write the derivative of F as

$$F'(q) = \int_{\theta_1(q)}^{\theta_2(q)} \frac{\partial^2 H}{\partial q^2}(q, \theta)d\theta$$

Thus, if we make the reasonable assumption that the virtual surplus is concave in q,[27] $\partial^2 H/\partial q^2$ will be negative and therefore F will be decreasing. This implies that if there is a $\tilde{q}$ such that $F(\tilde{q}) = 0$, then it is unique, and this completes our characterization of the solution.

The solution in this more complicated case is depicted in figure 2.6. In sum, we speak of *bunching* or pooling of types on the subintervals where q is constant, and there is less than perfect revelation. Obviously all the types $\theta \in [\theta_1, \theta_2]$ pay the same transfer t for their constant allocation.

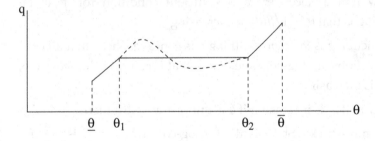

Figure 2.6
An optimum with bunching

---

27. We assume, for instance, that u is concave in q, C is convex and $\partial^2 u/\partial q^2$ increases in θ.

Exercises

Exercise 2.1

Assume that there are n types of consumers in the wine-selling example of section 2.2 and that $\theta_1 < \ldots < \theta_n$. Their respective prior probabilities are $\pi_1, \ldots, \pi_n$, with $\sum_{i=1}^n \pi_i = 1$. Show that the only binding constraints are the downward adjacent incentive constraints

$$\theta_i q_i - t_i \geq \theta_i q_{i-1} - t_{i-1}$$

for $i = 2, \ldots, n$ and the individual rationality constraint of the lowest type

$$\theta_1 q_1 - t_1 \geq 0$$

Exercise 2.2

In the context of section 2.3.2, assume that $u(q, \theta) = \theta q$ and C is convex.

1. Show that a necessary and sufficient condition for q^* to be increasing is that $\theta - 1/h(\theta)$ be increasing.

2. A function g is *log-concave* iff $\log g$ is concave. Show that all concave functions are log-concave. Show that if $(1 - F)$ is log-concave, then q^* is increasing.

3. Show that q^* is increasing if θ is uniformly distributed.

4. A bit more tricky: Show that if f is log-concave, then so is $(1 - F)$.

5. Conclude that q^* is increasing if θ is normally distributed.

Exercise 2.3 (difficult)

My characterization of the bunching optimum in section 2.3.2 implies a hidden assumption: bunching does not occur "at the bottom" (on some interval $[\underline{\theta}, \theta_1]$) nor "at the top" (on some interval $[\theta_2, \overline{\theta}]$). Modify the proof so that it covers these two cases as well.

Exercise 2.4

Denote $t(q)$ the optimal tariff in the continuous-type model of section 2.3 and $\theta(q)$ the inverse function to the optimal $q(\theta)$.

1. Prove that $t'(q) = \dfrac{\partial u}{\partial q}(q, \theta(q))$.

2. Assume that $u(q, \theta)$ is linear in q; prove that $t(q)$ is convex.

Exercise 2.5

Let us study the sufficient conditions for the optimal mechanism to be deterministic in the continuous-type model of section 2.3. Let the Agent's utility function be $u(q, \theta) - t$ and the Principal's utility function be $t - C(q)$. We assume that u is increasing in θ and has a positive cross-derivative, and that C is increasing and convex in q.

Denote by $(Q(\theta), T(\theta))$ a stochastic mechanism that is a lottery from which the (q, t) pair is drawn after the Agent announces his type.

1. Rewrite the arguments of section 2.3 to show that the $Q(\theta)$ in the optimal stochastic mechanism maximizes

$$I = \int_{\underline{\theta}}^{\overline{\theta}} EH(q(\theta), \theta)f(\theta)d\theta$$

under the second-order incentive constraint that

$$E\frac{\partial^2 u}{\partial q \partial \theta}(Q(\theta), \theta)\frac{dQ}{d\theta}(\theta) \geq 0$$

2. Assume that $EQ'(\theta) \geq 0$ everywhere. Let $q^e = EQ$. Use Jensen's inequality to show that if $\dfrac{\partial u}{\partial \theta}$ is convex in q, then the deterministic

mechanism schedule q^e satisfies the incentive constraint and improves the objective I.

3. Assume that $u(q, \theta) = q\theta$. Show that the optimal mechanism is deterministic.

References

Guesnerie, R., and J.-J. Laffont. 1984. A complete solution to a class of principal-agent problems with an application to the control of a self-managed firm. *Journal of Public Economics.* 25:329–69.

Kamien, M., and N. Schwartz. 1981. *Dynamic Optimization: The Calculus of Variations and Optimal Control in Economics and Management.* Amsterdam: North-Holland.

Laffont, J.-J. 1989. *The Economics of Uncertainty and Information.* Cambridge: MIT Press.

Maskin, E., and J. Riley. 1984. Monopoly with incomplete information. *Rand Journal of Economics* 15:171–96.

Milgrom, P., and C. Shannon. 1994. Monotone comparative statics. *Econometrica* 62:157–80.

Moore, J. 1988. Contracts between two parties with private information. *Review of Economic Studies* 55:49–70.

Mussa, M., and S. Rosen. 1978. Monopoly and product quality. *Journal of Economic Theory* 18:301–17.

Palfrey, T. 2002. Implementation theory. In *Handbook of Game Theory*, vol. 3, R. Aumann and S. Hart, eds. Amsterdam: North-Holland.

Rogerson, W. 1987. On the optimality of menus of linear contracts. Mimeo. Northwestern University.

Salanié, B. 2000. *The Microeconomics of Market Failures.* Cambridge: MIT Press.

Stiglitz, J., and A. Weiss. 1981. Credit rationing in markets with imperfect information. *American Economic Review* 71:393–410.

3

Adverse Selection:
Examples and Extensions

This chapter shows how the theory presented in chapter 2 can be applied to various economic problems. It also presents some of its main extensions.

3.1 Examples of Applications

3.1.1 Regulating a Firm

In modern economies much of production is carried out by firms that are natural monopolies[1] in their industries. This is arguably the case in the energy sector and the transportation sector, for instance. The government must, however, regulate these firms so that they do not behave as monopolies, be they public or private. The big difficulty is that regulators typically do not know all the characteristics of the firm. A lot of literature has therefore focused, since the seminal paper

---

1. For the sake of this discussion, just define a natural monopoly as a firm with subadditive costs:

$$\forall n, \forall (q_1, \ldots, q_n), \quad C\left(\sum_{i=1}^{n} q_i\right) < \sum_{i=1}^{n} C(q_i)$$

so that for purely technical reasons, it is socially efficient to set up the firm as a monopoly. Natural monopolies are connected with the presence of strong increasing returns and are often said to arise in industries with large fixed costs due to the importance of infrastructures, such as utilities and transportation.

by Baron-Myerson (1982), on the case where the firm is better informed of its costs than the regulator.

Let us take a firm that produces a marketed good for which demand is given by an inverse demand function $P(q)$. The cost of producing q units of the good is $C(q, \theta)$. The parameter θ is private information of the firm; its production, however, is observable. The firm is regulated by a public agency that gives it transfers t conditional on its production level. The objective of the regulator is to maximize social surplus, a weighted sum of the firm's profit $(t + P(q)q - C(q, \theta))$ and consumer surplus $(S(q) - P(q)q - t)$, where

$$S(q) = \int_0^q P(c)dc$$

The weights given to consumer surplus and profit depend on the regulator's redistributive objectives and are summed up in a coefficient k: one dollar of profit is socially worth as much as k dollars of consumer surplus. Moreover public transfers involve direct costs (e.g., the cost of tax collection) and economic distortions (since transfers are typically not lump sum) that jointly define the opportunity cost of public funds. It is therefore reasonable to assume that any transfer t occasions a social cost λt. The social surplus in this case is

$$W = k(t + P(q)q - C(q, \theta)) + S(q) - P(q)q - t - \lambda t$$

The regulator must find a direct truthful mechanism $(q(\theta), t(\theta))$ that maximizes the expectation of W (taken over all possible cost parameters θ) while giving each type of firm a nonnegative profit.

Our model differs from the standard model in that W depends on θ through the Agent's utility function. However, our techniques to solve it and the qualitative results we obtain are quite similar. So we will not attempt to solve the model here. The interested reader should consult the survey by Caillaud-Guesnerie-Rey-Tirole (1988) or the useful perspective given by Laffont (1994).

It should be noted here that Laffont-Tirole (1986) introduced a somewhat different model to analyze regulation. Think of an indivisible project, such as a railway network, run by a firm for the government. The project has gross value S. The firm's cost $C = \beta - e$ depend on both an efficiency parameter β and an effort level e, both of which are unobserved by the regulator, while the costs are observed. Effort has a cost $\psi(e)$ for the firm; ψ is assumed to be increasing and convex. If the government pays t to the firm, then its profit is $(t - C - \psi(e))$ and the government gets $(S - (1 + \lambda)t)$, where λ again measures the opportunity cost of public funds. Thus (unweighted) social welfare is

$$(S - (1 + \lambda)t) + (t - C - \psi(e)) = S - C - \psi(e) - \lambda t$$

The first-best is achieved in this model when the government can observe both C and β, and therefore also $e = \beta - C$. Then the government leaves zero rent to the firm: $t = C + \psi(e)$, and it orders the firm to put on effort e^* given by $\psi'(e^*) = 1$.

In the more realistic second-best, the government only has a prior (f, F) on $\beta \in [\underline{\beta}, \overline{\beta}]$. Since it observes C and decides to transfer t to the firm, it looks for the optimal direct revealing mechanism $(t(\beta), C(\beta))$. As in chapter 2, define $v(\beta)$ to be the rent the firm of type β obtains by truthfully announcing its type; then with a revealing mechanism we have

$$v(\beta) = \max_{\hat{\beta}} (t(\hat{\beta}) - C(\hat{\beta}) - \psi(\beta - C(\hat{\beta})))$$

as the firm of type β must incur effort $\beta - C(\hat{\beta})$ in order to reach cost $C(\hat{\beta})$. By the envelope theorem, we obtain

$$v'(\beta) = -\psi'(\beta - C(\beta))$$

A first consequence of this formula is that v is a decreasing function of β. Since it must be nonnegative everywhere to fulfill the individual rationality constraint, the government will fix $v(\overline{\beta}) = 0$: as always, the bad type has zero rent (remember that costs increase in β). Thus we have by integrating

$$v(\beta) = \int_\beta^{\bar{\beta}} \psi'(u - C(u))du$$

We can rewrite social welfare as

$$S - C - \psi(e) - \lambda t = S - C - \psi(e) - \lambda(v + C + \psi(e))$$
$$= S - \lambda v - (1 + \lambda)(C + \psi(e))$$

and thus the government must choose $C(.)$ in order to maximize

$$\int_{\underline{\beta}}^{\bar{\beta}} \left(S - \lambda \int_\beta^{\bar{\beta}} \psi'(u - C(u))du - (1 + \lambda)(C(\beta) + \psi(\beta - C(\beta))) \right) f(\beta)d\beta$$

This maximization problem can be solved by exactly the same techniques as in section 2.3.2. After integration by parts and pointwise maximization, we obtain (with effort denoted $e(\beta) = \beta - C(\beta)$)

$$\psi'(e(\beta)) = 1 - \frac{\lambda}{1 + \lambda} \frac{F(\beta)}{f(\beta)} \psi''(e(\beta)).$$

Thus effort is suboptimal: $e(\beta) \leq e^*$.

As usual, this optimal contract can be implemented by a nonlinear schedule $t = T(C)$, which can be interpreted here as a cost reimbursement schedule. Exercise 3.6 asks you to prove that under reasonable conditions, this function T is convex. Thus we can use Rogerson's 1987 result (quoted in footnote 12 of chapter 2); as Laffont-Tirole (1986) showed, the optimal incentive scheme can be implemented by offering the firm a menu of linear schemes $t = a + bC$, where there are as many (appropriately chosen) (a, b) pairs as there are efficiency parameters. The slope b of a scheme can be interpreted as its incentive power. The most efficient firms $(\beta = \underline{\beta})$ choose a fixed-price contract (a linear scheme with zero b) and provide the first-best effort e^*; less efficient firms choose a linear scheme with a higher b and make less effort. Thus the solution prescribes *price-cap* contracts only for the most efficient firms; the less efficient a firm is, the more its contract will look like a *cost-plus* contract. The bible in this field, the book by Laffont-Tirole (1993), is essentially based on this model, and uses it to study many important questions that are beyond the scope of this text.

3.1.2   Optimal Taxation

Consider an economy populated by consumers-producers indexed by a parameter θ distributed according to a probability distribution function f on $[\underline{\theta}, \overline{\theta}]$; all individuals have the same utility function

$$C - v(L)$$

where C denotes consumption, L denotes labor, and v is increasing and convex. An individual of parameter θ has a constant-returns-to-scale production function given by

$$Q = \theta L$$

The productivity of this individual, θ, equals his hourly wage in a competitive labor market.

In an autarkic economy where every agent consumes the product of his own labor, his labor supply is given by

$$v'(L) = \theta$$

and utility, consumption, and labor supply increase with θ, as should be expected.

The government wants to implement an allocation of consumption and labor $(L(\theta), C(\theta))$ that maximizes social welfare. Let us assume this is given by the "weighted utilitarian" criterion

$$\int_{\underline{\theta}}^{\overline{\theta}} \Big(C(\theta) - v(L(\theta)) \Big) g(\theta) d\theta$$

Here g is a probability density that typically differs from f in so far as the government has redistributive objectives. Then the government puts a higher weight on lower θ's, so that $G \geq F$: the cumulative distribution function of g first-order stochastically dominates that of f.

The government must, of course, take into account a scarcity constraint that implies that the economy cannot consume more than it produces:

$$\int_{\underline{\theta}}^{\overline{\theta}} C(\theta) f(\theta) d\theta \leq \int_{\underline{\theta}}^{\overline{\theta}} Q(\theta) f(\theta) d\theta$$

Real-life governments have very little information on individual productivities. The only thing they can do is use taxation systems that rely on observable variables. Labor inputs are typically unobserved by the government; on the other hand, gross income $Q = \theta L$ can reasonably be taken as observable. Thus the government must rely on a tax on income to achieve his goals.

Our model fits almost exactly within the standard model studied in chapter 2: an income tax can be assimilated to a nonlinear tariff $C = Q - T(Q)$, where T is the tax schedule. We just have to find a direct truthful mechanism $(Q(\theta), C(\theta))$ that maximizes social welfare under the scarcity constraint. The only new feature of this model is that there is no individual rationality constraint, since agents cannot refuse taxation (barring tax evasion). On the other hand, we now have a scarcity constraint whose integral form differentiates this model from the standard model and justifies that we solve it here.

First note that the utility of individual θ, rewritten as a function of the variables of the "contract," is

$$C - v\left(\frac{Q}{\theta}\right)$$

Since v is convex, the marginal rate of substitution of Q for C is increasing in θ, so the Spence-Mirrlees condition holds. The results we obtained in section 2.3.1 therefore apply directly (replacing q with Q and t with C); they show that the mechanism $(Q(\theta), C(\theta))$ is incentive compatible if, and only if,

$$\begin{cases} C'(\theta) = v'\left(\dfrac{Q(\theta)}{\theta}\right)\dfrac{Q'(\theta)}{\theta} & (IC_1) \\[2mm] Q'(\theta) \geq 0 & (IC_2) \end{cases}$$

The objective of the government's tax policy is to maximize

$$\int_{\underline{\theta}}^{\bar{\theta}} \left(C(\theta) - v\left(\frac{Q(\theta)}{\theta}\right)\right) g(\theta)d\theta$$

under the scarcity constraint and the first- and second-order incentive constraints. As in section 2.3.2 we can proceed by eliminating one of the two variables, here $C(\theta)$. To do this, we integrate by parts the first-order incentive constraint and get

$$C(\theta) = K + v\left(\frac{Q(\theta)}{\theta}\right) + \int_{\underline{\theta}}^{\theta} v'\left(\frac{Q(t)}{t}\right)\frac{Q(t)}{t^2}dt$$

Now we can go back to the notation $L(\theta) = Q(\theta)/\theta$. The scarcity constraint, which must obviously be an equality, gives us

$$\int_{\underline{\theta}}^{\bar{\theta}} \theta L(\theta)f(\theta)d\theta = K + \int_{\underline{\theta}}^{\bar{\theta}} \left(v(L(\theta)) + \int_{\underline{\theta}}^{\theta} v'(L(t))\frac{L(t)}{t}dt\right)f(\theta)d\theta$$

Using Fubini's theorem (see footnote 25 of chapter 2), we get

$$K = \int_{\underline{\theta}}^{\bar{\theta}} \left((\theta L(\theta) - v(L(\theta))f(\theta) - \frac{L(\theta)}{\theta}v'(L(\theta))(1 - F(\theta))\right)d\theta$$

This completes the elimination of $C(\theta)$. There just remains to maximize the government's objective, which can be simplified because

$$C(\theta) - v(L(\theta)) = K + \int_{\underline{\theta}}^{\bar{\theta}} v'(L(t))\frac{L(t)}{t}dt$$

The simplest approach consists in ignoring, as in section 2.3.2, the second-order constraint $Q'(\theta) \geq 0$ at first. Again, using Fubini's theorem we write the government's objective as

$$K + \int_{\underline{\theta}}^{\bar{\theta}} (1 - G(\theta)) \frac{L(\theta)v'(L(\theta))}{\theta} d\theta$$

Now substituting in the expression of K, we obtain

$$\int_{\underline{\theta}}^{\bar{\theta}} \left((\theta L(\theta) - v(L(\theta)))f(\theta) - (G(\theta) - F(\theta)) \frac{L(\theta)v'(L(\theta))}{\theta} \right) d\theta$$

Note that this integral shows the virtual surplus

$$\theta L(\theta) - v(L(\theta)) - \frac{G(\theta) - F(\theta)}{f(\theta)} \frac{L(\theta)v'(L(\theta))}{\theta}$$

So maximizing the virtual surplus at every point gives

$$\theta - v'(L(\theta)) = \frac{G(\theta) - F(\theta)}{\theta f(\theta)} (v''(L(\theta))L(\theta) + v'(L(\theta)))$$

This optimality condition may seem complicated, but it can be fairly easily interpreted. First, remember that in autarky, labor supply is given by $v'(L) = \theta$. Its elasticity is readily computed; it is

$$\varepsilon = \frac{v'(L)}{Lv''(L)}$$

Second, if the income tax paid is linked to gross income by a differentiable tax schedule $T(Q)$, then to find the labor supply, we maximize $\theta L - T(\theta L) - v(\theta L)$ so that $v'(L) = \theta(1 - T'(Q))$. The optimality condition is consequently written as

$$T' = (1 - T')\left(1 + \frac{1}{\varepsilon}\right)\frac{G - F}{\theta f}$$

but it is best rewritten as the product of three terms:

$$\frac{T'}{1 - T'} = \left(1 + \frac{1}{\varepsilon}\right)\frac{1 - F}{\theta f}\frac{G - F}{1 - F} \qquad (T)$$

Note that the left-hand side of this equation is clearly increasing in the marginal tax rate T'. This tells us that the marginal tax rate depends on the elasticity of labor supply, on the shape of the distribution of productivities, and on the government's redistributive objectives.

Of course, the $Q(\theta) = \theta L(\theta)$ characterized here may decrease over some interval. Where it does, it violates the second-order incentive condition, and the result is a bunching phenomenon: at some interval consumers will get the same allocation (Q, C). Outside this interval the solution coincides with that given by the optimality condition. As a technical aside, it is easily seen that the solution coincides with the autarkic solution at both ends (in $\underline{\theta}$ and $\bar{\theta}$); this is typical of continuous-type models with an integral constraint on a finite range.

Optimal taxation is a very large field, and I cannot do it justice here. The reader can turn to part II of my textbook, Salanié (2003), for a more extensive survey of the theory.

3.1.3 The Insurer as a Monopolist

We will study in this subsection the problem facing an insurer who is a monopolist and serves a population that contains several risk classes.[2] We can assume that all individuals in this population are identical, as far as observable characteristics are concerned. Let us take, for instance, a policy (a contract) that insures against the risk of

---

2. The analysis here is adapted from Stiglitz (1977). It differs from the more famous studies of the insurance market whose firms are assumed to act competitively.

disability a population of forty-year-old males living in Boston who do office work and who have not had heart trouble. The problem is the obvious element of heterogeneity in the target population: each individual knows the state of his health better than the insurer does.[3] If the insurer only designs a policy for the average risk in the population, he may attract mostly only high-risk individuals and incur major losses. This is where the term *adverse selection* comes from. To "hedge against" this possibility, the insurer must therefore consider offering as many different policies as there are risk classes.

More formally, let W denote the initial wealth of each insured Agent. The effect of an accident is to reduce this wealth by an amount d that represents the *pretium doloris*, the discounted loss of wages over the rest of the working life, and so on. An insurance policy, or contract, consists of a premium q paid by the insurees and a reimbursement R that they receive upon incurring a disability due to an accident. The final wealth therefore is

$$W_A = W - d - q + R$$

in the event of a disabling accident and

$$W_N = W - q$$

otherwise. The expected utility of an Agent is

$$U = pu(W_A) + (1 - p)u(W_N)$$

if he belongs to the risk class whose probability of having an accident is p; u is an increasing concave function.

Now suppose that two risk classes coexist in the population: the high risks, whose probability of having an accident is p_H, and the low risks, whose probability is $p_L < p_H$. First note that this model

---

3. Alternatively, there may exist variables that are observable but that law forbids insurers to use in computing the terms of the contract. This is often for ethical reasons.

differs from the standard model in that the reservation utility of an Agent of class i is

$$p_i u(W - d) + (1 - p_i)u(W)$$

This utility depends on the Agent's risk class, which is unknown to the insurer. Also the Agent's utility is not quasi-separable in premium and reimbursement.

A Spence-Mirrlees condition nevertheless holds. The marginal rate of substitution between the premium and the reimbursement is

$$-\frac{\partial U/\partial q}{\partial U/\partial R} = \frac{pu'(W_A) + (1 - p)u'(W_N)}{pu'(W_A)}$$

which is a decreasing function of p. It should therefore be possible to separate the high risks from the low risks by offering them a better coverage in return for a higher premium.

The most important difference from the model of chapter 2 is that this is a common values model, as opposed to the private values model. The profit of the Principal (the insurer) depends on the risk class of the insuree as well as on the contract:

$$\pi = q - pR$$

We will assume that the insurance company is risk-neutral. This assumption is reasonable because shareholders of insurance companies generally have a diversified portfolio. The first-best consists in insuring completely every class of Agents so that their final wealths do not depend on the occurrence of an accident.

The analytical treatment of our model is more complicated than that of the standard model because both reservation utilities and profits are type-dependent. But we can just as effectively study the risks graphically by tracing indifference curves on the plane (W_N, W_A), where the 45-degree line corresponds to complete insurance (since wealth is the same whether or not an accident has happened), and point O, with coordinates $(W, W - d)$, represents the no insurance situation. Our objective is to check that the indifference curves of the insurees are decreasing and convex. The slope of the indifference curve of risk class p is

$$-\frac{1-p}{p}\frac{u'(W_N)}{u'(W_A)}$$

Because the slope of the indifference curve of low risks is steeper than that of high risks, the Spence-Mirrlees condition is confirmed. Correspondingly isoprofit curves are straight lines; the isoprofit line for the given risk class p has the slope

$$-\frac{1-p}{p}$$

and it is tangent to the indifference curve of that class on the complete insurance line. As figure 3.1 shows, utilities increase in when going northeast and profits increase when going southwest.

The second-best optimum is obtained by finding a pair of contracts $C_L = (q_L, R_L)$ and $C_H = (q_H, R_H)$ that maximize the expected

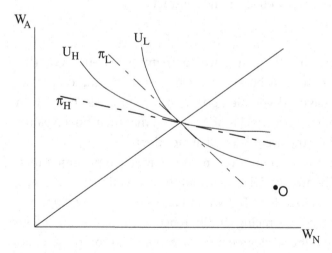

Figure 3.1
The insurance model

profit of the Principal under the usual incentive constraints and that give each class at least as much utility as with no insurance. Again, solving this program analytically is arduous, and most properties of the solution can be obtained graphically.

At least one of the two risk classes must be indifferent between the contract that is designed for it and no insurance; otherwise, the insurer could profitably increase the premia and reduce the reimbursements. We want to observe graphically that C_L can give at least as much utility to the low risks as no insurance so that it can be preferred to no insurance by the high risks; the low risks must then be indifferent between C_L and no insurance.

Again, a little playing with graphic analysis should convince us that C_H gives maximal profits to the insurer when it is located in a point where the indifference curve of the high risks is tangent to the corresponding isoprofit line, and we know that this can only happen on the complete insurance line. We get figure 3.2 where the high risks are completely insured, and again, C_L is designed for low risks and C_H for high risks.

Unlike the low risks, the high risks are completely insured and receive an informational rent,[4] so they are indifferent between C_L and C_H. As in the standard model the graphic analysis leaves one parameter to be determined: the location of C_H on the diagonal, or equivalently the location of C_L on the indifference curve between O and the complete insurance line. It is easy to see that in order to maximize profits, C_L must be closer to O when the proportion of high risks in the population increases. Indeed, beyond a certain proportion of high risks, as Stiglitz (1977) showed, C_L will coincide with O

---

4. Note that in the standard model, one expects the "good" Agent to receive an informational rent. Here it seems natural to define the low risks as the "good" agents, but it is the high risks who get the rent, and so on. This apparent paradox is due to the peculiar features of the insurance problem: here the reservation utilities decrease with the type.

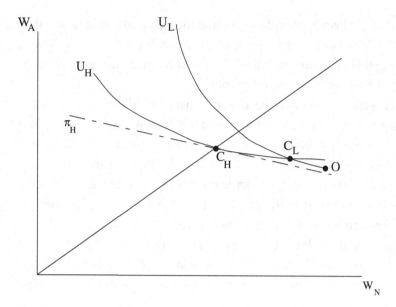

Figure 3.2
The optimal insurance contract

so that the low risks get no insurance: any contract that attracts low risks will also attract the high risks. This is actually the extreme form of adverse selection: Only the high risks can find insurance! Note further that while it is clear from figure 3.2 that the insurer always takes positive profits on the low risks, this is not necessarily the case with the high risks. When there are many low risks in the population, they will get almost complete insurance, and the insurer will make losses on the high risks.[5] In that case the low risks in effect cross-subsidize the high risks. Although C_H causes losses in that configuration, there is nothing unstable about it. The insurer could withdraw C_H, but the high risks could all then buy the contract C_L and create losses on them, drastically depleting the insurer's profits.

---

5. This is not the case illustrated in figure 3.2, since the π_H isoprofit line lies below O.

3.2 Extensions

We briefly study in this section a few main extensions of the Principal–Agent theory introduced in chapter 2. We take a look at competition among Principals or among Agents, risk-averse Agents, taking into account multidimensional characteristics, the presence of asymmetric information on both sides, and type-dependent participation utilities. This section does not give a representative summary of the literature. It reflects my personal biases. Still it should give the reader an idea of recent advances.

3.2.1 Perfect Competition in Contracts

Let us go back to the discrete model of section 2.2. How much profit π_i does the seller make on each type i of consumer? First note that he makes a positive profit on type 1, since

$$\pi_1 = \theta_1 q_1 - C(q_1) = \int_0^{q_1} (\theta_1 - C'(q))dq$$

and $C'(q) < C'(q_1) < \theta_1$ on $[0, q_1]$. Next consider the difference $\pi_2 - \pi_1$, and write it as

$$\pi_2 - \pi_1 = (\theta_2 - \theta_1)q_2 + \int_{q_1}^{q_2} (\theta_2 - C'(q))dq$$

Again, $C'(q) \leq \theta_2$ on $[0, q_2]$, so both terms are positive. The seller can make even more profit on type 2 Agents.[6] Type 2 Agents are therefore more attractive to potential entrants in the wine market. If the Principal's monopoly power were to disappear, an entrant could propose the contract located on B in figure 3.3, capture the sophisticated

---

6. Again, these results are proved here analytically, but they can be obtained easily by just looking at the figures.

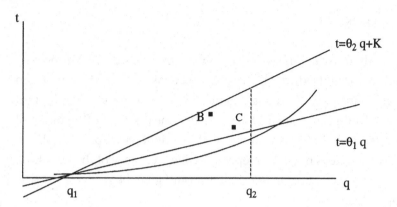

Figure 3.3
Competitive entry

consumers while leaving the frugal consumers to the Principal, and make positive profits.

The Principal who stands to lose a good share of his profits in the event is unlikely to be passive. He can react, for instance, by offering to the sophisticated consumers contract C, which only leaves to the entrant the frugal consumers, but this is not the end of the story. What can be learned about the competitive equilibria?[7]

The Rothschild-Stiglitz Equilibrium
To define a competitive equilibrium, we reach some notion of what makes a competitive configuration stable. The equilibrium concept proposed by Rothschild-Stiglitz (1976) in the context of insurance markets applies generally to all adverse selection models. We will call a "profitable entrant" a contract that makes positive profits if the other existing contracts are left unmodified. A Rothschild-Stiglitz equilibrium is a set of contracts where none takes losses and no additional contract can make profits if the original contracts are left

---

7. Our analysis here is only of free entry equilibria; Champsaur-Rochet (1989) study the duopoly case. Another important hidden assumption of the presentation here that an Agent cannot split his demand between competing Principals.

unchanged. In this sense it is a Nash equilibrium in a game among Principals where the strategies of the players are contracts.

The Irrelevance Result

It may be surprising, but adverse selection does not change the set of competitive equilibria in the model we studied in chapter 2. If we accept perfect competition as a working hypothesis, adverse selection is in fact irrelevant. To see this, first note that when the Agent's characteristic θ is known to the Principals, competition will push their profits down to zero. The only competitive equilibrium with perfect information is therefore one in which the Principals offer a family of contracts $(q^*(\theta), t^*(\theta))$ that solves $\max_{(q,t)}(\theta q - t)$ subject to $t - C(q) \geq 0$. The solution is that given by the first-best quantity $q^*(\theta)$ and $t^*(\theta) = C(q^*(\theta))$ where the whole surplus $S^*(\theta)$ goes to the Agent.

Now suppose that the Principals do not know the Agent's type. I claim that the family of contracts $(q^*(\theta), t^*(\theta))$ is the *unique* Rothschild-Stiglitz equilibrium. Such an equilibrium is easy to prove since $(q^*(\theta), t^*(\theta))$ extracts all the surplus for Agent θ, this is the contract he will choose from the family, which makes it incentive-compatible. Any other contract will give him lower utility, and there is no way an entrant can make a profit by offering a different contract.

It is only slightly harder to prove that no other Rothschild-Stiglitz equilibrium exists. Suppose, on the contrary, that one exists; then some Agent's type θ must be getting less utility than $S^*(\theta)$. Take a small positive ε, and let an entrant propose the contract $(q(\theta, \varepsilon), t(\theta, \varepsilon))$ that solves $\max_{(q,t)}(\theta q - t)$ subject to $t - C(q) \geq \varepsilon$. This contract makes $\varepsilon > 0$ profit on every type that chooses it, and Agent θ chooses it for small enough ε. By continuity, the entrant's contract gets the Agent close to the maximal level of utility $S^*(\theta)$. Thus this is a profitable entrant, which destabilizes the candidate equilibrium.

This general result was proved by Fagart (1996). How can it be reconciled with the famous results of Rothschild and Stiglitz? They started from the insurance model discussed in section 3.1.3 and introduced competition. Their observations were as follows:

• There exists no *pooling* equilibrium in which the two types buy the same contract.

• There can exist only one separating equilibrium, which gives complete insurance to the high risks.

• This separating configuration may not be an equilibrium if the high-risk insurance buyers are relatively few in number.

Their most striking conclusion was that there can exist no competitive equilibrium in insurance markets. However, and as I have already noted in section 3.1.3, the insurance model differs from the standard adverse selection model in several ways. The crucial one is that it has common values: the type of the insuree (his risk) enters the insurers' profit functions. Then the competitive equilibrium with perfect information, which gives full insurance to every Agent at a fair actuarial price, is not incentive compatible and cannot be a Rothschild-Stiglitz equilibrium.

The Rothschild-Stiglitz equilibrium concept has been widely criticized, mainly because it assumes that incumbent firms do not react when an entrant arrives to take a bite out of their profits. Other equilibrium concepts have been proposed to restore equilibrium in competitive insurance markets. They differ according to how they assume the incumbents react to the entry (by withdrawing contracts that start showing losses, by designing new contracts, etc.) and how they describe the entrant's behavior. In our model of chapter 2 private values, a contract makes profits or losses independently of the type of the Agent who buys it. Therefore the irrelevance result holds, no matter how we attempt to alter (within reason) the equilibrium effect.[8]

---

8. The situation is different in insurance markets, since there a contract may make profits when it is bought by low risks and losses when it is bought by high risks.

*3.2.2 Multiple Principals

There are at least two other ways to model competition among (a small number of) Principals. The first one is analyzed in the paper by Champsaur-Rochet (1989), who consider the case of a duopoly. Champsaur and Rochet start from the vertical differentiation model with continuous types studied by Mussa-Rosen (1978). In that model a monopoly chooses to offer a range of qualities to different buyer types. Champsaur and Rochet show that when two firms compete in prices and qualities, it is optimal for them to offer two distinct ranges of qualities so that one firm can specialize in the higher range and the other in the lower range.

The second possible model of competition among Principals is that of an Agent who faces two or more Principals, each offering a direct truthful mechanism. The Agent must choose his announcements so as to maximize his utility while the Principals play a Nash equilibrium: each Principal chooses the best contract given the choices offered by the other Principals. This model is called a *common agency* model, or a *multiprincipals* model. Its general study was started by Martimort (1992) and Stole (1990), and it has proved useful in many areas of economics, mainly in studies of political economy and imperfect competition.

As can be expected, the outcomes of this model differ greatly depending on whether the activities regulated by the Principals are complements or substitutes in the Agent's utility function. Take the simple case where the Agent is a firm and two Principals, respectively, control its production and its pollution level. In this case the two activities are complements and noncooperative behavior of the Principals creates distortions and reduces the Agent's rent. A polar case would be where two activities are substitutes, such as when the Agent is a multinational and the Principals are two governments that tax its production in two different countries. Then the noncooperative behavior of the Principals both reduces distortions and increases the Agent's rent.

While these results are intuitive, the formal analysis of the multi-principals model is complex. Consider an Agent who trades quantities q_1 and q_2 with two Principals, with accompanying transfers t_1 and t_2. The Agent has utility function $u(q_1, q_2, \theta) - t_1 - t_2$ and Principal $i = 1, 2$ has utility $t_i - C(q_i)$. We assume that the cross-derivatives $u''_{\theta q_1}$ and $u''_{\theta q_2}$ are positive, and the Agent's type is continuously distributed over $[\underline{\theta}, \overline{\theta}]$.

In the case where information is symmetric (θ is known to both Principals before the contract is signed), it is easy to see that the optimal contract implements the same quantities whether or not the Principals collude. In the more interesting case where the Principals do not observe θ but share a common prior about its value, collusion can be analyzed much as the general model in section 2.3. The revelation principle applies to the contract $(q_1(\theta), q_2(\theta), t(\theta))$, where t is the transfer from the Agent to the colluding Principals. Exercise 3.5 shows that the optimal quantity schedules are given by the two equations for $i = 1, 2$:

$$u'_{q_i}(q_1(\theta), q_2(\theta), \theta) = C'(q_i(\theta)) + \frac{1 - F(\theta)}{f(\theta)} u''_{\theta q_i}(q_1(\theta), q_2(\theta), \theta) \quad \text{(CP)}$$

As usual, both quantities are distorted downward.

The noncooperative case when the two Principals play a Nash equilibrium in contracts is more complex, and it is probably the most complicated formal analysis you will find in this book. A first difficulty is that the revelation principle does not apply: since, in general, the cross-derivative $u''_{q_1 q_2}$ is nonzero, the response by the Agent to a contract from Principal 1 depends on the contract offered by Principal 2. Thus the Principals can do better than employ direct revealing mechanisms. To see this, imagine that a general game in mechanisms played by the two Principals implements an equilibrium $(q_1(\theta), q_2(\theta), t_1(\theta), t_2(\theta))$. For any θ then, it must be that both $u(q_1(s), q_2(\theta), \theta) - t_1(s)$ and $u(q_1(\theta), q_2(s), \theta) - t_2(s)$ are maximal in $s = \theta$. But when $u''_{q_1 q_2}$ is nonzero, it does not follow that $u(q_1(s), q_2(s'), \theta) - t_1(s) - t_2(s')$ is maximal in $s = s' = \theta$.

Interestingly, Martimort-Stole (2002) show that it is still possible to restrict the game to competition in nonlinear tariffs in which Principals $i = 1, 2$ simultaneously offer a schedule $T_i(q_i)$ and the Agent picks two quantities (q_1, q_2) that maximize his utility. Let us therefore take T_2 as given and look at the interaction between the Agent and Principal 1. For simplicity, we will neglect the many technical difficulties that crop up in the mathematics and concentrate on the main argument. Note first that since Principal 2 offered T_2, the Agent's utility function in his interaction with Principal 1 is

$$U^1(q_1, \theta; T_2) = \max_{q_2} (u(q_1, q_2, \theta) - T_2(q_2)) \qquad (P_2)$$

Let $Q_2(q_1, \theta; T_2)$ denote the value of q_2 at the optimum of this program. One difficulty that is more than technical is that the cross-derivative of U^1 in (q_1, θ) may not have a constant sign, jeopardizing any hope of using a Spence-Mirrlees condition to simplify the analysis of the incentive problem between Principal 1 and the Agent. By the envelope theorem applied to (P_2), we have

$$\frac{\partial U^1}{\partial \theta}(q_1, q_2, \theta) = \frac{\partial u}{\partial \theta}(q_1, Q_2(q_1, \theta; T_2), \theta)$$

from which we can compute

$$\frac{\partial^2 U^1}{\partial q_1 \partial \theta} = u''_{q_1 \theta} + u''_{q_2 \theta} \frac{\partial Q_2}{\partial q_1}$$

However, the implicit function theorem shows that the derivative of Q_2 with respect to q_1 has the sign of $u''_{q_1 q_2}$, which we left unrestricted. When $u''_{q_1 q_2}$ is negative (the case of substitutes), strange things can happen. We omit this first major hurdle.

Note that given T_2, the incentive problem between Principal 1 and the Agent with utility function U^1 can be solved by the standard techniques of section 2.3. It implements a quantity schedule q_1 that solves

$$\frac{\partial U^1}{\partial q_1}(q_1(\theta), \theta; T_2) = C'(q_1(\theta)) + \frac{1 - F(\theta)}{f(\theta)} \frac{\partial^2 U^1}{\partial q_1 \partial \theta}(q_1(\theta), \theta; T_2) \qquad (D)$$

This is not elegant, as it relies on the derivative of the "reduced form" utility function U^1. Already we know from the envelope theorem applied to (P_2) that

$$\frac{\partial U^1}{\partial q_1}(q_1, \theta; T_2) = u'_{q_1}(q_1, Q_2(q_1, \theta; T_2), \theta)$$

We already computed the cross-derivative of U^1 in (q_1, θ). Further, from the implicit function theorem applied to (P_2), we have

$$\frac{\partial Q_2}{\partial q_1} = \frac{u''_{q_1 q_2}}{T''_2 - u''_{q_2 q_2}}$$

We just have to eliminate T''_2. This is done by denoting $(q_1(\theta), q_2(\theta))$ the quantity schedules in equilibrium and rewriting the first-order condition for (P_2) as $u'_{q_2}(q_1(\theta), q_2(\theta), \theta) = T'_2(q_2(\theta))$. Differentiating this identity in θ, we get

$$T''_2 - u''_{q_2 q_2} = \frac{u''_{q_2 \theta} + u''_{q_1 q_2} q'_1}{q'_2}$$

We can substitute in (D) and eventually obtain a differential equation for the two unknown functions $(q_1(\theta), q_2(\theta))$:

$$u'_{q_1}(q_1(\theta), q_2(\theta), \theta) = C'(q_1(\theta)) + \frac{1 - F(\theta)}{f(\theta)} \left(u''_{q_1 \theta} + u''_{q_2 \theta} \frac{u''_{q_1 q_2} q'_2}{u''_{q_2 \theta} + u''_{q_1 q_2} q'_1} \right)$$

Solving the incentive problem between the Agent and Principal 2 will give us another differential equation.

A study of this system can reveal some interesting facts. Note, for instance, that $1 - F(\theta)$ is zero in $\underline{\theta}$, so the differential system has a singularity there. The form of the differential equations themselves suggests some properties of their solutions. For instance, the only difference from the cooperative case of colluding Principals is where $u''_{q_1 q_2} \neq 0$; compare equation (CP). Now take the case where q_1 and q_2 are complements in the Agent's utility function ($u''_{q_1 q_2} > 0$); the added positive term serves to increase the distortion downward of q_1, which occurs in the relationship between an Agent and a single Principal. It can be shown rigorously that this conclusion holds in general.

3.2.3 The Theory of Auctions

The previous subsection covered competition among Principals. The theory of auctions belongs to the dual topic of competition among Agents. I will not try to cover here such a vast field;[9] I will only present one of the simplest models of auctions.

Auctions are used by sellers who want to sell one or several objects to agents whose valuations for the good are hidden from them; thus they can be seen as a device to extract information from the bidders. Auctions are traditionally classified into two groups: *independent private values auctions* and *common value auctions*. The sale of a durable good such as a painting or a house is the typical example of an independent private values auction: the value of the good for each potential buyer is known only to himself, and these values are statistically independent. The situation is quite different in a common values auction: the value of the good is the same for each

---

9. Among the several good recent books on auctions, see Klemperer (2004), Krishna (2002), and Milgrom (2004).

potential buyer, but neither the buyer nor the seller fully knows this value; each buyer only observes a signal of his reservation value. The sale of the rights to drill in an oil tract is the most often quoted example. Note that these two types of auctions can actually be studied together inside a more general setup (Milgrom-Weber 1982).

Auctions are one of the oldest and most widely used economic mechanisms. They are still intensively used for traditional purposes such as the selling of timber, the pricing of Treasury bonds in the United States, and the selection of firms to operate public utilities. More recent, multibillion dollar examples are the spectrum auction organized by the Federal Communications Commission in 1994 in the United States and the 2000 UMTS auctions in various European countries.

The most usual mechanisms are[10]

• the ascending auction (*English auction*), where bidders raise the price until only one of them remains;

• the descending auction (*Dutch auction*), where an auctioneer quotes decreasing prices until a bidder claims the good;

• sealed bid type of auctions where bidders submit sealed bids and the winner is the bidder who quoted the highest bid. In the *first-price sealed bid auction* the winner pays the sum he quoted, and in the *second-price sealed bid auction* the winner pays the value of the second-highest bid.

We will study here only the first-price sealed bid in an independent private values auction. We have for this auction n potential buyers whose valuation of the good is drawn from a continuous distribution of probability distribution function f and of cumulative

10. There are many other, more or less exotic auctions; for example, see Riley-Samuelson (1981).

distribution function F on $[\underline{\theta}, \overline{\theta}]$. We denote by $(\theta_1, ..., \theta_n)$ the valuations of the n buyers and by $(\theta_{(1)}, ..., \theta_{(n)})$ the corresponding *order statistics*: $\theta_{(1)}$ is the highest of all θ_i, $\theta_{(2)}$ the second-highest, and so on.

We are interested in symmetric equilibria with increasing bids. It can be shown that there exists no other equilibrium (in this very simple setting) if the bids are bounded below, for example, by 0. So we assume that the buyers $2, ..., n$ submit bids $(b_2, ..., b_n)$ that are linked to their respective valuations through an increasing function B where $b_i = B(\theta_i)$. Buyer 1 will win the auctioned good if and only if he submits a higher bid, namely if and only if

$$\forall i = 2, ..., n, \quad b_1 \geq B(\theta_i)$$

This happens with probability

$$\Pr\left(\forall i = 2, ..., n, \theta_i \leq B^{-1}(b_1)\right) = F(B^{-1}(b_1))^{n-1}$$

Buyer 1 gets a surplus $(\theta_1 - b_1)$. Suppose that buyers are risk-neutral; then the expected utility of buyer 1 is

$$(\theta_1 - b_1)F(B^{-1}(b_1))^{n-1}$$

Buyer 1 must maximize this expression in b_1. We let $\pi_1(\theta_1)$ denote the value of the optimum:

$$\pi_1(\theta_1) = \max_{b_1}\left((\theta_1 - b_1)F(B^{-1}(b_1))^{n-1}\right)$$

By the envelope theorem, we get

$$\frac{d\pi_1}{d\theta_1}(\theta_1) = F(B^{-1}(b_1))^{n-1}$$

To find the symmetric Nash equilibria, in which all bidders adopt the same increasing strategy B, we must have $b_1 = B(\theta_1)$, whence

$$\frac{d\pi_1}{d\theta_1}(\theta_1) = F(\theta_1)^{n-1} \qquad (D)$$

The expected utility of a buyer with the lowest possible valuation must be zero:[11] $\pi_1(\underline{\theta}) = 0$. Therefore, after integrating the differential equation (D), we obtain

$$\pi_1(\theta_1) = \int_{\underline{\theta}}^{\theta_1} F(\theta)^{n-1} d\theta$$

Note that $\pi_1(\theta_1)$ is the informational rent of the buyer of valuation θ_1. Thus we have again a property we obtained in the previous chapter: the informational rent of the buyer with the lowest possible valuation $\underline{\theta}$ is zero, and that of the other buyers is positive and increases with their type.

Since

$$\pi_1(\theta_1) = (\theta_1 - B(\theta_1))F(\theta_1)^{n-1}$$

we finally get the equilibrium strategy

$$B(\theta_1) = \theta_1 - \frac{\int_{\underline{\theta}}^{\theta_1} F(\theta)^{n-1} d\theta}{F(\theta_1)^{n-1}}$$

which indeed is an increasing function, as we assumed earlier.

The equilibrium therefore is separating. In equilibrium, bidders submit a bid that is lower than their valuation for the good: They *shade* their bid. In order to win, it is sufficient to submit a bid that is just higher than the second-highest bid; therefore the best strategy is to guess that bid and to just slightly better it. We can confirm this intuition by integrating by parts

$$\int_{\underline{\theta}}^{\theta_1} F(\theta)^{n-1} d\theta = \theta_1 F(\theta_1)^{n-1} - \int_{\underline{\theta}}^{\theta_1} (n-1)\theta F(\theta)^{n-2} f(\theta) d\theta$$

We can write the successful bid function B as

11. Since the function B is increasing, this buyer indeed wins with zero probability.

$$B(\theta_1) = \frac{\int_{\underline{\theta}}^{\theta_1} (n - 1)\theta F(\theta)^{n-2} f(\theta) d\theta}{F(\theta_1)^{n-1}}$$

It is easy to check that $(n - 1)F(\theta)^{n-2}f(\theta)/F(\theta_1)^{n-1}$ is the probability distribution function of the conditional distribution of $\theta_{(2)}$ given that $\theta_{(1)} = \theta_1$. We then have

$$B(\theta_1) = E(\theta_{(2)} | \theta_{(1)} = \theta_1)$$

This shows that every potential buyer assumes he will win and computes his bid by estimating the second-highest valuation.

Now, to get the seller's point of view, we integrate once more to obtain the expectation of the winning bid:

$$EB(\theta_{(1)}) = E\theta_{(2)}$$

This equality actually has two consequences. First, because $\theta_{(2)}$ is an increasing function of the number of potential buyers n, the valuations will spread as the bidders become more numerous. The competition between buyers that comprises the auction mechanism allows the seller to extract an expected revenue $EB(\theta_{(1)})$ that increases with the number of bidders. If that number goes to infinity, $\theta_{(2)}$ converges to the highest possible valuation $\bar{\theta}$, and in the limit the appropriates the entire surplus.

Second, the equation that gives the seller's expected revenue happens to hold for all four independent private values auction mechanisms listed earlier, the seller's expected revenue does not depend on the auction mechanism he uses where (as we assumed) agents are risk-neutral. The proof of this property, which is often called the *revenue equivalence theorem*, is due to Vickrey (1961). The equivalence of revenue implies that the reason a seller decides on a particular auction must be considered in a more general model than that presented here. The introduction of risk-averse buyers or collusive strategies, for instance, throws off the revenue equivalence theorem.

Even in the symmetric, independent private values setting of our example, the choice of an optimal auction can generate some argument. There are two views on studying the optimality of an auction. First, there is the socially efficient auction, one that maximizes social surplus. Since the latter is just $(\theta_i - \theta_0)$ when the seller's valuation for the good is θ_0 and he sells to buyer i, a socially efficient auction is just one that sells the good to the buyer with the highest valuation.[12] Thus the first-price sealed-bid auction is socially efficient. Second, there is the interest of the seller himself in designing an auction that will give him the highest expected utility. The literature has focused on this more difficult topic, and by "optimal," it is meant "optimal for the seller," as we do so here. The optimal auction turns out to be socially efficient when buyers are symmetric, meaning that their valuations are drawn from the same probability distribution. However, this is not true when buyers are asymmetric.[13]

Finding the optimal auction is equivalent to finding the optimal direct truthful mechanism $(x_i(\theta), t_i(\theta))_{i=1,\dots,n}$, where x_i is the probability that buyer i gets the good, t_i is his expected payment, and θ is the n-uple of valuations. So we will first focus, as did Riley-Samuelson (1981), on the more restricted question of the optimal reserve price the seller must fix in the first-price sealed-bid auction.

Assume therefore that before the auction starts, the seller announces that he will not award the good if all bids are lower than some reserve price b_r. From the characterization of the equilibrium bids above, it is easy to see that the successful bid is now written as

$$B(\theta_1) = \theta_1 - \frac{\int_{b_r}^{\theta_1} F(\theta)^{n-1} d\theta}{F(\theta_1)^{n-1}}$$

---

12. Or leaves it to the seller if $\theta_0 > \theta_{(1)}$.
13. The optimal auction takes into account the virtual valuations of buyers, which depend on the hazard rates of the probability distributions. With asymmetric buyers it is easy to see that comparing virtual valuations is not equivalent to comparing valuations.

for $\theta_1 \geq b_r$ (underbids occur if $\theta_1 < b_r$). Since $B(b_r) = b_r$, this implies that the good will be sold only if the highest valuation exceeds b_r. Now let θ_0 be the seller's valuation for the good. Exercise 3.4 asks you to show that the optimal reserve price is given by

$$b_r - \frac{1 - F(b_r)}{f(b_r)} = \theta_0$$

The left-hand side of this equation is called the *virtual valuation* due to the buyer's valuation b_r, just as we defined a virtual surplus in chapter 2. If the hazard rate of F is nondecreasing, then the virtual valuation rises with the buyer's valuation, and there is a unique solution b_r. Note that if the optimal b_r is larger than the seller's valuation, there may be unrealized gains from trade: cases where the highest valuation of the buyers is larger than θ_0 and yet smaller than b_r, so the good remains unsold.

Now let us recall our original question. What is an optimal auction if an auction can take different forms? Myerson (1981) shows that the answer is remarkably simple: An auction with an optimally set reserve price is optimal. There is no gain for the seller in choosing complicated auction mechanisms. Myerson's paper is technically demanding, however, and Bulow-Roberts (1989) gives a much simpler introduction to optimal auctions.

Before we leave the domain of auctions, we should include a surprising result by Cremer-McLean (1988). In our discussion above the seller is allowed to appropriate most of the surplus when the number of bidders is large. Suppose that we change one small detail in the model of independent private values: we now assume that the valuations of the bidders are correlated. Then, as Cremer-McLean show, the seller can generically extract all the surplus, even when only two bidders are involved, and no matter how small the correlation is of the private values of the bidders.

This development in auction theory is a consequence of a general result of Riordan-Sappington (1985). It takes us back to our standard adverse selection model with one Principal and one Agent. Recall that the Agent has utility function $\theta q - t$ and is one of two possible types, $\theta_1 < \theta_2$. Now suppose that the Principal can observe a public signal s correlated with θ after production of q has occurred but before t is paid. Then transfers (but not production) can be made conditional in both θ and s. The signal can take two values s_1 and s_2. Let P be the conditional probability $\Pr(s_2 \mid \theta_1)$, and p be $\Pr(s_2 \mid \theta_2)$; we assume without loss of generality that $P > p$. We let the Principal offer the following contract, where q_i^* is the first-best quantity for θ_i and λ is a positive number:

$$\begin{cases} q(\theta_1) = q_1^* \\ t(\theta_1, s_1) = \theta_1 q_1^* - p\lambda \\ t(\theta_1, s_2) = \theta_1 q_1^* + (1 - p)\lambda \\ q(\theta_2) = q_2^* \\ t(\theta_2, s_1) = \theta_2 q_2^* + P\lambda \\ t(\theta_2, s_2) = \theta_2 q_2^* - (1 - P)\lambda \end{cases}$$

By construction, this contract gives a truthful Agent exactly his reservation utility of zero. Now suppose that Agent θ_2 declares he is type θ_1. Then he should get expected utility $\theta_2 q(\theta_1) - Pt(\theta_1, s_2) - (1 - P)t(\theta_1, s_1)$, which equals $(\theta_2 - \theta_1)q_1^* - (P - p)\lambda$. Thus, for λ large enough, this deviation from the truth is not profitable. A similar argument applies to deviations by Agent θ_1. So it is easy to see that the Principal extracts all the surplus.

The intuition behind this contract is simple: a deviator is likely to emit a "wrong" signal. So punishing Agents whose signals do not have the value that agrees with their announcement but rewarding the other Agents deters deviations. This applies directly to auctions in which private values are correlated, as the bids of the other buyers give information to the Principal on any buyer's valuation.

While this result is striking, its practical importance is debatable. The problem is that the size of the required signal-contingent transfers, λ, tends to infinity as the signal gets less informative (as $P - p$ becomes small). This may conflict with limited liability constraints, among other things.

3.2.4 Collusion

A typical organization contains several hierarchical layers: workers only interact with their employers through middle managers, for instance. This helps employers alleviate the incentive problem by using the information provided to them by the people who supervise the workers. Daily observation suggests that this remedy is not perfect, however. Workers can "bribe"[14] their supervisors not to reveal damaging information. The study of the properties of mechanisms designed to prevent collusion between several members of an organization has become a very active area of research since the pioneering work of Tirole (1986).

Let us return to our canonical model of two types, $\theta_1 < \theta_2$, where we know that the optimal quantities are $q_2 = q_2^*$ (the high type gets the first-best quantity) and

$$C'(q_1) = \theta_1 - \frac{1 - \pi}{\pi}(\theta_2 - \theta_1)$$

with the low type's quantity distorted downward. Recall that the incentive problem lies in preventing θ_2 from posing as θ_1. This is achieved by leaving θ_2 an informational rent $U_2 = (\theta_2 - \theta_1)q_1$. Now introduce a Supervisor who observes a signal s with probability p that the Agent is of type θ_2. The Agent knows that this signal was observed in this instance. However, the Principal only learns the signal if the Supervisor chooses to reveal it to him. We assume that the

---

14. Such bribes are rarely monetary in a corporate context. Then they often consist in ensuring for the supervisor a quiet life in exchange for a lax supervision.

signal is *hard information*: the Principal can regard the signal as reliable evidence that the Agent is of type θ_2.

If the Supervisor always acts in the Principal's interests, he will reveal the signal whenever he observes it. Therefore the Principal can implement a contract $(q_1, t_1, q_2, t_2, q_{2s}, t_{2s})$, with a novelty in the contract that specifies (q_{2s}, t_{2s}) when the Supervisor shows s to the Principal. It is fairly obvious in this case that the Principal extracts all the surplus: the Agent gets $U_{2s} = 0$. Thus the Agent of type θ_2 receives only a rent of $(\theta_2 - \theta_1)q_1$ with probability $(1 - p)$ when s is not observed. As for the Principal's profit, it is easy to see that the optimal q_1 is now given by

$$C'(q_1) = \theta_1 - (1 - p)\frac{1 - \pi}{\pi}(\theta_2 - \theta_1)$$

which is still distorted downward, but less than before. The Principal benefits from employing a Supervisor.

What if the Supervisor observes s, and the Agent tries to bribe him to keep quiet before he can reveal the signal to the Principal. The bribe will increase Agent θ_2's utility by $(\theta_2 - \theta_1)q_1$ with probability, so any monetary equivalent smaller than $(\theta_2 - \theta_1)q_1$ that will do as a bribe. Our analysis now will take into account the possibility of such collusive behavior of the Agent and the Supervisor. We can assume that the two parties agree by way of a *side-contract*. This side-contract will reduce the ability of the Principal to extract information from the Supervisor. To avoid such collusion, the Principal can in turn reward the Supervisor for every report of s.

The optimal contract is always the contract that deters collusion. If collusion should occur, at the optimum the Principal can always alter the contract by making quantity transfers independent of the Supervisor's report—and collusion will be deterred because it is no longer useful to the Agent. This is known as the *collusion-proofness principle*. So, to deter collusion, the Principal must be sure to reward the Supervisor for reporting s, by an amount that is exactly equal to the maximal bribe that the Agent can offer the Supervisor to keep quiet: Anything short of this will open the door to collusion, and anything more will be a waste of money. But we know that the Agent can afford to bribe the Supervisor with as much as $(\theta_2 - \theta_1)q_1$. To inject some realism, we can allow for the possibility that bribes, being illegal, are more costly to the Supervisor than to the Agent; it is one way to take into account the risk of exposure. So we let $0 < k < 1$ be the relevant parameter. The Principal then gives exactly $k(\theta_2 - \theta_1)q_1$ to the Supervisor when he reports s. Introducing this into the Principal's program shows that this time q_1 is given by

$$C'(q_1) = \theta_1 - (1 - p(1 - k))\frac{1 - \pi}{\pi}(\theta_2 - \theta_1)$$

Note that the distortion on q_1 (and thus the efficiency loss) is smaller than in the absence of a Supervisor (which obtains when $k = 1$) but larger than when the Supervisor behaves as the Principal wishes.

Collusion is an important issue in the study of organizational behavior. Many papers have applied and enriched this model. In a recent example Laffont-Martimort (1997) study the case of two firms in a regulatory duopoly that collude to hide their true costs from the regulator. More recently Mookherjee-Tsumagari (2004) study the case of a buyer who is supplied by two firms that collude on their costs; they study whether it is optimal for the buyer to delegate decisions to one of the suppliers or to a supervisor. All papers in this literature assume that side-contracts between the colluding parties are enforceable. Yet in the Principal-Supervisor-Agent model above, the Supervisor might accept the bribe from the Agent and then reveal s to the Principal for a fee. One can think of several ways such deviations can be prevented (repeated interactions, retaliation strategies); Tirole (1992) explores some of these preventive measures.

3.2.5   Risk-Averse Agents

We have assumed so far that a contract between the Principal and the Agent is signed after the Agent learns his private information. In some situations it may be more realistic to assume that the Agent learns his private information after the contract is signed but before it is executed. Consider, for instance, a chain monopoly in which the unknown variable is the strength of demand. Before the sales campaign starts, manufacturer and retailer sign a contract that specifies a nonlinear tariff to be used between them. After the contract is signed, the retailer gradually learns the strength of demand, but the manufacturer can only acquire this information by observing the orders the retailer places with him. The Agent here still has an informational advantage, but it comes from knowing he will soon be better informed than the Principal.

Salanié (1990) studies just such a model. The formal difference from the standard model here is that the Agent does not know his type when the contract is signed. So his participation constraint is written in an expected utility form:

$$\int_{\underline{\theta}}^{\overline{\theta}} U\Big(u(q(\theta), \theta) - t(\theta)\Big) f(\theta) d\theta \geq U(0)$$

where U is the Agent's von Neumann-Morgenstern utility function.

This makes solving the model much more difficult.[15] Nevertheless, the solution has interesting properties. Figure 3.4 gives the shape of the optimal allocation $q(\theta)$ as a function of the strength of demand θ for several values of the Agent's absolute risk-aversion index σ.

For any given θ, the optimal allocation is a decreasing function of the risk-aversion parameter: smaller production imposes less risk

---

15. The Pontryagin minimum principle should be used here, and it yields (even in the simplest specification) a nonlinear second-order differential equation in q with fixed ends.

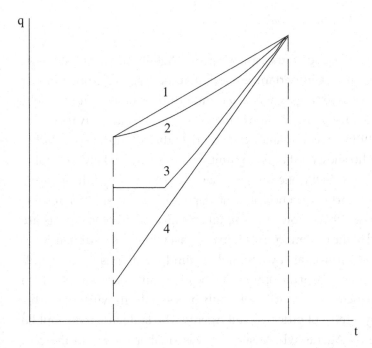

Figure 3.4
The optimal allocation with a risk-averse agent: (1) $\sigma = 0$; (2) σ small; (3) σ large;
(4) σ infinite

for the Agent. Another interesting feature of the solution is that it
involves bunching for a large but finite risk-aversion. This is in contrast with the two polar cases of zero or infinite risk-aversion, in
which the optimal allocation fully separates types. The standard
model is obtained by letting σ be infinite, so the participation constraint then is

$$\forall \theta, \quad u(q(\theta), \theta) - t(\theta) \geq 0$$

as in chapter 2. Thus focusing on the standard model, in which
bunching can be excluded with a monotone hazard rate condition,
may induce us to underestimate the extent of bunching.[16]

---

16. Laffont-Rochet (1998) study a formally analogous model in a regulatory context.

*3.2.6   Multidimensional Characteristics

So far we have studied the case where the Agent's private type is one-dimensional. It is important to check that the results obtained in that case extend to settings in which θ is multidimensional. Unfortunately, a multidimensional extension of the study can become fairly involved. The multidimensional analysis started with Laffont-Maskin-Rochet (1985), who showed that the optimum is then more likely to display bunching than in the one-dimensional case. The book by Wilson (1993) is another early reference. Recent papers obtained sharper results. Armstrong (1996) shows that for all specifications, some Agents are excluded at the optimum. This is in contrast with the one-dimensional case in which it is always possible to find conditions such that all Agents participate at the optimum. The intuition is fairly simple: if the Principal increases his tariff uniformly by a small ε, he will increase his profits by a term of order ε on all Agents who still participate, but he will lose all Agents whose surplus was smaller than ε. In the case where θ is multidimensional, the probability that an Agent has surplus lower than ε is a higher-order term in ε. Thus it pays to slightly increase the tariff, even if the Principal thereby excludes some Agents.

The paper by Rochet-Choné (1998) reaches several distressing conclusions for the two-dimensional problem:

• When the correlation between the one-dimensional components of the characteristic is strongly negative, upward or transverse incentive constraints may be binding at the optimum.

• The solution may be stochastic.

• Most strikingly, bunching appears to be a generic property in multidimensional problems; no simple condition on the primitives of the problem (e.g., a multidimensional generalization of the monotone hazard rate condition) can exclude it.

Thus the nice properties obtained in the one-dimensional case do not appear to carry over to general multidimensional problems. This is clearly a challenge for the theory, especially given that the analysis becomes quite involved. Some particular cases, however, are easier to study and can help convey some intuition about the properties of the solution. Following Armstrong-Rochet (1999), we will examine here a discrete two-dimensional case.

Since types and quantities are two-dimensional, we generalize the Principal's utility function to $t - C(q_1) - C(q_2)$ and that of the Agent, $\theta = (\theta_1, \theta_2)$, to $\theta_1 q_1 + \theta_2 q_2$. For $i = 1, 2$, θ_i may either be $\bar{\theta}$ (with probability π) or $\underline{\theta} < \bar{\theta}$. For simplicity, we will mostly focus on the case where θ_1 and θ_2 are independently distributed. For further reference we designate q^* and $\bar{q}^*$ the first-best quantities.

The revelation principle obviously holds in multidimensional as well as in one-dimensional settings. The Principal needs only to offer a contract that assigns a transfer and two quantities for every announcement of the two-dimensional type by the Agent. A moment's reflection shows that since the model is perfectly symmetric in the two dimensions, the contract can be written as

$$
\begin{cases}
(\underline{\theta}, \underline{\theta}) \longrightarrow t_{11}, (q_{11}, q_{11}) \\
(\underline{\theta}, \bar{\theta}) \longrightarrow t_{12}, (q_{12}, q_{21}) \\
(\bar{\theta}, \underline{\theta}) \longrightarrow t_{12}, (q_{21}, q_{12}) \\
(\bar{\theta}, \bar{\theta}) \longrightarrow t_{22}, (q_{22}, q_{22})
\end{cases}
$$

We denote U_{11}, $U_{12}(= U_{21})$, and U_{22} the corresponding utility levels for the Agent. There are seven unknowns here, twelve incentive constraints, and four individual rationality constraints. Fortunately, symmetry and intuition can help us a lot here. We know that in one-dimensional problems only the upward incentive constraints and the individual rationality constraint of the low type bind. So we want to focus on the *relaxed* program in which we only account for upward incentive constraints and for the individual rationality constraint of the lowest type $(\underline{\theta}, \underline{\theta})$. We will check later that the solution to the relaxed program satisfies all other constraints.

There are only five upward incentive constraints, and given symmetry, we only need to look at three of them. They are represented by dashed lines in figure 3.5. These three incentive constraints are

$$
\left\{
\begin{array}{l}
2\bar{\theta}q_{22} - t_{22} \ge \bar{\theta}(q_{12} + q_{21}) - t_{12} \\
\bar{\theta}q_{21} + \underline{\theta}q_{12} - t_{12} \ge (\bar{\theta} + \underline{\theta})q_{11} - t_{11} \\
2\bar{\theta}q_{22} - t_{22} \ge 2\bar{\theta}q_{11} - t_{11}
\end{array}
\right.
$$

Here the first constraint is the horizontal one in figure 3.5, while the second and third are the vertical and the diagonal constraints. The individual rationality constraint is just $2\underline{\theta}q_{11} - t_{11} \ge 0$. The Principal's objective is $\pi^2(t_{11} - 2C(q_{11})) + 2\pi(1 - \pi)(t_{12} - C(q_{12}) - C(q_{21})) + (1 - \pi)^2(t_{22} - 2C(q_{22}))$. It is, of course, increasing in transfers. But the four constraints can be rewritten as

$$
\left\{
\begin{array}{ll}
t_{22} - t_{12} \le 2\bar{\theta}q_{22} - \bar{\theta}(q_{12} + q_{21}) & \text{(M1)} \\
t_{12} - t_{11} \le \bar{\theta}q_{21} + \underline{\theta}q_{12} - (\bar{\theta} + \underline{\theta})q_{11} & \text{(M2)} \\
t_{22} - t_{11} \le 2\bar{\theta}(q_{22} - q_{11}) & \text{(M3)} \\
t_{11} \le 2\underline{\theta}q_{11} & \text{(M4)}
\end{array}
\right.
$$

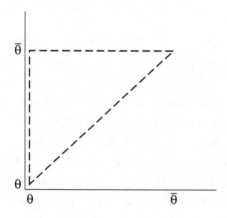

Figure 3.5
Incentive constraints in multidimensional screening

To make transfers as large as possible, M4 must clearly be binding at the optimum, and M2 as well; moreover either M1 or M3 must be binding. Thus we have

$$\begin{cases} t_{11} = 2\underline{\theta}q_{11} \\ t_{12} = \overline{\theta}q_{21} + \underline{\theta}q_{12} - (\overline{\theta} - \underline{\theta})q_{11} \\ t_{22} = 2\overline{\theta}q_{22} - (\overline{\theta} - \underline{\theta})\max(q_{11} + q_{12}, 2q_{11}) \end{cases}$$

Given this, maximizing the Principal's objective immediately gives $C'(q_{21}) = C'(q_{22}) = \overline{\theta}$, or $q_{21} = q_{22} = \overline{q}^*$. Intuition, again, suggests that we look for the other components of the solution in the region where $q_{11} < q_{12}$. Then we have to maximize (dropping already maximized parts)

$$\pi^2(2\underline{\theta}q_{11} - 2C(q_{11})) + 2\pi(1 - \pi)(\underline{\theta}q_{12} - (\overline{\theta} - \underline{\theta})q_{11} - C(q_{12}))$$
$$- (1 - \pi)^2(\overline{\theta} - \underline{\theta})(q_{11} + q_{12})$$

If we ignore the constraint that quantities cannot be negative, simple calculation yields

$$\begin{cases} C'(q_{11}) = \underline{\theta} - \dfrac{1 - \pi^2}{2\pi^2}(\overline{\theta} - \underline{\theta}) \\ C'(q_{12}) = \underline{\theta} - \dfrac{1 - \pi}{2\pi}(\overline{\theta} - \underline{\theta}) \end{cases}$$

It is easy to check, using $0 < \pi < 1$ and the convexity of C, that $q_{11} < q_{12}{}^{[17]}$, and with a little work, it is easy to check that the solution satisfies all the constraints that we neglected in the relaxed program. (I leave this to the reader as an exercise.) We have effectively characterized the complete solution. It does not imply any bunching because the optimal quantity packages all differ in one dimension at least (as $q_{12} \neq q_{21}$). The low type $(\underline{\theta}, \underline{\theta})$ gets no informational rent, the

---

17. Since the function being maximized is strictly quasi-concave, there cannot be another candidate solution in the complementary region.

intermediate types $(\underline{\theta}, \overline{\theta})$ and $(\overline{\theta}, \underline{\theta})$ get a rent $(\overline{\theta} - \underline{\theta})q_{11}$, and the high type $(\overline{\theta}, \overline{\theta})$ gets the largest rent $(\overline{\theta} - \underline{\theta})(q_{11} + q_{12})$.

Armstrong and Rochet show that when the two dimensions of the types are only weakly correlated, the qualitative properties of the solution remain the same. Larger correlations give rise to different phenomena. We know, for instance, that with perfect correlation, the only binding incentive constraint is the diagonal one. This suggests, and it can be proved, that for large positive correlation this incentive constraint will also bind. Bunching can also emerge in such cases.

3.2.7 Bilateral Private Information

Some economists take the theory of contracts to task because much of it focuses on models in which only one party possesses private information. They argue that in the real world, private information tends to be widely dispersed throughout the economy, and that in most two-party relationships both parties have their share of private information. Clearly, we should study models in which the private information is distributed more symmetrically than it is in the models of chapter 2. The next paragraphs include examples of two such models. We will first consider a mechanism design problem between a seller and a buyer, both of whom have private information on their own valuation. Then we will study an extension of the Principal–Agent adverse selection model in which the Principal has some private information too.

The Inefficiency of Trading Mechanisms

Myerson-Satterthwaite (1983) consider a transaction on a 0–1 good between a seller of the valuation c and a buyer of valuation v. Efficiency requires that trading occur if, and only if, v is greater than c. Only the seller knows c and only the buyer knows v. The valuations c and v are independently distributed with respective probability distribution functions f_1 on $[\underline{c}, \overline{c}]$ and f_2 on $[\underline{v}, \overline{v}]$, both of which are positive on their whole domains. Let us study the most favorable case, where there exists a Center that wants to implement efficient trade. The problem is to find an efficient trading mechanism that is incentive compatible and individually rational. Thus we look for two functions $x(c, v)$ (the probability of trading the good) and $t(c, v)$ (the transfer from the buyer to the seller).

• The mechanism should be efficient. $x(c, v) = d(c, v)$, where $d(c, v) = 1$ if $v \geq c$ and $d(c, v) = 0$ otherwise.

• The mechanism should be incentive compatible for both the seller and buyer. Define

$$
\begin{cases}
X_S(c) = \displaystyle\int_{\underline{v}}^{\bar{v}} x(c, v) f_2(v) dv \\[2mm]
T_S(c) = \displaystyle\int_{\underline{v}}^{\bar{v}} t(c, v) f_2(v) dv \\[2mm]
X_S(v) = \displaystyle\int_{\underline{c}}^{\bar{c}} x(c, v) f_1(c) dc \\[2mm]
T_S(v) = \displaystyle\int_{\underline{c}}^{\bar{c}} t(c, v) f_1(c) dc
\end{cases}
$$

Then $T_S(c') - cX_S(c')$ must be maximal in $c' = c$ and $vX_B(v') - T_B(v')$ must be maximal in $v' = v$;

• The mechanism should be individually rational for both the seller and the buyer. For all c and v, $U_S(c)$ and $U_B(v)$, the corresponding expected utilities must be nonnegative.

Similar formulas were used in chapter 2. The difference here is that each party ignores the type of the other party and computes his expected utility by integrating over it.

We first consider two trivial cases. First, if $\bar{v} < \underline{c}$, it is common knowledge that there are no gains from trade. Then $x(c, v) = t(c, v) = 0$ solves our problem. Things are almost as simple if it is common knowledge that there are gains from trade: $\bar{c} < \underline{v}$. Then any mechanism that prescribes $x(c, v) = 1$ and $t(c, v) = T$, with $\bar{c} \leq T \leq \underline{v}$, is efficient, incentive compatible, and individually rational.

The interesting case comes when there is a positive probability of gains from trade ($\underline{c} < \overline{v}$) but also a positive probability of no gains from trade ($\underline{v} < \overline{c}$). Myerson-Satterthwaite show that there exists no efficient trading mechanism that is both incentive compatible and individually rational.

For those who know the literature on Vickrey-Clark-Groves mechanisms, this can be easily proved. As usual with quasi-linear utility functions, the pivot mechanism is individually rational, incentive compatible, and efficient here. However, the pivot mechanism does incur a deficit. When trade occurs ($v > c$), the seller should receive v while the buyer pays c; thus it is not a feasible mechanism. We can invoke the payoff equivalence theorem to show that any incentive compatible mechanism that is individually rational and is efficient must have a deficit at least as large as the pivot mechanism.

This proof is too advanced for most readers, so instead we consider below a self-contained proof. We let x be incentive compatible. Then, by the envelope theorem, we have $U'_S(c) = -X_S(c)$ and integrate:

$$U_S(c) = U_S(\overline{c}) + \int_c^{\overline{c}} X_S(t)dt$$

By symmetry, we get

$$U_B(v) = U_B(\underline{v}) + \int_{\underline{v}}^v X_B(u)du$$

The sum of expected utilities cannot exceed the total surplus available, so

$$\int_{\underline{c}}^{\overline{c}} U_S(c)f_1(c)dc + \int_{\underline{v}}^{\overline{v}} U_B(v)f_2(v)dv$$

$$\leq \int_{\underline{c}}^{\overline{c}} \int_{\underline{v}}^{\overline{v}} (v - c)x(c,v)f_1(c)f_2(v)dcdv$$

We combine the last three equations and get

$$U_S(\bar{c}) + U_B(\underline{v})$$

$$\leq \int_{\underline{c}}^{\bar{c}} \int_{\underline{v}}^{\bar{v}} (v - c)x(c, v)f_1(c)f_2(v)dcdv$$

$$- \int_{\underline{c}}^{\bar{c}} f_1(c)dc \int_{c}^{\bar{c}} X_S(t)dt - \int_{\underline{v}}^{\bar{v}} f_2(v)dv \int_{\underline{v}}^{v} X_B(u)du$$

Simple computations show that

$$\int_{\underline{c}}^{\bar{c}} f_1(c)dc \int_{c}^{\bar{c}} X_S(t)dt = \int_{\underline{c}}^{\bar{c}} f_1(c)dc \int_{c}^{\bar{c}} \int_{\underline{v}}^{\bar{v}} x(t, u)f_2(u)dtdu$$

$$= \int_{\underline{c}}^{\bar{c}} \int_{\underline{v}}^{\bar{v}} x(c, v)F_1(c)f_2(v)dcdv$$

A similar formula holds for the integral of $X_B(v)$. So we end up with

$$U_S(\bar{c}) + U_B(\underline{v})$$

$$\leq \int_{\underline{c}}^{\bar{c}} \int_{\underline{v}}^{\bar{v}} x(c, v)\left(\left(v - \frac{1 - F_2(v)}{f_2(v)}\right) - \left(c - \frac{F_1(c)}{f_1(c)}\right)\right)f_1(c)f_2(v)dcdv \qquad \text{(MS)}$$

Note that the right-hand side of this equation gives the virtual surpluses of the buyer and the seller. This should not be a surprise at this stage. For the mechanism to be individually rational, the left-hand side of (MS) must be nonnegative. We are going to prove now that the right-hand side is negative when evaluated for the efficient mechanism $x = d$. This is not so obvious. We first have to define $z(t) = -t(1 - F_2(t))$. Then $z'(t) = tf_2(t) - (1 - F_2(t))$, and it follows that for any c,

$$\int_{\underline{v}}^{\bar{v}} d(c, v)\left(v - \frac{1 - F_2(v)}{f_2(v)}\right)f_2(v)dv$$

$$= \int_{\max(c,\underline{v})}^{\bar{v}} (vf_2(v) - (1 - F_2(v)))dv$$

$$= \max(c, \underline{v})(1 - F_2(c)).$$

We can rewrite the formula as

$$\int_{\underline{c}}^{\bar{c}} \int_{\underline{v}}^{\bar{v}} d(c,v)\left(v - \frac{1 - F_2(v)}{f_2(v)}\right) f_1(c) f_2(v) dc dv$$

$$= \int_{\underline{c}}^{\bar{c}} f_1(c)(1 - F_2(c)) \max (c, \underline{v}) dc$$

It is easily seen that what we have is just the expectation over (c, v) of $d(c, v) \max (c, \underline{v})$. A similar argument for the other term on the right-hand side of (MS) shows that it is the expectation of $d(c, v) \min (v, \bar{c})$. Now note that $\max (c, \underline{v}) - \min (v, \bar{c})$ is always negative, except possibly when it equals $(c - v)$, but in the last case its product with $d(c, v)$ is zero. Thus the right hand-side of (MS) is negative when the intervals $[\underline{c}, \bar{c}]$ and $[\underline{v}, \bar{v}]$ overlap. Clearly, the efficient mechanism must violate the individual rationality constraints.

Note that we have assumed nothing whatsoever about the trading mechanism to be chosen (by the Principal–Agent paradigm, some form of bargaining between buyer and seller, a rule imposed by a third party, etc.). This is a very strong inefficiency result. It indicates that the celebrated Coase "theorem," which states that in the absence of transaction costs agents can always bargain away any inefficiency, does not extend to environments with bilateral private information.

The Informed Principal

We return now to a more specific Principal–Agent model. In real life the Principal often has some private information. We will study here only the case where the values are private; the reader can consult Maskin-Tirole (1992) for the analysis of the common values case. Again, we turn to the standard model of the discriminating wine seller. If the seller's production cost depends on a parameter λ, which he is the only one to observe, then we are in an informed Principal private values model, since λ does not figure in the Agent's utility function. Let us denote utility functions as

$$V(q, t, \lambda)$$

for the Principal and

$$U(q, t, \theta)$$

for the Agent. Each party has in this case private information.

A direct truthful mechanism is a menu of contracts (q, t) indexed by parameters θ and λ such that when both parties announce their type simultaneously, truthtelling is their best strategy. We let $(q(\theta; \lambda), t(\theta; \lambda))$ be the menu of contracts that is optimal in the uninformed Principal model when λ is public information. The type λ Principal can always propose this menu of contracts when his private information is λ and thus guarantee himself the same utility as when λ is public information. As Maskin-Tirole (1990) show, for a generic subset of utility functions, the Principal can actually do better and obtain a higher utility than if he were to reveal his information before proposing the contract. To see why, let P be the probability distribution of the different types of Principal for the Agent. Since the Agent does not know the Principal's type when the contract is signed and only learns it after θ and λ are simultaneously revealed, the incentive and individual rationality constraints of the Agent in the Principal's program must be written as expectations over P. Now, if λ were public information, these constraints would have to hold for all values of λ. Thus the Principal's program is less constrained when he only reveals his characteristic after the contract is signed. He thus gets a higher utility thanks to his private information, even though the Agent does not particularly care for the Principal's type.

However, in the case of quasi-linear utilities which we covered in chapter 2, it can be shown that the Principal gains nothing by withholding his private information. Our endowing the Principal with privileged information on his type does not modify the properties of the optimum in the adverse selection model when both parties have quasi-linear utilities. To see this, suppose that among the family of optimal mechanisms for all types of Principal there is one where he reveals his type to the Agent before signing the contract. Recall from our earlier discussion that the Principal can benefit in hiding his private information only if he can achieve a higher expected utility by relaxing a constraint by a small ε in the contract for type λ at the price of tightening another one by ε for another type, so as to keep the same constraint in expectation over Principal types. By definition, then the gain from relaxing a constraint (or the loss from tightening it) is proportional to its multiplier. If both parties have quasi-linear utilities $V(q, \lambda) + t$ and $U(q, \theta) - t$, the first-order optimality conditions on transfers imply that the multipliers for all constraints do not depend on the value of λ. Thus, at the first order, the beneficial effect of relaxing a constraint is exactly canceled by the loss from tightening another.

3.2.8   Type-Dependent Reservation Utilities

So far the Agent's reservation utility has not depended on his type—in fact it was normalized at zero. This is not always realistic. For instance, if the Agent can interact with other Principals, then his reservation utility will reflect this outside option, which presumably depends on his type. We let therefore $\underline{U}(\theta)$ denote Agent's θ's reservation utility. We take the model of section 2.3 with continuous types, Agent's utility function $\theta q - t$ and Principal's utility function $t - C(q)$. Clearly, nothing changes in the analysis of the incentive constraints: a quantity schedule q is incentive-compatible if, and only if, it is nondecreasing in θ, and the corresponding utility profile $V(\theta)$ then satisfies $V'(\theta) = q(\theta)$. The only thing new here is that the individual rationality constraints $V(\theta) \geq \underline{U}(\theta)$ can bind for other types than $\underline{\theta}$. This needn't be the case, as we will see. We let Q be the optimal quantity schedule when the Agent's reservation utility is zero. If the Principal now faces Agents whose reservation utility satisfies $\forall \theta, \underline{U}'(\theta) \leq Q(\theta)$, then the individual rationality constraint will only bind in $\underline{\theta}$ and Q will still be optimal.

Jullien (2000) studied the general case where the reservation utility profile increases too fast for Q to remain optimal. He shows that the optimal quantity schedule can be distorted upward as well as downward, and that types interior to the interval $[\underline{\theta}, \overline{\theta}]$ can be excluded from trading with the Principal at the optimum. This is in contrast to the standard model where quantities are only distorted downward and exclusion can only occur "at the bottom."

Although Jullien's analysis is fairly complicated, we can get the gist of it by a simple case where quantities are distorted upward for every type. So we can assume for now that $\underline{U}$ is so steep that the individual rationality constraint only binds in $\overline{\theta}$. Then the analysis goes as in section 2.3, with a few differences:

$$V(\theta) = \underline{U}(\overline{\theta}) - \int_{\theta}^{\overline{\theta}} q(t)dt$$

The virtual surplus becomes

$$\theta q - C(q) + \frac{F(\theta)}{f(\theta)}q,$$

From this formula we obtain the optimal quantity

$$C'(\tilde{q}(\theta)) = \theta + \frac{F(\theta)}{f(\theta)}$$

which clearly is distorted upward. Given any reservation utility profile that increases faster than $\tilde{q}$, the individual rationality constraint only binds in $\overline{\theta}$.

3.2.9   Auditing the Agent

Incentive constraints are costly for the Principal. One way for the Principal to relax these constraints is to invest resources in ascertaining the Agent's type when he suspects that the Agent is lying. In our canonical two-type model, the nexus of the incentive problem is that the high type θ_2 may want to pass for the low type. So suppose that the Principal "audits" the Agent's type when he announces it as

θ_1. The audit technology is imperfect: it yields no information at all on the Agent's type with probability $(1 - p)$. The Principal can then choose the quality p of his audit by paying $c(p)$, where c is an increasing, convex function. If the Agent is observed to be lying (he announced θ_1 and the audit shows him to be θ_2), the Principal fines him P.

The revelation principle holds here as usual: the optimal contract makes the Agent reveal his type. The incentive constraint for the high type now becomes

$$\theta_2 q_2 - t_2 \geq \theta_2 q_2 - t_1 - pP$$

Clearly, a harsh penalty could relax the incentive constraint, and frequent penalties require a more costly audit technology. So the Principal should fine the Agent rarely (p very small) but severely (pP very large). To avoid this conclusion,[18] the literature assumes that there are limits to the fines: for instance, they cannot exceed the Agent's wealth A. For this reason the Principal's expected utility has a new term $(1 - \pi)(pA - c(p))$ and the optimal audit technology is obtained by setting $c'(p) = A$. This policy involves no change in quantities relative to the analysis in chapter 2, but the conclusion can be altered if the maximal penalty A depends on q_1 or t_1. Auditing, of course, improves the Principal's expected utility if $c'(0) < A$.

The optimal use of auditing was first studied by Townsend (1979). Gale-Hellwig (1985) applied it to a lender–borrower relationship and showed that the optimal contract is a standard debt contract that prescribes a fixed repayment if things go well and a file for bankruptcy with an audit if otherwise.[19] A difficulty with this literature is that since the Agent reveals his type with probability one in equilibrium, it makes no sense for him to be audited ex post. Inar-

---

18. Which is reminiscent of the Beckerian analysis of crime.
19. Bolton-Scharfstein (1990) used a formally analogous model to investigate predation. The lender relaxes the incentive constraint by threatening to refuse refinancing the loan if the borrower claims that times are bad.

guably in some situations the Principal should be able to commit to an auditing strategy. Khalil (1997) studies the case where a commitment to auditing is credible. The revelation principle fails and the high-type Agent randomizes between lying and revealing his type. Surprisingly, the optimal contract involves upward distortions of both the low type's quantity q_1 and the investment of the Principal in auditing quality p.

Exercises

Exercise 3.1

Go back to the optimal taxation model of section 3.1.2. Let $T(\theta) = Q(\theta) - C(\theta)$ be the tax paid by Agent θ. Assume that the optimum is fully separating.

1. Show that the marginal tax rate $T'(\theta)$ is given by

$$T'(\theta) = Q'(\theta)\left(1 - \frac{v'(L(\theta))}{\theta}\right)$$

2. Use formula (T) to show that $T'(\underline{\theta}) = T'(\overline{\theta}) = 0$ and that $T'(\theta) > 0$ everywhere else.

3. How does this compare with the tax schedules in your country?

Exercise 3.2

Show directly that in the standard model, any Rothschild-Stiglitz equilibrium is efficient (use figures in your argument).

Exercise 3.3

Wilson (1977) argued that in a competitive equilibrium an incumbent firm should be able to withdraw a contract that has become unprofitable because of a profitable entry. A Wilson competitive equilibrium therefore is a set of profitable contracts such that no entrant can propose a contract that remains profitable after all unprofitable contracts are withdrawn. It can be shown that a Wilson equilibrium always exists in the competitive insurance model, and that it coincides with the Rothschild-Stiglitz equilibrium when the latter exists.

Show that the Wilson equilibrium coincides with the Rothschild-Stiglitz equilibrium in the standard model.

Exercise 3.4

In this exercise you will derive the optimal reserve price in the simple auction of section 3.2.3. You may admit the formula for the equilibrium bid as a function of b_r.

1. Let $P(\theta_1)$ be the expected payment of agent 1 when $\theta_1 \geq b_r$. Show that

$$P(\theta_1) = \theta_1 F(\theta_1)^{n-1} - \int_{b_r}^{\theta_1} F(\theta)^{n-1} d\theta$$

2. Now let R be the expected revenue of the seller, which equals $n\int_{b_r}^{\overline{\theta}} P(\theta_1) f(\theta_1) d\theta_1$. Integrating by parts, show that

$$R = n\int_{b_r}^{\overline{\theta}} \left(\theta f(\theta) + F(\theta) - 1\right) F^{n-1}(\theta) d\theta$$

3. Show that the seller's expected utility is $(\theta_0 F^n(b_r) + R)$, and differentiate with respect to b_r so as to obtain the formula given in section 3.2.3.

Exercise 3.5

We study here the multiprincipals model with asymmetric information but colluding Principals.

1. Denote $V(\theta) = \max_{s} (u(\theta, q_1(s), q_2(s)) - t(s))$. Prove that for any incentive-compatible contract, $V'(\theta) = u'_\theta(\theta, q_1(\theta), q_2(\theta))$. Use the individual rationality constraint to get an expression for $V(\theta)$.

2. Prove that if $u''_{\theta q_1} > 0$ and $u''_{\theta q_2} > 0$, the second-order incentive constraints state that q_1 and q_2 must be nondecreasing. Neglect these constraints from now on.

3. Prove that the expected profit of the colluding Principals is

$$\int_{\underline{\theta}}^{\bar{\theta}} (u(\theta, q_1(\theta), q_2(\theta)) - C(q_1(\theta)) - C(q_2(\theta)))f(\theta)$$
$$- (1 - F(\theta))u'_\theta(\theta, q_1(\theta), q_2(\theta)))d\theta$$

4. Conclude that at the optimum

$$u'_{q_i}(\theta, q_1(\theta), q_2(\theta)) = C(q_i(\theta)) + \frac{1 - F(\theta)}{f(\theta)} u''_{\theta q_i}(\theta, q_1(\theta), q_2(\theta))$$

for $i = 1, 2$.

Exercise 3.6

We want to prove that the optimal nonlinear tariff $t = T(C)$ is convex in Laffont-Tirole's 1986 model if $\psi''' \geq 0$ and F is log concave (the logarithm of F is concave).

1. Using the first-order incentive condition, show that $T'(C) = 1 - \psi'(\beta(C) - C)$, where $\beta(C)$ is the inverse function to $C(\beta)$.

2. Use the equation that defines the optimal $C(\beta)$ to prove that under the two conditions above, $e(\beta) = \beta - C(\beta)$ is a nonincreasing function.

3. Use 2 and the second-order incentive condition to deduce that $0 < \beta'(C) < 1$, and discuss this conclusion.

References

Armstrong, M. 1996. Multiproduct nonlinear pricing. *Econometrica* 64:51–75.

Armstrong, M., and J.-C. Rochet. 1999. Multi-dimensional screening: A user's guide. *European Economic Review* 43:959–79.

Baron, D., and R. Myerson. 1982. Regulating a monopolist with unknown cost. *Econometrica* 50:911–30.

Bolton, P., and D. Scharfstein. 1990. A theory of predation based on agency problems in financial contracting. *American Economic Review* 80:93–106.

Bulow, J., and J. Roberts. 1989. The simple economics of optimal auctions. *Journal of Political Economy* 97:1060–90.

Caillaud, B., R. Guesnerie, P. Rey, and J. Tirole. 1988. Government intervention in production and incentives theory: A review of recent contributions. *Rand Journal of Economics* 19:1–26.

Champsaur, P., and J.-C. Rochet. 1989. Multiproduct duopolists. *Econometrica* 57:533–57.

Cremer, J., and R. McLean. 1988. Full extraction of the surplus in dominant strategy auctions *Econometrica* 56:1247–57.

Dewatripont, M. 1989. Renegotiation and information revelation over time: The case of optimal labor contracts. *Quarterly Journal of Economics* 104:589–619.

Fagart, M.-C. 1996. Concurrence en contrats, anti-sélection et structure d'information. *Annales d'Economie et de Statistique* 43:1–27.

Gale, D., and M. Hellwig. 1985. Incentive-compatible debt contracts: The one-period problem. *Review of Economic Studies.* 52:647–63.

Jullien, B. 2000. Participation constraints in adverse selection models. *Journal of Economic Theory.* 93:1-47.

Khalil, F. 1997. Auditing without commitment. *Rand Journal of Economics.* 28:629–40.

Klemperer, P. 2004. *Auctions: Theory and Practice.* Princeton: Princeton University Press.

Krishna, V. 2002. *Auction Theory.* San Diego: Academic Press.

Laffont, J.-J. 1994. The new economics of regulation ten years after. *Econometrica* 62:507–37.

Laffont, J.-J., and D. Martimort. 1997. Collusion under asymmetric information. *Econometrica* 65:875–911.

Laffont, J.-J., E. Maskin, and J.-C. Rochet. 1987. Optimal nonlinear pricing with two-dimensional characteristics. In *Information, Incentives, and Economic Mechanisms: In Honor of L. Hurwicz,* T. Groves, R. Radner, and S. Reiter, eds. Saint-Paul: University of Minnesota Press.

Laffont, J.-J., and J.-C. Rochet. 1998. Regulating a risk-averse firm. *Games and Economic Behavior* 25:149–73.

Laffont, J.-J., and J. Tirole. 1986. Using cost observation to regulate firms. *Journal of Political Economy* 94:614–41.

Laffont, J.-J., and J. Tirole. 1993. *A Theory of Incentives in Procurement and Regulation.* Cambridge: MIT Press.

Martimort, D. 1992. Multi-principaux avec sélection adverse. *Annales d'Economie et de Statistique* 28:1–38.

Martimort, D., and L. Stole. 2002. The revelation and delegation principles in common agency. *Econometrica* 70:1659–73.

Maskin, E., and J. Tirole. 1990. The Principal–Agent relationship with an informed Principal. I: Private values. *Econometrica* 58:379–409.

Maskin, E., and J. Tirole. 1992. The Principal–Agent relationship with an informed Principal. II: Common values. *Econometrica* 60:1–42.

Milgrom, P. 2004. *Putting Auction Theory to Work.*Cambridge: Cambridge University Press.

Milgrom, P., and R. Weber. 1982. A theory of auctions and competitive bidding. *Econometrica* 50:1089–1122.

Mookherjee, D., and M. Tsumagari. 2004. The organization of supplier networks: Effects of delegation and intermediation. *Econometrica* 72, 1179–1219.

Mussa, M., and S. Rosen. 1978. Monopoly and product quality. *Journal of Economic Theory* 18:301–17.

Myerson, R. 1981. Optimal auction design. *Mathematics of Operation Research* 6:58–73.

Myerson, R., and M. Satterthwaite. 1983. Efficient mechanisms for bilateral trading. *Journal of Economic Theory* 28:265–81.

Riley, J., and W. Samuelson. 1981. Optimal auctions. *American Economic Review* 71:381–92.

Riordan, M., and D. Sappington. 1988. Optimal contracts with public ex post information. *Journal of Economic Theory* 45:189-99.

Rochet, J.-C, and P. Choné. 1998. Ironing, sweeping and multidimensional screening. *Econometrica* 66:783–826.

Rothschild, M., and J. Stiglitz. 1976. Equilibrium in competitive insurance markets. *Quarterly Journal of Economics* 90:629–49.

Salanié, B. 1990. Sélection adverse et aversion pour le risque. *Annales d'Economie et de Statistique* 18:131–49.

Salanié, B. 2003. *The Economics of Taxation.* MIT Press: Cambridge.

Stiglitz, J. 1977. Monopoly, nonlinear pricing, and imperfect information: The insurance market. *Review of Economic Studies* 44:407–30.

Stole, L. 1990. Mechanism design under common agency. Mimeo.

Tirole, J. 1986. Hierarchies and bureaucracies: On the role of collusion in organizations. *Journal of Law, Economics, and Organizations* 2:181–214.

Tirole, J. 1992. Collusion and the theory of organizations. In J.-J. Laffont, ed., *Advances in Economic Theory*, vol. 2, Cambridge: Cambridge University Press.

Townsend, R. 1979. Optimal contracts and competitive markets with costly state verification. *Journal of Economic Theory* 21:265–93.

Vickrey, W. 1961. Counterspeculation, auctions, and competitive sealed tenders. *Journal of Finance* 16:8–37.

Wilson, C. 1977. A model of insurance markets with incomplete information. *Journal of Economic Theory* 16:167–207.

Wilson, R. 1993. *Nonlinear Pricing*. Oxford: Oxford University Press.

4   Signaling Models

In adverse selection models the uninformed party takes the initiative by offering to an informed party a menu of contracts among which the different types of informed agents can choose according to their private characteristics. In real life it is sometimes difficult to determine whether the initiative resides with the informed party or with the uninformed party. The institutional context matters greatly and considerably varies across situations. Most economic relationships moreover are repeated, and this makes it difficult to observe the extensive form of the game. It is therefore important to also study games in which the informed party plays first by sending a signal that may reveal information relating to its type. The uninformed party then tries to decipher these signals by some (endogeneously determined) interpretative scheme.

We will study three types of models in this chapter. The first model is due to Akerlof (1970); it shows that a market may function badly if the informed party has no way to signal the quality of the good it is selling. In the second model, due to Spence (1973), the signal that is sent by the informed party has a cost that depends on its type so that higher types are more likely to send higher signals. This signal may then help the uninformed party to discriminate among the different types. We analyze last the Crawford-Sobel (1982) model, which shows that even if the signal is purely extrinsic (if it has no cost for the informed party) and thus constitutes *cheap talk*, both parties may still coordinate on equilibria that reveal some information.

A typical feature of signaling models of the Spence and Crawford-Sobel type is that contrary to adverse selection models, they possess a large number of equilibria. While this multiplicity can be eliminated by way of perfect Bayesian equilibrium refinements in the Spence model, it is a robust feature of the Crawford-Sobel model.

In parts of this chapter we will encounter intuitions of game theory that are more advanced than in the rest of the book. The appendix at the end of the book provides some equilibrium concepts for the readers who may not be familiar with them.

4.1 The Market for Secondhand Cars

In a classic paper Akerlof (1970) showed that uncertainty as to the quality of a good can hinder the functioning of the market. Suppose that two types of cars coexist on the market for secondhand cars: good cars and bad cars, so-called lemons in American slang. A good car is worth g to the seller and $G > g$ to the buyer, while a lemon is worth l to the seller and $L > l$ to the buyer; naturally, $G > L$ and $g > l$. The proportion of good cars is q and that of lemons is $(1 - q)$. Note that since the value of any car to the buyer exceeds its value to the seller, with perfect information both types of cars are traded.

We will assume that the supply of cars is finite but the number of potential buyers is infinite. Under these conditions the price of good cars will settle in G and that of lemons in L if both sellers and buyers can observe the quality of a given car. If both are equally ignorant about the quality of the cars, then the equilibrium price will be $(qG + (1 - q)L)$ whatever the car. In these two polar cases, all cars find a buyer.

It is definitely easier for the seller to observe the quality of a car. So we will assume that the seller knows the quality of the cars he has in stock while the buyer is clueless about the quality of these cars. What will be the equilibrium price p on the market?

First note that sellers only offer good cars if the price p settles above g; otherwise, they lose money. If the price is lower than g, the buyers therefore will know that the cars being offered are lemons, so they will buy if, and only if, the price is not above L. Now, if the price p is not below g, and both types of cars are put up for sale, then buyers must consider that a car is worth $(qG + (1 - q)L)$.

There are therefore only two possible equilibria:

- $p = L < g$ and only lemons are sold.
- $p = qG + (1 - q)L \geq g$ and both types of cars are sold.

The second equilibrium coincides with that of the model where neither buyer nor seller is informed of the quality, so there is no revelation of quality in equilibrium. But this can only be an equilibrium if $qG + (1 - q)L \geq g$; otherwise, the equilibrium must be the first one,[1] whereby the lemons are chosen over good cars.

The presence of such informational asymmetries can clearly hinder the functioning of the market. Because all types of cars are traded to the point where only low-quality goods are traded,[2] we have another striking example of adverse selection.

4.2   Costly Signals

The dysfunctioning in the secondhand car market analyzed by Akerlof come from the inability of sellers of used cars to signal the quality of their good. If independent laboratories could publish the results of tests run on used cars, the informational asymmetry that affects the buyers directly and sellers indirectly might be reduced.

---

1. Since $qG + (1 - q)L < g$ implies that $L < g$, the first equilibrium exists.
2. In a model with continuous types for some parameter values only the worst car will be traded, and the market essentially unravels. Mas-Colell-Whinston-Green (1995, ch. 13) gives also a labor market example.

We will not pursue this line of inquiry here. Rather, we will return to
Akerlof's model in section 4.4. For now, we want to look at Spence's
model, which aims at describing how employers can infer the productivity of job searchers holding diplomas.

Every potential employee has a private information on his pro-
ductivity $\theta \in \{\theta_1, \theta_2\}$, where $\theta_1 < \theta_2$; if he studies for e years and is
hired at wage w, his utility will be $u(w) - C(e, \theta)$. His productivity
may not depend on his education,[3] but obtaining the diploma is
more costly to him if he is by nature not very productive:[4]

$$u' > 0, \quad u'' < 0$$

$$\frac{\partial C}{\partial e} > 0, \quad \frac{\partial C}{\partial \theta} > 0, \quad \frac{\partial^2 C}{\partial e^2} > 0, \quad \frac{\partial^2 C}{\partial e \partial \theta} < 0$$

This last assumption on the cross-derivative above can be justified
by common sense that the ability to pursue higher studies and productivity are positively correlated because they both depend on a
common factor—the general readiness to do work. It is important to
recognize, however, that education can only serve as a signal; it does
not enhance productivity.

The productivity of job searchers is their private information,
whereas their diplomas are public information.[5] The condition on
the cross-derivative of C thus is a Spence-Mirrlees condition. It has
the same role as in chapter 2, as it allows us to entertain the thought
that employers can discriminate among job candidates by virtue of
their diplomas.

Suppose that our potential employers are identical and that they
compete, à la Bertrand, in the market for labor. Each worker is there-

3. Education is not essential here, but it makes the model results more interesting.
4. In what follows, we do not distinguish between the number of years of schooling
and the level of diploma awarded.
5. We can assume that a job searcher who refuses to show his diploma will not be
hired.

fore paid his expected marginal productivity. A job searcher who enters the market with a diploma e is thus offered a wage[6]

$$w(e) = \mu(e)\theta_1 + (1 - \mu(e))\theta_2$$

if employers think that the candidate is θ_1 with probability $\mu(e)$. We will denote by μ_0 the a priori of employers on the worker's productivity.

This is a game of incomplete information in that when taking their decisions, employers do not know a worker's type. We will therefore look for the perfect Bayesian equilibria of this game.

Following the definition given in the appendix, a perfect Bayesian equilibrium in pure strategies consists of a vector of strategies (e_1^*, e_2^*, w^*) and a system of beliefs μ^* as follows:

• A job searcher chooses the number of years he will spend in school e by anticipating the wage function w^* that prevails on the labor market,

$$\forall i = 1, 2, \quad e_i^* \in \arg \max_e (u(w^*(e)) - C(e, \theta_i))$$

• An employer hires job searchers with a diploma e at a wage

$$w^*(e) = \mu^*(e)\theta_1 + (1 - \mu^*(e))\theta_2$$

• The beliefs $\mu^*(e)$ are consistent with e^* strategies:

For $\quad e_1^* \neq e_2^*$

*if $\quad e = e_1^*,\quad$ then $\quad \mu^*(e) = 1$

*if $\quad e = e_2^*,\quad$ then $\quad \mu^*(e) = 0$

for $\quad e_1^* = e_2^*$

*if $\quad e = e_1^* = e_2^*,\quad$ then $\quad \mu^*(e) = \mu_0$

---

6. Strictly speaking, there is no contract in the model, but a system of norms (the connection between diploma and wage) and an institution (Bertrand competition) that ensures that these norms are respected by employers.

Note that this definition in no way restricts the belief $\mu^*(e)$ that diploma e is not chosen in equilibrium $(e \neq e_1^*$ and $e \neq e_2^*)$. We only know that the wage $w^*(e)$ must lie between θ_1 and θ_2. As we will see, this degree of freedom gives rise to multiple perfect Bayesian equilibria; there will be both a continuum of separating equilibria and a continuum of pooling equilibria.[7]

4.2.1 Separating Equilibria

In a separating equilibrium the low-productivity agent chooses to study for e_1^* years and the high-productivity agent studies for $e_2^* > e_1^*$ years. Employers can therefore infer something about the agent's productivity by looking for evidence of a diploma. A low-productivity agent gets a wage equal to θ_1, so a costly education is of no use to him. He therefore does not need to pursue a diploma at all: $e_1^* = 0$. A high-productivity agent who studies for $e_2^* > 0$ years gets a wage θ_2. For this to be an equilibrium, the low-productivity agent must not envy the high-productivity agent his allocation; in other words, we must have

$$u(\theta_1) - C(0, \theta_1) \geq u(\theta_2) - C(e_2^*, \theta_1)$$

which tells us that e_2^* should not be below a certain $\underline{e}$. Since θ_2 should not envy θ_1's allocation, symmetrically we have

$$u(\theta_2) - C(e_2^*, \theta_2) \geq u(\theta_1) - C(0, \theta_2)$$

so e_2^* should be smaller than some $\bar{e}$. Figure 4.1 shows one of the many wage functions that sustain such an equilibrium.[8]

---

7. I have focused on pure strategies equilibria here. Exercises 4.1 and 4.3 ask the reader to study semiseparating equilibria in which one of the two types randomizes between two education levels.

8. Note that if e_2^* is high enough,

$$u(\theta_2) - C(e_2^*, \theta_2) < u(\mu_0\theta_1 + (1 - \mu_0)\theta_2) - C(0, \theta_2)$$

so the high-productivity agent will be better off if all schools close and there is no way to signal his productivity. Nevertheless, schools exist in this model, and refusing to study will leave the high-productivity worker worse off.

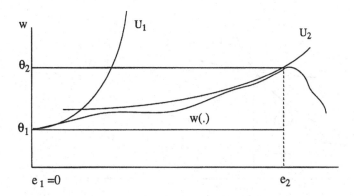

Figure 4.1
A separating equilibrium

4.2.2 Pooling Equilibria

In a pooling equilibrium, Agent types θ_1 and θ_2 choose the same diploma e^*. Employers therefore have no reason to update their beliefs and offer both a wage $\mu_0\theta_1 + (1 - \mu_0)\theta_2$. This configuration suggests that the low-productivity agent gets wage θ_1. The diploma held in a pooling equilibrium therefore is bounded above by $\bar{\bar{e}}$ such that

$$u(\mu_0\theta_1 + (1 - \mu_0)\theta_2) - C(\bar{\bar{e}}, \theta_1) = u(\theta_1) - C(0, \theta_1)$$

Figure 4.2 shows the case where $e^* > 0$. All workers are better off if education is banned, since they get one wage $\mu_0\theta_1 + (1 - \mu_0)\theta_2$ and save themselves the cost of schooling.

4.2.3 The Selection of an Equilibrium

There therefore exists a continuum of separating equilibria indexed by $e_2^* \in [\underline{e}, \bar{e}]$ and a continuum of pooling equilibria indexed by $e^* \in [0, \bar{\bar{e}}]$. Employers make zero profits in all these equilibria

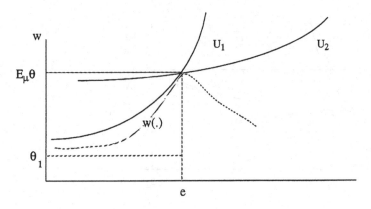

Figure 4.2
A pooling equilibrium

because they compete à la Bertrand. However, the utility of employees decreases in e, the Pareto optimum therefore is the pooling equilibrium where $e^* = 0$. All other equilibria are then Pareto dominated by it.

Multiple equilibria stem from the fact that out-of-equilibrium beliefs (i.e., the beliefs of employers on the productivity of an employee whose diploma is unusual) are not constrained by the definition of perfect Bayesian equilibria. The wage functions that employers offer are therefore only fixed for diplomas chosen in equilibrium. There are always out-of-equilibrium beliefs that sustain a given equilibrium, and this translates into the freedom with which we can trace the graph for a function w^*. This type of equilibrium (where expectations are perfectly rational) gives rise to what is known as *self-fulfilling prophecies*. It can even be shown that allowing education to affect productivity does not affect the number of equilibria.

There are two reasons why multiple equilibria are undesirable. The first is that multiplicity severely limits the predictive power of theory. The second one is that comparative statics, the favorite exercise of economists, usually rests on the continuity of a locally unique equilibrium with respect to the primitives of the model.

The only way to reduce the number of equilibria and thus to obtain more precise predictions is to restrict the beliefs $\mu^*(e)$—and therefore the wages $w^*(e)$—out of equilibrium. For instance, the wage functions shown in figures 4.1 and 4.2 do not seem realistic because they are lower for high diplomas. However, it would be easy to redraw the figures so that $w^*(e)$ increases in e. We need a stronger refinement if we are to select a unique equilibrium.

The "intuitive" criterion that allows us to eliminate all but one of these equilibria is due to Cho-Kreps (1987).[9] Fortunately, it demonstrates that no pooling equilibrium can satisfy the intuitive criterion. To see this, let e^* be a pooling perfect Bayesian equilibrium, and pick e on the segment between A and B on figure 4.3. Then we have both

$$u(\mu_0\theta_1 + (1 - \mu_0)\theta_2) - C(e^*, \theta_1) < u(\theta_2) - C(e, \theta_1)$$

and

$$u(\mu_0\theta_1 + (1 - \mu_0)\theta_2) - C(e^*, \theta_2) > u(\theta_2) - C(e, \theta_2)$$

The first inequality tells us that if employers assume that workers with e years of education have high productivity θ_2, the deviation from e^* to e is the dominating strategy for type θ_1. On the other hand, the second inequality tells us that this is not a dominating strategy for type θ_2. The intuitive criterion therefore tells us that we must have $\mu^*(e) = 0$ and $w^*(e) = \theta_2$ for such an e. But then the second inequality above tells us that type θ_2 would benefit from deviating to e, and the pooling in e^* cannot be an intuitive equilibrium. By a similar argument, we find that the only separating equilibrium that satisfies the intuitive criterion must leave type θ_1 indifferent between $e = 0$ and $e = e^*$ (see figure 4.4).

---

9. With three types one needs more refinements in order to select a unique equilibrium.

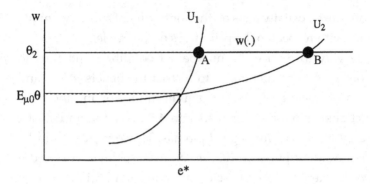

Figure 4.3
Pooling equilibria and the intuitive criterion

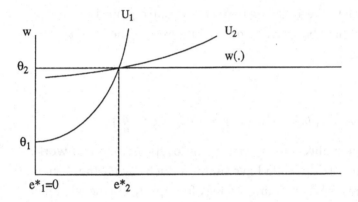

Figure 4.4
The intuitive equilibrium

Therefore the only intuitive equilibrium is a separating equilibrium, which give $e = 0$ and $w = \theta_1$ to the low-productivity agent and $e = \underline{e}$ and $w = \theta_2$ to the high-productivity agent, with

$$u(\theta_2) - C(\underline{e}, \theta_1) = u(\theta_1) - C(0, \theta_1)$$

This separating equilibrium is called the *least-cost separating equilibrium*, since the high-productivity agent chooses the minimum diploma that allows him to signal his type without attracting the low-productivity agent. It is the most efficient separating perfect Bayesian equilibrium, in that it entails the least wasteful education. It also does not depend on a prior μ_0.

The least-cost separating equilibrium is like the optimum of adverse selection models in two ways:[10]

• Only one of the two incentive constraints is active. It is the constraint that prevents the low-productivity agent from posing as a high-productivity agent.

• Only one of the two types (the low-productivity agent) receives an efficient allocation ($e = 0$).

Thus the results we get are in the end similar to those we obtained for adverse selection models. However, we paid a price by first deferring to refinements of perfect Bayesian equilibria that are not universally accepted.

4.3   Costless Signals

In Spence's model the fact that we can separate the agents (e.g., by the intuitive equilibrium) is due to the existence of a signal (education) whose cost varies with the type of the worker.

However, Crawford-Sobel (1982) show that it is possible to obtain semiseparating equilibria—alongside bunching equilibria—even if the signal has no cost for the agent who sends it. Their model belongs to the cheap talk family. Because sending the signal is costless, it may seem a priori that meaningful communication among agents cannot be readily achieved. The surprising result, as we will see in this section, is that while there always exists a *babbling* equilibrium of signals that convey no information whatsoever, there are equilibria that reveal some information.

---

10. Note that while adverse selection models typically lead to underproduction (of quality in the wine market example), Spence's model exhibits overproduction (of education, which is a wasteful activity in this model).

We first will consider a simple example of how preplay communication can enhance the efficiency of an interaction. Then we will study the Crawford-Sobel model.

4.3.1   A Simple Example

Consider N villagers $i = 1, ..., N$. Each villager is privately informed of the cost he will incur if he goes hunting with the pack.[11] This cost, denoted c_i, is a priori uniformly distributed on $[0, 1 + \varepsilon]$, where ε is some positive number; c_i is independently distributed across villagers. If all agree to hunt together, upon capturing a stag they each will get a value 1. However, if just one villager of the groups opts to stay home, the others will not be able to catch the stag.[12]

Clearly, the N villagers face a coordination problem. The risk for hunter i is that he goes hunting, incurs cost c_i, and gets 0 value because one of his fellows has preferred to stay at home. In fact no one will hunt in the only Nash equilibrium of this game. To see this, let π be the equilibrium probability that any villager goes hunting. The expected value of hunting for a single villager i is just the probability that all other villagers go hunting, which is π^{N-1}. Each villager will go hunting if, and only if, his private cost c_i is lower than π^{N-1}. A *cutoff rule* can be thus defined so that each villager will go hunting if, and only if, his private cost is lower than $c = \pi^{N-1}$. In equilibrium, π is just the probability that c_i is lower than c. This gives

$$\pi = \frac{c}{1 + \varepsilon} = \frac{\pi^{N-1}}{1 + \varepsilon}$$

---

11. This cost may depend on his second-best options, such as farming or educating children.

12. The "stag hunt" story goes back to Jean-Jacques Rousseau, who used it in 1755 to illustrate the conflict between individualism and the need for cooperation in primitive societies.

whose only solution is $\pi = c = 0$. Thus no one will go hunting, which is very inefficient, since when ε is small, the probability that c_i is lower than 1 is close to 1.

Fortunately, a little preplay communication can clarify the game considerably. Let the game have two stages now:

• In the first stage each villager announces "yes" or "no" to all the others.

• In the second, each villager decides whether or not to go hunting.

We claim that this game has an equilibrium in which, in the first stage, each villager announces "yes" if, and only if, his private cost c_i is lower than 1. Then:

• If all villagers announced "yes," they all go hunting.

• If at least one announces "no," one goes hunting.

This is easily seen by reasoning backward. Moreover this equilibrium is almost efficient for ε small because all go hunting with probability close to 1. The trick is that the villagers all know after stage one whether any of their companions will defect and stay home. So there is no risk that any villager will incur a private cost c_i in going on the hunt and not catching the stag. Also note that the announcements "yes" or "no" are purely conventional; they could be replaced with "yellow" or "blue" or anything else.

In this situation a babbling equilibrium also exists, where no information is conveyed if, for instance, all hunters say "yes" whatever their costs, and play a Nash equilibrium that in the second stage generates the same "no hunting" outcome.

4.3.2 The General Model

Crawford-Sobel's model is a little more abstract and general than Spence's model, but it has the same basic structure. It introduces two agents,[13] who we will call the sender and the receiver. The sender S observes the state of the world, which is a parameter $m \in [0, 1]$; the receiver R only observes a signal $n \in [0, 1]$ sent to him by S. The signal should help him refine his prior μ, a cumulative distribution function on the state of the world m.

Once he receives the signal n, the receiver forms a posterior given by a conditional cumulative distribution function $r(m| n)$ on the state of the world. He next takes a decision $y(n)$ that affects the utilities $U^S(y, m)$ and $U^R(y, m)$ of both agents.

We assume the following:

• U^S is concave in y and has a maximum in $y = y^S(m)$, and y^S is increasing.

• U^R is concave in y and has a maximum in $y = y^R(m)$ that differs from $y^S(m)$ for all m.

For example, U^R and U^S might be

$$\begin{cases} U^S(y, m) = -(y - m)^2 \\ U^R(y, m) = -(y - m - a)^2 \end{cases}$$

where a is a constant so that $y^S(m) = m$ and $y^R(m) = m + a$. We will come back to this example later in this section.

The difference $| y^S - y^R |$ measures the divergence between the objectives of the two agents; it will limit the possibilities for communicating. S will only want to reveal information to R if the latter then takes a decision that suits S well enough.

The "contract" here is purely implicit: the sender anticipates that the receiver will react to the signal n by the decision $y(n)$ just because it is in the receiver's interest.

The perfect Bayesian equilibria of this game consist of a vector of strategies (y^*, q^*) and a system of beliefs r^* such that:

---

13. Exercise 4.4 shows how to build an N sender–one receiver model that nests the stag hunt story.

• S believes that if he sends the signal n, R will choose $y = y^*(n)$, so he sends $n = q^*(m) \in \arg \max_n U^S(y^*(n), m)$.

• R observes $n \in q^*([0, 1])$, and forms a posterior $r^*(m| n)$, which he computes by restricting the prior μ to the set of states of the world that may have led S to send n. That is, if $(q^*)^{-1}(n)$, he chooses

$$y = y^*(n) \in \arg \max_y \int_0^1 U^R(y, m) \, dr^*(m| n)$$

or equivalently

$$y = y^*(n) \in \arg \max_y \int_{(q^*)^{-1}(n)} U^R(y, m) \, d\mu(m)$$

We will focus on "partition equilibria" in which the interval $[0, 1]$ is divided into p subintervals (denoted $[m_{i-1}, m_i]$ for $i = 1, ..., p$, with $m_0 = 0$ and $m_p = 1$) and where the signal sent by the sender depends on only the subinterval state the world happens to be in:

$$\exists n_1 < ... < n_p, \quad \forall i = 1, ..., p, \quad q^*([m_{i-1}, m_i]) = \{n_i\}$$

It can be shown that all other perfect Bayesian equilibria can be turned into a partition equilibrium by a change of variables that does not affect the economic interpretation of the results. More precisely we can associate to each equilibrium a partition of $[0, 1]$ into $(A_1, ..., A_p)$ such that

$$\forall i = 1, ..., p, \quad q^*(A_i) = \{n_i\}$$

where the sequence $(n_1, ..., n_p)$ may not be increasing.

Crawford and Sobel show that there exists an integer N such that for all $p = 1, ..., N$, there is a partition equilibrium with p subintervals. Figure 4.5 shows such an equilibrium for the case where $p = 3$.

To see how these equilibria are determined, we return to the example above in which utilities are quadratic. We assume that the

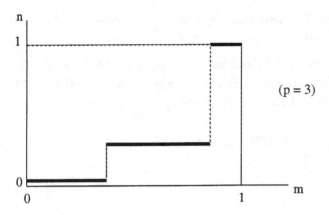

Figure 4.5
A partition equilibrium

prior μ is uniformly distributed on $[0, 1]$. For a given sequence m_i, the receiver who gets the signal n_i maximizes over y,

$$\int_{m_{i-1}}^{m_i} -(y - m - a)^2 \, dm$$

The immediate result is

$$y_i = y^*(n_i) = \frac{m_{i-1} + m_i}{2} + a$$

From the shape of the sender's utility function, the limit conditions

$$\forall i = 1, \ldots, p - 1, \quad U^S(y_{i+1}, m_i) = U^S(y_i, m_i)$$

will guarantee that the receiver sends n_i if $m \in [m_{i-1}, m_i]$. These conditions give

$$\left(\frac{m_{i-1} - m_i}{2} + a \right)^2 = \left(\frac{m_{i+1} - m_i}{2} + a \right)^2$$

whence

$$m_{i+1} = 2m_i - m_{i-1} - 4a$$

We know that the solution to this difference equation must take the form $m_i = \lambda i^2 + \mu i + \nu$. The difference equation gives $\lambda = -2a$, and the initial and final conditions $m_0 = 0$ and $m_p = 1$ give $\nu = 0$ and $\mu = 1/p + 2ap$. We thus get the solution

$$m_i = \left(\frac{1}{p} + 2ap \right) i - 2ai^2$$

Clearly, the sequence (m_i) must be increasing for the solution to be valid. If, say, a is positive, we can rewrite the difference equation as

$$m_{i+1} - m_i = m_i - m_{i-1} - 4a$$

and therefore the sequence $(m_0, \ldots, m_p)$ is increasing if, and only if,

$$m_1 - m_0 - 4a(p - 1) > 0$$

or

$$\frac{1}{p} - 2ap + 2a > 0$$

Because the left-hand side of this inequality is decreasing in p and goes to $-\infty$ in $+\infty$, it defines an integer N such that the sequence increases if, and only if, $p \leq N$.

In this example we have thus all the properties of the Crawford-Sobel model. There always exists a noninformative equilibrium, which is the babbling equilibrium. When $p = 1$, the sender sends a message that does not depend on the state of the world and the receiver does not change his prior.

The informativeness of the signal depends on the number p. In our example this number takes all values from 1 to an integer N, which increases when the absolute value of a decreases. There are therefore N more and more informative equilibria up to the N partition equilibria, that reveal more information. It can be shown that this N partition equilibrium Pareto-dominates all others because it allows the agents to coordinate on a more appropriate action. The closer the utilities (the smaller the $|a|$), the higher is N. The infor-mativeness of the equilibrium is only limited by the divergence of the players' objectives.

It should be noted that the signal is purely extrinsic here: It has no effect on the primitives of the model. So it is another instance of what we call a cheap talk model. Instead of exchanging a signal in [0, 1], the players can perfectly well communicate by an entirely dif-ferent code. What matters is that the receiver build up an interpreta-tion scheme that reflects a preplay communication game. The minimum requirements are that the players share a language and agree on the description of the game.

4.4   Other Examples

There are many products about which buyers cannot easily form an opinion on their reliability. This is learned often only over time by experience. A seller who wants to draw the attention of buyers to the reliability of his product can nevertheless announce that the product is covered by a warranty. This policy brings costs due to the mainte-nance and repair of the product, but these costs are low when the good is reliable. The underlying model therefore is formally analo-gous to that of Spence,[14] and the offering of warranties is a way out of the Akerlof paradox studied at the beginning of this chapter. Recall that in the Cho-Kreps intuitive equilibrium, the sellers whose product is not reliable do not offer any warranty and the sellers whose product is reliable offer the minimum warranty that allows them to stand out among their competitors.

Another example of a signaling model à la Spence is due to Leland-Pyle (1977). They consider risk-averse entrepreneurs who end up financing risky projects. Each entrepreneur is privately informed of the expected return μ on his project. By holding equity

---

14. This similarity can be seen by replacing the type θ with the reliability of the product, the signal e with the characteristics of the warranty, and the wage w with the price of the good.

in the project, an entrepreneur increases his exposure to risk but also his expected profits; the latter effect is greater when μ is large. The entrepreneurs with higher quality projects then signal their type by holding a larger fraction of equity.

Suppose that a journalist in the financial press has bullish inside information on the profits of a firm but advises his readers to sell this firm's shares. If readers follow his advice, the price of the shares will drop, and he will be able to buy the shares at much lower cost and resell them once the firm's high profits are announced. This scenario can in fact be cast in the Crawford-Sobel model form. The to-be-announced profits of the firm represent the state of the world m, the information published by the journalist (the sender) is the signal n, and the decision to sell y taken by the readers (the collective receiver) is the number of shares they sell. There are no limits to the greed of the journalist; his objective is entirely contrary to what he tells the readers because their losses will be his profits. The only equilibrium of the game, as a result, will be noninformative, with the savvy readers placing no trust at all in the journalist's recommendation. The only way a journalist can use his privileged information is by sometimes telling the truth so that he can establish a reputation for honesty. The journalist's struggle between greed and a desire to be credible will determine the quality of information that will be transmitted in equilibrium.[15]

Yet another application of the cheap talk model is by Aghion-Tirole (1997). In this interesting variant, a manager and a worker are initially uninformed about the value of potential projects but can acquire information at some cost. By paying e, the manager (resp. the worker) is informed with probability $p_M(e)$ (resp. $p_W(e)$). The values of projects differ for the two agents, as they derive different private benefits from them. At the beginning of the relationship, the right to choose which project will be implemented (the *formal authority*) is allocated to either agent. Then they decide how much information to

---

15. A variant of this model is studied by Benabou-Laroque (1992).

acquire. If the agent who does not have formal authority receives some information, then he may communicate it to the other party. It may be, for instance, that the manager keeps formal authority but remains uninformed. Then, if there is enough congruence between their objective functions, the manager optimistically rubberstamps the recommendation of the worker, who is then said to have *real authority*. Aghion and Tirole use this model to study when formal authority should be delegated by the manager to the worker.

4.5 The Informed Principal

To conclude the discussion of signaling models, let us return to the informed Principal model. This model has a close connection to signaling models because in both cases the party who moves first is informed. We saw in chapter 3 that when the private characteristic of the Principal does not directly concern the Agent, and the utilities are quasi-linear, the Principal has nothing to gain by revealing his type. In Spence's model, for instance, the private characteristic of the worker is his productivity, but it is a characteristic that influences the profits of the employer. An analogous model is that of the informed Principal with common values. The worker here acts as the Principal and the employer as the Agent. It is clearly important for the Principal that he can signal his type to the Agent. The game the two parties play is, however, not quite the same as the one we analyzed in this chapter because the signal (education) is chosen before the wage contract is signed in Spence's model and after it is signed in the informed Principal model with common values. The analysis of the latter model can be found in Maskin-Tirole (1992). The least-cost separating equilibrium plays an important role in both cases: in Spence's model, it is the only intuitive equilibrium; in Maskin-Tirole, it is the lower bound (for the Pareto criterion) of the set of equilibrium allocations.[16]

---

16. The set may be reduced to a singleton if the prior probability of the low type is high enough.

Exercises

Exercise 4.1

Show, by using figures, that the Spence model has two types of semi-separating equilibria:

• Equilibria in which θ_1 chooses an education level e_1 and θ_2 randomizes between e_1 and a higher education level e_2.
• Equilibria in which θ_2 chooses an education level e_2 and θ_1 randomizes between e_2 and a lower education level e_1.

Exercise 4.2

In Spence's model, show that all perfect Bayesian equilibria are sequential (use the definition of sequential equilibria in the appendix to exhibit appropriate supporting beliefs).

Exercise 4.3

Show that the "intuitive" criterion eliminates all semiseparating equilibria in Spence's model.

Exercise 4.4

Consider a variant of the Crawford-Sobel model in which there are N senders $i = 1, ..., N$ and one receiver, with utility functions

$$U_i^S(y, m_i) = y(1 - m_i)$$

$$U^R(y, m_1, ..., m_N) = \sum_{i=1}^{N} U_i^S(y, m_i)$$

where y is a 0–1 variable. The prior on m_i is independently distributed as a uniform distribution on $[0, 1 + \varepsilon]$.

1. How does this fit the stag hunt example? (*Hint:* The receiver is the benevolent chief of the village, and $y = 1$ if and only if he has decided to send everybody hunting.)

2. We saw in section 4.3.1 that it is reasonable to look for equilibria in which each sender i announces "yes" if, and only if, $m_i \leq m$ and "no" otherwise. Show that in any such equilibrium, there cannot be a switch from $y = 1$ to $y = 0$ if one villager changes his "no" to a "yes."

3. Show that m must be equal to 1.

4. (*Slightly more difficult*) Compute the equilibrium probability that all go hunting, and show that it converges to 1 as ε becomes arbitrarily small.

References

Aghion, P., and J. Tirole. 1997. Formal and real authority in organizations. *Journal of Political Economy* 105:1–29.

Akerlof, G. 1970. The market for lemons: Quality uncertainty and the market mechanism. *Quarterly Journal of Economics* 89:488–500.

Benabou, R., and G. Laroque. 1992. Using privileged information to manipulate markets: Insiders, gurus, and credibility. *Quarterly Journal of Economics* 107:921–58.

Cho, I.-K., and D. Kreps. 1987. Signaling games and stable equilibria. *Quarterly Journal of Economics* 102:179–221.

Crawford, V., and J. Sobel. 1982. Strategic information transmission. *Econometrica* 50:1431–51.

Leland, H., and D. Pyle. 1977. Asymmetries, financial structure, and financial intermediation. *Journal of Finance* 32:371–87.

Mas-Colell, A., M. Whinston, and J. Green. 1995. *Microeconomic Theory*. Oxford: Oxford University Press.

Maskin, E., and J. Tirole. 1992. The principal–agent relationship with an informed principal. II: Common values. *Econometrica* 60:1–42.

Spence, M. 1973. Job market signaling. *Quarterly Journal of Economics* 87:355–74.

5   Moral Hazard

Well, then, says I, what's the use you learning to do right when it's troublesome to do right and ain't no trouble to do wrong, and the wages is just the same? I was stuck. I couldn't answer that. So I reckoned I wouldn't bother no more about it, but afterwards always do whichever come handiest at the time.
—**Mark Twain,** *Adventures of Huckleberry Finn.*[1]

We speak of *moral hazard* when

• the Agent takes a decision ("action") that affects his utility and that of the Principal;

• the Principal only observes the "outcome," an imperfect signal of the action taken;

• the action the Agent would choose spontaneously is not Pareto-optimal.

Because the action is unobservable, the Principal cannot force the Agent to choose an action that is Pareto-optimal. He can only influence the choice of action by the Agent by conditioning the Agent's utility to the only variable that is observable: the outcome. This in turn can only be done by giving the Agent a transfer that depends on the outcome.

---

1. Quoted by Holmstrom-Milgrom (1987).

Examples of moral hazard abound, and it is difficult to imagine an economic relationship that is not contaminated by this problem.[2] If a perfect relationship could exist, the Principal would be able to observe all the decision variables of the Agent that relate to his utility; this would be extremely costly in terms of supervisory measures.

Moral hazard is present everywhere within firms, since employers rarely can control all decisions of their employees. The term *effort* is often used to designate the employee inputs that are not directly observable, the employer can only base wages on production or some other observable variable that induces employees not to shirk. This term effort is confusing in that it suggests that moral hazard in firms consists only in employees avoiding work. However, moral hazard exists as soon as the objectives of the parties differ. A good example is the relationships between shareholders and managers. Because the managers are autonomous agents, they will have objectives that are not necessarily the same as those of the shareholders (who above all want the firm's value to be maximized).

In the area of property insurance, the moral hazard is due to an insurer not being able to observe the precautions against theft, fire, and so forth, of the insured despite the positive effects of such effort on the insurer's profits.

In service activities, moral hazard is present where the effort of the service provider bears on the outcome of a task. Simple examples include the relationship between a car-owner and his mechanic, or between a patient and his doctor.

Last, in the economics of development, moral hazard is often studied to describe the relationships between landowners and their farmers. In sharecropping, for example, agreements stipulate that the harvest will be shared between both parties, thus making it important for the landlord to get the farmer to put in effort.

---

2. The moral hazard model actually is often called the "agency problem" and identified with the Principal–Agent model.

The first-best situation is therefore defined by the situation where the Principal can observe every action of the Agent. Then he can rcommend that the Agent choose the most efficient action,[3] and the wages that provide for optimal risk sharing. It is often assumed that in these models the Principal is risk-neutral; for instance, the Principal faces many independent risks and thus can diversify the risks associated to his relationship with the Agent.[4] In contrast, the Agent normally exhibits risk-aversion (it is more difficult for him to diversify his risks). Optimal risk sharing then requires that the Principal perfectly ensure the Agent by paying him a constant wage and by bearing all risks involved in their common activity.

In the second-best situation the Principal can only observe a variable correlated with the Agent's action: the outcome. If the Principal is risk-neutral, the first-best optimum consists in giving the Agent a constant wage. In second-best circumstances this will tempt the Agent to choose selfishly the action that is the least costly for him, and in general, this is not optimal.[5] Solving the moral hazard problem thus implies that the Principal offers the Agent a contract with trade-offs between risk sharing and incentives:

• Risk sharing so that the Agent's wage do not depend too heavily on the outcome.

• Incentives so that the Principal can base the Agent's wage on the outcome.

Now, when the Agent is risk-neutral, this trade-off is nonexistent. The Agent does not mind bearing all the risk, so the issue of risk-sharing is irrelevant. We sometimes say in that case that the moral hazard problem is solved by "selling the firm to the Agent." However, this case has little practical interest.

---

3. Or, equivalently, the Principal can fine the Agent if he does not choose the efficient action.

4. This is by no means always the most natural assumption, as the patient–doctor relationship shows. However, it is not crucial to the analysis.

5. This is the meaning of the *Huckleberry Finn* quotation that opens this chapter.

5.1   A Simple Example

We start with the simplest framework: a two action, two outcome model. The Agent can choose between working, $a = 1$, and not working, $a = 0$. The cost of action a is normalized to a so that the Agent's utility, if he gets wage w and chooses action a, is $u(w) - a$, where u is strictly concave. The Principal can only observe whether the Agent succeeds or fails at his task. If the Agent works, his probability of succeeding is P and the Principal gets a payoff x_S. If he does not work, the probability of success falls to $p < P$, and the Principal's payoff is $x_F < x_S$.

In the more interesting case the Principal must induce the Agent to work. Then he has to give the Agent wages w_S (in case of success) and w_F (in case of failure) such that the Agent's effort is rewarded:

$$Pu(w_S) + (1 - P)u(w_F) - 1 \geq pu(w_S) + (1 - p)u(w_F)$$

so the incentive constraint is

$$(P - p)(u(w_S) - u(w_F)) \geq 1$$

Because the Principal must (obviously) pay a higher wage when the Agent works, the difference $(w_S - w_F)$ increases as P gets closer to p. As this occurs, it becomes difficult to distinguish a worker from a nonworker. Then we say that the incentive to work must become more *high powered*.

We must also take into account an individual rationality constraint. By this we mean that the Agent must find it worthwhile to work rather than to quit and get his outside option $\underline{U}$. This gives

$$Pu(w_S) + (1 - P)u(w_F) - 1 \geq \underline{U}$$

This inequality must clearly be an equality. Otherwise, the Principal can decrease both $u(w_S)$ and $u(w_F)$ by the same small transfer ε, which would not affect the incentive constraint and would increase his own utility, since (assuming he is risk-neutral) this is

$$P(x_S - w_S) + (1 - P)(x_F - w_F)$$

Proving that the incentive constraint is an equality is slightly more involved. If it were a strict inequality, we could subtract $(1 - P)\varepsilon/u'(w_S)$ from w_S and add $P\varepsilon/u'(w_F)$ to w_F. The incentive constraint would still hold for ε small. By construction, $u(w_S)$ would decrease by $(1 - P)\varepsilon$ and $u(w_F)$ would increase by $P\varepsilon$ so that the individual rationality constraint would still be satisfied. Moreover the wage bill $Pw_S + (1 - P)w_F$ of the Principal would decrease by $P(1 - P)\varepsilon(1/u'(w_S) - 1/u'(w_F))$, which is positive because $w_F < w_S$ and u is strictly concave.[6]

Because both inequalities are linear equalities in $(u(w_F), u(w_S))$ and we have just two unknowns, we can easily solve for $u(w_S)$ and $u(w_F)$. This gives

$$\begin{cases} u(w_F) = \underline{U} - \dfrac{p}{P - p} \\ u(w_S) = \underline{U} + \dfrac{1 - p}{P - p} \end{cases}$$

from which we can proceed to compute the Principal's expected utility

$$W_1 = P(x_S - w_S) + (1 - P)(x_F - w_F)$$

However, this is a very special case. We only relied on the maximization of W_1 to prove that both constraints are binding at the optimum.

It might well be that the Principal finds it too costly to get the Agent to work and decides to let him shirk instead. In this case he

---

6. More diagram-oriented readers can also easily see this by drawing a curve in the $(u(w_F), u(w_S))$ plane.

will give the Agent a constant wage $w_S = w_F = w$ such that $u(w)$
$= \underline{U}$, and he will get an expected utility

$$W_0 = px_S + (1 - p)x_F - w$$

The difference between W_0 and W_1 can then be rewritten as

$$W_1 - W_0 = (P - p)(x_S - x_F) + w - Pw_S - (1 - P)w_F$$

Since the wages do not depend on x_S and x_F, it appears that if success
is much more attractive than failure for the Principal ($x_S - x_F$ is high),
he will choose to get the Agent to work. (The reader is asked in exercise 5.1 to prove that then $x_S - w_S > x_F - w_F$ at the optimum, with the
surplus from success shared between the Agent and the Principal.)

5.2   The Standard Model

We consider here the standard model in a discrete version. The
Agent can choose between n possible actions: $a_1, \ldots, a_n$. These
actions produce one among m outcomes, which we denote $x_1, \ldots, x_m$.

The outcome a priori is a signal that brings information on the
action the Agent chooses. To simplify matters, we identify it as surplus from the Principal–Agent relationship.[7] (We will return to this
assumption in section 5.3.4.)

The stochastic relationship between the chosen action and the outcome is often called a "technology." The idea here is that when the
Agent chooses action a_i, the Principal observes outcome x_j with a
probability p_{ij} that is positive.[8] Because the only variable that is pub-

7. For instance, in an employer–employee relationship, a will be the effort and x the
resulting production or profit.
8. If some of the probabilities p_{ij} were zero, the Principal could use this information to
exclude some actions. Suppose that action a_i is the first-best optimal action and that
$p_{ij} = 0$ for some j. The Principal then can fine the Agent heavily when the outcome is
x_j, since the fact that he observes x_j signals that the Agent did not choose the optimum
action a_i. This type of strategy will even allow the Principal to implement the first-best:
if moreover $p_{kj} > 0$ for all $k \neq i$, then the choice of any a_k other than a_i will expose the
Agent to a large fine, thus effectively deterring him from deviating. This was noted
early on by Mirrlees (1975, published 1999); it is the reason why I exclude this case.

licly observed is the outcome, contracts must take the form of a wage that depends on the outcome. If the Principal observes the outcome x_j, he will pay the Agent a wage w_j and keep $x_j - w_j$ for himself.

A general specification for the Agent's von Neumann–Morgenstern utility function would be $u(w, a)$. However, the choice of action would then affect the agent's preferences toward risk, which would complicate the analysis.[9] Therefore we will assume that the Agent's utility is separable in income and action. Moreover it is always possible to renormalize the actions so that their marginal cost is constant.

Thus in the standard model we take the Agent's utility function to be

$$u(w) - a$$

where u is increasing and concave. We can assume that the Principal is risk-neutral, as done in most of the literature. The Agent's von Neumann–Morgenstern utility function then is

$$x - w$$

5.2.1 The Agent's Program

When the Principal offers the Agent a contract w_j, the Agent chooses his action by solving the following program:

$$\max_{i=1,\dots,n} \left(\sum_{j=1}^{m} p_{ij} u(w_j) - a_i \right)$$

If the Agent chooses a_i, then the $(n-1)$ incentive constraints

$$\sum_{j=1}^{m} p_{ij} u(w_j) - a_i \geq \sum_{j=1}^{m} p_{kj} u(w_j) - a_k \quad (IC_k)$$

must hold for $k = 1, \dots, n$ and $k \neq i$.

---

9. Then it may be optimal for the Principal to give higher wages if it reduces the Agent's disutility of effort, so that the individual rationality constraint may not be binding at the optimum.

We can assume that the Agent will accept the contract only if it gives him a utility no smaller than some $\underline{U}$, which represents the utility the Agent can obtain by breaking his relationship with the Principal for his next-best opportunity. The participation constraint (the individual rationality constraint) can in this case be written

$$\sum_{j=1}^{m} p_{ij} u(w_j) - a_i \geq \underline{U} \quad (IR)$$

if the Agent's preferred action is a_i.

5.2.2 The Principal's Program

The Principal should choose the contract $w_1, \ldots, w_m$ that maximizes his expected utility, while taking into account the consequences of this contract on the Agent's decision:

$$\max_{(w_1,\ldots,w_m),\, i} \sum_{j=1}^{m} p_{ij}(x_j - w_j)$$

under

$$\begin{cases} (IC_k) & k = 1, \ldots, n \text{ and } k \neq i \quad (\lambda_k) \\ (IR) & (\mu) \end{cases}$$

where a_i is the action chosen at the optimum and the numbers in parentheses represent the (nonnegative) multipliers associated with the constraints. The maximization therefore is with respect to wages (w_j) and action a_i, which the Principal indirectly controls.

If we fix a_i, the Lagrangian of the maximization problem is

$$\mathcal{L}(w, \lambda, \mu) = \sum_{j=1}^{m} p_{ij}(x_j - w_j) + \sum_{k=1; k \neq i}^{n} \lambda_k \left(\sum_{j=1}^{m} p_{ij} u(w_j) - a_i \right. $$
$$\left. - \sum_{j=1}^{m} p_{kj} u(w_j) + a_k \right) + \mu \left(\sum_{j=1}^{m} p_{ij} u(w_j) - a_i - \underline{U} \right)$$

Differentiating it with respect to w_j and regrouping terms yields

$$\frac{1}{u'(w_j)} = \mu + \sum_{k=1, k \neq i}^{n} \lambda_k \left(1 - \frac{p_{kj}}{p_{ij}} \right) \qquad (E)$$

At the first-best, we would get the efficient risk-sharing; the ratio of marginal utilities of the Principal and the Agent would be constant, which implies that the wage itself is constant:

$$\frac{1}{u'(w_j)} = \mu_0$$

where μ_0 is chosen so that the constraint (IR) is an equality.

The difference between the two equations (IC_k) and (IR) above comes from the fact that some multipliers λ_k are positive. That is, incentive constraints may be active, so some actions a_k give the Agent the same expected utility as a_i. In equilibrium at least one of the λ_k must be positive (otherwise, we can neglect the incentive constraints, and the moral hazard problem will be moot); w_j then depends on j through the terms p_{kj}/p_{ij}.

The p_{kj}/p_{ij} terms play a fundamental role in the analysis of moral hazard. They can be interpreted by analogy with mathematical statistics. The Principal's problem likewise consists, in part, of inferring the action the Agent will choose given the observed outcome. In statistical terms the Principal must estimate the "parameter" a from the observation of "sample" x. This parameter can be obtained by way of the maximum likelihood estimator, which is the a_k such that k maximizes the probability p_{kj}. The next two statements are therefore equivalent:

a_i is the maximum likelihood estimator of a given x_j

and

$$\forall k, \quad \frac{p_{kj}}{p_{ij}} \leq 1$$

By analogy then the p_{kj}/p_{ij} quantities can be called "likelihood ratios," and because of this analogy we can interpret equation (E).

Fix the optimal action a_i. Because all multipliers λ_k are nonnegative and the function $1/u'$ is increasing, the wage w_j associated with outcome j will be higher when a greater number of likelihood ratios p_{kj}/p_{ij} are smaller than 1. This wage is therefore higher when a_i is the maximum likelihood estimator of a given x_j. Because the wage w_j depends on a *weighted* sum of the likelihood ratios, this argument is, of course, not airtight.[10] Still the intuition is important and basically right: the Principal will give the Agent a high wage when he observes an outcome from which he can infer that the action taken was the optimal one; however, he will give the Agent a low wage if the outcome shows it unlikely that the Agent chose the optimal action.

Before we study the properties of the optimal contract, let us consider briefly an alternative approach popularized by Grossman-Hart (1983). They solve the Principal's maximization program in two stages:

• For any action a_i, they minimize the cost to implement it for the Principal. This amounts to minimizing the wage bill

$$\sum_{j=1}^{m} p_{ij} w_j$$

under the incentive constraints and the participation constraint.

• They then choose the action that maximizes the difference between the expected benefit from action a_i, or

$$\sum_{j=1}^{m} p_{ij} x_j$$

and the cost-minimizing wage bill.

---

10. The reader should check that with only two actions ($n = 2$), the argument holds as given in the text.

The Grossman-Hart approach is clearly equivalent to the approach we used above, and in some ways it may be more enlightening

5.2.3 Properties of the Optimal Contract

Let $x_1 < ... < x_m$ and $a_1 < ... < a_n$. We are interested here in how the wage w_j depends on the outcome j. We know that when the action is observable and the Principal is risk-neutral, w_j is constant. If, more generally, the Principal is risk-averse with a concave von Neumann-Morgenstern utility function v, then the ratios of marginal utilities

$$\frac{v'(x_j - w_j)}{u'(w_j)}$$

are independent of j at the first-best wage.[11] We see that the first-best wage w_j must be an increasing function of j. This property is likewise desirable for the second-best wage schedule. It is natural for the wage to be higher when the surplus to be shared is higher. Recall that we obtained such a result for the two-action, two-outcome example in section 5.1.

It turns out that, it is only possible to show that in general (see Grossman-Hart 1983),

1. w_j cannot be uniformly decreasing in j,

2. neither can $(x_j - w_j)$,

3. $\exists (j, l), w_j > w_l$ and $x_j - w_j \geq x_l - w_l$.

The proofs are fairly complex and will be omitted here. However, these results are obviously far removed from what commen sense tells us. For instance, they do not exclude an optimal wage schedule in which wages decrease in part of the range. The usefulness of these three results for our purpose appears when there are only two

---

11. This is known in the literature as Borch's rule.

possible outcomes: success or failure. The optimal wage schedule
can then be written as

$$\begin{cases} w_1 = w \\ w_2 = w + s(x_2 - x_1) \end{cases}$$

The Agent receives a basis wage w and a bonus proportional to the
increase in the surplus if he accepts the contract. Result 3 above
shows that the bonus rate s must satisfy $0 < s \leq 1$: wages increase
with the outcome but not so fast that they exhaust the whole
increase in the surplus.

When there are more than two outcomes, we cannot obtain more
positive results without adding structure to the technology that produces the outcome (the probabilities p_{ij}). The outcome has a dual
role in this model: it represents the global surplus to be shared, and
it also signals to the Principal the action taken by the Agent. The
shape of the solution is therefore determined by the properties of
this signal which is what we already saw in our study of likelihood
ratios.

Let us return to (E), the equation that defines the optimal contract:

$$\frac{1}{u'(w_j)} = \mu + \sum_{k=1, k \neq i}^{n} \lambda_k \left(1 - \frac{p_{kj}}{p_{ij}} \right)$$

As the left-hand side of (E) increases in w_j, w_j will increase in j if, and
only if, the right-hand side of (E) increases in j as well. In other
words, we need to assume that a high action increases the probability of getting a high outcome at least as much as it increases the
probability of getting a low outcome:

$$\forall k < i, \forall l < j, \quad \frac{p_{ij}}{p_{il}} \geq \frac{p_{kj}}{p_{kl}}$$

This condition is called the *monotone likelihood ratio condition* (MLRC).
It amounts to assuming that for all $k < i$, the likelihood ratio p_{ij}/p_{kj}

increases with the outcome j. Excercise 5.6 asks you to prove that MLRC implies another commonly used comparison of probability distributions, first-order stochastic dominance. First order dominance just states that as a increases, the cumulative distribution function of outcomes moves to the right: however one defines a good outcome, the probability of a good outcome increases in a.

Since the multipliers λ_k are nonnegative, MLRC allows us to state that the $\lambda_k(1 - p_{kj}/p_{ij})$ terms in (E) are increasing in j if $k < i$, and decreasing otherwise. We are done if we can find a condition whereby the multipliers λ_k are all zero when k is greater than i, that is, when the only active incentive constraints are those that prevent the Agent from choosing actions less costly than the optimal action.

Note that if $i = n$, in which case the Principal wants to implement the most costly action, then we are indeed done. When there are two possible actions—when the choice is work or not work and the Principal wants the Agent to work—the MLRC is enough to ensure that the wage increases in the outcome. In the general case Grossman and Hart proposed[12] the *convexity of the distribution function condition* (CDFC),[13] the cumulative distribution function of the outcome should be convex in a on $\{a_1, \dots, a_n\}$. More precisely, for $i < j < k$ and $\lambda \in [0, 1]$ such that

$$a_j = \lambda a_i + (1 - \lambda)a_k$$

the CDFC says that

$$\forall l = 1, \dots, m, \quad P_{jl} \le \lambda P_{il} + (1 - \lambda)P_{kl}$$

One rough interpretation of this new condition is that returns to the action are stochastically decreasing, but this must be taken with a bit

---

12. Both (MLRC) and (CDFC) appear in earlier work by Mirrlees.
13. Some authors call this a *concavity of the distribution function condition,* meaning that the *decumulated* distribution function (one minus the cumulative distribution function) is concave.

of skepticism. CDFC really has no clear economic interpretation, and its validity is much more doubtful than that of MLRC.[14] The main appeal of CDFC is that it allows us to obtain the result we seek, as we will now show.

Let a_i be the optimal action. It is not difficult to see that there must exist a $l < i$ such that the multiplier λ_l is positive. If all λ_k were zero for $k < i$, then the optimal wage would be the same if the choice of possible actions were restricted to $A = \{a_i, \ldots, a_n\}$. But the optimal wage would then be constant, since a_i is the least costly action in A. Now a constant wage can only implement action a_1 and not a_i in the global problem, so this conclusion makes no sense.

Consider the problem in which the Agent is restricted to choosing an action in $\{a_1, \ldots, a_i\}$, and let w be the optimal wage. In this problem a_i is the costliest action and MLRC therefore implies that w_j increases in j. We will show that w stays optimal if we allow the Agent to choose from the unrestricted set of actions $\{a_1, \ldots, a_n\}$. Assume, to the contrary, that there exists a $k > i$ such that the Agent prefers to choose a_k:

$$\sum_{j=1}^{m} p_{kj} u(w_j) - a_k > \sum_{j=1}^{m} p_{ij} u(w_j) - a_i$$

and let l be the index of an action less costly than a_i and whose associated multiplier λ_k is nonzero so that

$$\sum_{j=1}^{m} p_{lj} u(w_j) - a_l = \sum_{j=1}^{m} p_{ij} u(w_j) - a_i$$

There exists a $\lambda \in [0, 1]$ such that

$$a_i = \lambda a_k + (1 - \lambda) a_l$$

---

14. Take, for instance, a slightly different model in which there is a continuous set of outcomes given by $x = a + \varepsilon$, where ε is some random noise with probability distribution function f. Then returns to the action are constant; however, CDFC is equivalent here to f being nondecreasing, not a very appealing property.

We can therefore apply CDFC:

$$\forall j = 1, \ldots, m, \quad P_{ij} \le \lambda P_{kj} + (1 - \lambda)P_{lj}$$

We deduce from this

$$\sum_{j=1}^{m} p_{ij}u(w_j) - a_i = \sum_{j=1}^{m-1} P_{ij}(u(w_j) - u(w_{j+1})) + u(w_m) - a_i$$

$$\ge \lambda\left(\sum_{j=1}^{m-1} P_{kj}(u(w_j) - u(w_{j+1})) + u(w_m) - a_k\right)$$

$$+ (1 - \lambda)\left(\sum_{j=1}^{m-1} P_{lj}(u(w_j) - u(w_{j+1})) + u(w_m) - a_l\right)$$

$$= \lambda\left(\sum_{j=1}^{m} p_{kj}u(w_j) - a_k\right)$$

$$+ (1 - \lambda)\left(\sum_{j=1}^{m} p_{lj}u(w_j) - a_l\right)$$

which is absurd by the definition of a_k and a_l. The wage schedule w therefore is the optimal solution in the global problem, and this concludes our proof because w is increasing.

The general logic that should be drawn from this analysis is that the structure of the simplest moral hazard problem is already very rich and that it is therefore dangerous to trust one's intuition too much. It is not necessarily true, for instance, that the second-best optimal action is less costly for the Agent than the first-best optimal action. It may not be true either that the expected profit of the Principal increases as the Agent becomes more "productive" (in the sense of first-order stochastic dominance) whatever action he chooses.[15] The literature contains many negative results of this sort.

---

15. Exercise 5.3 provides a counterexample.

5.3   Extensions

5.3.1   Informativeness and Second-Best Loss

Since the Principal must provide incentives to the Agent, his expected profit is lower in the second-best than it is in the first-best. We will show here that this loss in utility is greater when the technology is less informative.

Consider an (m, m) stochastic matrix[16] R, and assume that the probabilities p transform into numbers p' such that

$$\forall i,j, \quad p'_{ij} = \sum_{k=1}^{m} R_{jk} p_{ik}$$

Here the p' also are probabilities, since each column of R sums to one. In addition we let the outcomes x transform into x' so that the expected surplus stays constant for each action:[17]

$$\forall i, \quad \sum_{j=1}^{m} p'_{ij} x'_j = \sum_{j=1}^{m} p_{ij} x_j$$

We can understand the purpose of this transformation by imagining the following two-step experiment: The Principal does not observe the outcome x_k obtained according to the distribution p_{ij} given the choice of an action a_i, but only an outcome x'_j that is obtained by drawing from the outcomes x' with the probability distribution associated with the kth column of R. This transformation of the probabilities corresponds to less information (a *coarsening*) in the sense of Blackwell. This is because, in statistical terms, inferences drawn on a after observing x' with probabilities p' will be less precise than those drawn from observing x when the probabilities are p.

---

16. A stochastic matrix is a square matrix such that all of its elements are nonnegative and the elements in each column sum to 1.
17. This can be achieved by letting $x' = Sx$, where S is the inverse of the transpose of R.

Let a_i be an action and w' a wage schedule that implements it in the (p', x') model. Now recall the (p, x) model, and consider the wage schedule w given by

$$u(w_j) = \sum_{k=1}^{m} R_{kj}u(w'_k)$$

Going back to the two-step experiment invoked above, it is easy to see that this wage schedule implements a_i in the (p, x) model. We have indeed

$$\sum_{j=1}^{m} p_{ij}u(w_j) = \sum_{j=1}^{m}\sum_{k=1}^{m} p_{ij}R_{kj}u(w'_k)$$

$$= \sum_{k=1}^{m} p'_{ik}u(w'_k)$$

This implementation is less costly for the Principal than that obtained by w' in the (p', x') model, since it imposes less risk to the (risk-averse) Agent. This result, which appears in both Gjesdal (1982) and Grossman-Hart (1983), shows that the optimal action can be implemented at less cost in the more informative model. The problem is that the relation "being more informative than" is only a very partial order in the set of possible technologies, so this conclusion has little practical interest. It does allow us nevertheless to exhibit another of the many links between the moral hazard problem and the principles of statistical inference.

5.3.2 A Continuum of Actions

If the values of a are used in a continuous interval $[\underline{a}, \bar{a}]$, the incentive constraints will be too numerous to be tractable. One must then take the "first-order approach," which consists in neglecting all non-local incentive constraints.

Let $p_j(a)$ be the probability of x_j given a; the Agent maximizes

$$\sum_{j=1}^{m} p_j(a)u(w_j) - a$$

in a. The first-order condition then is

$$\sum_{j=1}^{m} p_j'(a)u(w_j) = 1$$

The first-order approach consists in neglecting all other conditions. The local second-order condition

$$\sum_{j=1}^{m} p_j''(a)u(w_j) \leq 0$$

is ignored along with the global conditions.

Models with a continuous set of actions were among the first considered in the literature. The question of the validity of the first-order approach was featured prominently from Mirrlees (1999) on, despite it being over only a technical point. Rogerson (1985) showed that this approach is valid under CDFC and MLRC, and that the wage then automatically increases with the outcome. Recall, however, that CDFC is not an entirely satisfactory condition; Jewitt (1988) proposed using weaker conditions on technology at the cost of requiring new conditions on the Agent's utility function.

Nevertheless, the use of a continuous-action model with two outcomes—success and failure, for instance—can make some comparative statics easier to prove. Exercises 5.4 and 5.5 give two examples that extend this discussion; see also sections 5.3.3 and 5.3.8.

5.3.3   The Limited Liability Model

The focus of this chapter on moral hazard has been so far the model where the Agent is risk-averse and the Principal faces a trade-off between incentives and risk-sharing. A popular alternative is the model where the Agent is risk-neutral, but there is a limit to the punishments the principal can inflict on the Agent when the outcome is bad. There are many good reasons for having limits; the obvious reason is that the Agent cannot face monetary fines that exceed his wealth.[18]

The limited liability model thus brings an interesting twist to the continuous-action, two-outcome model. Here we denote (w_S, w_F) the wages of the Agent and (x_S, x_F) the gross surplus, and assume that the probability of success $p(a)$ is increasing and concave. Then (as shown in exercise 5.4) the first-order approach applies and the Agent chooses the action such that

$$p'(a)(w_S - w_F) = 1$$

In addition to the individual rationality constraint

$$p(a)w_S + (1 - p(a))w_F - a \geq \underline{U}$$

the Agent now also has a limited liability constraint of the form $w_F \geq \underline{w}$ (by which we can infer $w_S \geq \underline{w}$ due to the incentive constraint).

Recall that the incentive constraint is $w_S = w_F + 1/p'(a)$; substituted into the individual rationality constraint, it yields $w_F \geq G(a)$, where

$$G(a) = \underline{U} + a - \frac{p(a)}{p'(a)}$$

is a decreasing function. The Principal's expected utility can thus be written as $(F(a) - w_F)$, where

$$F(a) = p(a)x_S + (1 - p(a))x_F - \frac{p(a)}{p'(a)}$$

This expression is then maximized over (a, w_F) under the individual rationality constraint and the incentive constraint. These two constraints reduce to

$$w_F \geq \max(\underline{w}, G(a))$$

---

18. Innes (1990) introduced this model to study a financial contracting problem.

This may look complicated, but the solution is quite simple. For simplicity, we take the generic case where F has a unique maximum in a_1 and $(F - G)$ has a unique maximum in a_2. Note that by defintion, $p'(a_2)(x_S - x_F) = 1$ and a_2 is the first-best effort. There are three possible constrained maxima:

- $a = a_1$, $w_F = \underline{w}$, with $G(a_1) \le \underline{w}$
- $w_F = G(a) = \underline{w}$
- $a = a_2$, $w_F = G(a_2)$, with $G(a_2) \ge \underline{w}$

Because G is decreasing, it is easy to see that $a_1 < a_2$, and the second case above happens for $G(a_2) < \underline{w} < G(a_1)$.

To sum up, when $\underline{w}$ is small, the limited liability constraint does not bind and the optimal effort is of course the first best effort a_2, since the Agent is risk-neutral. As $\underline{w}$ increases, we enter a regime where the optimal effort $G^{-1}(\underline{w})$ decreases, and for $\underline{w}$ large, the optimal effort settles in a_1. In the first two regimes, the Agent has no rent: his expected utility is $\underline{U}$. In the third regime, he gets a rent $(\underline{w} - G(a_2))$. By symmetry, the expected utility of the Principal is not affected by the limited liability constraint in the first regime; it decreases in the third regime, where it is $(F(a_2) - \underline{w})$. The reader can prove as an exercise that if F is increasing to the left of a_2 (e.g., if F is quasi-concave), then the expected utility of the Principal $(F(G^{-1}(\underline{w})) - \underline{w})$ also decreases in the second regime.

*5.3.4   An Infinity of Outcomes

Several studies have used an infinite (usually continuous) set of outcomes. Most do not prove the existence of an optimum, since it is a tricky problem to do so in this case. The contract w must be treated as a function. Since the Principal maximizes with respect to w, he must choose a function in a functional space. So the problem belongs to functional analysis. It only has a solution, in general, if the objective is continuous in w (which raises no particular problem) and if the space in which the function w is chosen is compact. Unfortunately, most natural function spaces are not compact, so one must impose restrictions on the shape of the contracts to keep a compact functional space (Page 1987). These restrictions (e.g., the equicontinuity of admissible w functions), however, cannot be easily intuited.

5.3.5 The Multisignal Case

The Principal may not only observe the outcome x that measures the global surplus but also a signal y that has no intrinsic economic value but brings information on a. For instance, the employer may observe the production of his employees through reports from middle management. How should the employer use this information?

Simple calculations show that (E) transforms into

$$\forall(j,y), \quad \frac{1}{u'(w_j^y)} = \mu + \sum_{k=1, k \neq i}^{n} \lambda_k \left(1 - \frac{p_{kj}^y}{p_{ij}^y} \right)$$

which characterizes the way the wage w depends on j and y (here p_{ij}^y denotes the probability of the pair (x_j, y) given a_i). The Principal will therefore condition the wage on y if and only if p_{kj}^y / p_{ij}^y depends on y, but in statistical terms, that is exactly the definition for x not being a sufficient statistic of (x, y) for a.[19]

This property underlies the *sufficient statistic theorem* (see Holmstrom 1979): the Principal conditions the wage on a sufficient statistic for all the signals he receives, whether extrinsic or intrinsic. Thus the conscientious employer will condition wages on middle management reports as well as on production if the reports convey information on the Agent's action that is not evident in his output. Kim (1995) generalizes both this result and the informativeness result of section 5.3.1 in the context of noninclusive information systems.

---

19. Intuitively this just means that the pair (x, y) contains more information on a than x alone.

Sometimes the Principal can obtain information on a by auditing the Agent's action at a cost. Dye (1986) studies the optimal monitoring strategy when MLRC and CDFC both hold, so that the optimal wage schedule keeps increasing. He shows that if auditing brings perfect information on a, the optimal monitoring policy consists in only auditing the Agent when his performance is lower than a threshold.

5.3.6   Imperfect Performance Measurement

It is often not the case that the Principal's payoff and the signal that he observes coincide, as was assumed thus far. The Principal often observes a signal that is imperfectly correlated with the surplus from the relationship. Baker (1992) shows that the optimal incentives then are lower-powered and implement less effort than when signal and surplus coincide. The reader is asked to prove this result in a more general model in exercise 5.5.

5.3.7   Models with Several Agents

In practice, there are many interactions between the Principal and the Agent that are difficult to isolate. For instance, the Principal may have a group of employees that work together as a team. In teamwork often only the team's global production can be measured, and the Agent's wage depends on global production. This clearly may induce Agents to free-ride on the effort of others, as proved by Holmstrom (1982). More generally, if a worker's effort additionally influences the production of some of his colleagues, then his wage should depend on their production as well as his own if individual production can be observed (Mookherjee 1984). This is a simple consequence of the sufficient statistic theorem.

Now consider a group of employees who accomplish similar tasks such that the production of each Agent depends on his effort, a noise that is common to all employees, and an idiosyncratic noise. Imagine, for instance, a group of workers who work in the same shop on partly independent tasks and who use the same machine tools; sellers of the same product to different clients also fit the picture. The sufficient statistic theorem then shows that the wage of each employee should depend on the productions of all, since observing all productions allows the employer to reduce uncertainty as to the common noise. As observed by Holmstrom (1982), competition among Agents here only has value insofar as it brings better information to the Principal: it would be useless if there was no common noise.

One frequently observes (especially in firms that rely on internal promotion) various practices of relative evaluation of employees that condition their utility on the way they are ranked by their superiors. This may be the only solution for the Principal if more specific measures of output are unverifiable. Green-Stokey (1983) have shown that in the model of the previous paragraph, these "tournaments" are almost optimal when there are many employees doing the same task; then the ranks of employees effectively become an almost sufficient statistic of their productions when employees are very numerous.

A slightly different model is that where Agents have tasks that are affected by independent observational noises, where each Agent may spend some of his time helping colleagues accomplish their tasks. If the wage given to Agent i only depends on how he accomplishes his own task, then he will not be induced to help his colleagues. However, it may be that the optimal contract consists in getting Agents to help each other. Itoh (1991) studies how the Principal can create the conditions for teamwork in such a model.

In all these results we assume that Agents adopt strategies that form a Nash equilibrium: Our conclusions would change drastically in situations where the Agents coordinate their actions, and even adopt collusive strategies.

5.3.8   Models with Several Principals

Agents' actions often affect many Principals whose preferences conflict. Think of firms regulated or taxed by several government bod-
ies or service workers who perform tasks for several employers. We
study here what Bernheim-Whinston (1986) call the "common
agency" model. The model also goes under the name "multiprincipals with symmetric information."[20]

For simplicity, we study here a continuous-action, two-outcome
model with one Agent and two Principals P_x and P_y. When he
expends effort a, the Agent succeeds in a project with probability $p(a)$
and fails with probability $1 - p(a)$. Both Principals are risk-neutral;
success (resp. failure) yields x_S (resp. x_F) to P_x and y_S (resp. y_F) to P_y.
If, for instance, $x_S - x_F > y_S - y_F$, then P_x is quicker than P_y in
extracting effort from the Agent because success has more value for
him.

We assume that the Principals play cooperatively, so that they
jointly get $S = x_S + y_S$ from success and $F = x_F + y_F$ from failure.
Exercise 5.4 shows that they choose to implement an effort level a^*
that is an increasing function of $(S - F)$:

$$a^* = G(S - F)$$

In addition exercise 5.5 shows that they jointly offer a wage schedule

$$(w_S(a^*), w_F(a^*))$$

where w_S (resp. w_F) is an increasing (resp. decreasing) function.

Bernheim-Whinston (1986) show that except in special cases (when
the Agent is risk-neutral), the Nash equilibrium of the game in
which each Principal simultaneously offers a wage schedule to the
Agent has a different outcome. In our model we go one step further:
the Nash equilibrium always implements a lower level of effort.

---

20. As opposed to the asymmetric information case studied in chapter 3.

We let P_y offer the wage schedule (w_y^S, w_y^F) to the Agent. In a Nash equilibrium, P_x must offer a wage schedule (w_x^S, w_x^F) that is a best response, given that the Agent optimally chooses his effort a. We then have

$$\begin{cases} w_x^S + w_y^S = w_S(a) \\ w_x^F + w_y^F = w_F(a) \end{cases}$$

Since P_x maximizes his expected utility

$$p(a)(x_S - w_x^S) + (1 - p(a))(x_F - w_x^F)$$

we rewrite this as

$$p(a)(x_S - w_S(a) + w_y^S) + (1 - p(a))(x_F - w_F(a) + w_y^F)$$

The reader is encouraged to apply exercise 5.4 to prove that at the optimum the Principal P_x gets $a_x = G(x_S + w_y^S - x_F - w_y^F)$. By similar reasoning, P_y gets $a_y = G(y_S + w_x^S - y_F - w_x^F)$. At the Nash equilibrium, we have $a_x = a_y = a$. This has two interesting consequences:

• Since G is increasing, its arguments in the two equations are equal. Rearranging gives

$$(x_S - x_F) - (w_x^S - w_x^F) = (y_S - y_F) - (w_y^S - w_y^F)$$

This means that Principal P_x gets the same increase in net surplus from a success as Principal P_y does, even if success is more or less valuable to him than to P_y.

• At the Nash equilibrium, $w_x^S - w_x^F < x_S - x_F$ and $w_y^S - w_y^F < y_S - y_F$ (otherwise, the Principals do not care for success). But this implies that

$$x_S + w_y^S - x_F - w_y^F < x_S + y_S - x_F - y_F = S - F$$

if the increasing function G is applied to both sides of the equation, $a < a^*$. The Principals thus implement a lower level of effort when they act noncooperatively.

The intuition for this second result is simple. Because the Agent acts on the basis of the sum of the incentives provided by the two Principals, these incentives have the character of a public good. In a noncooperative equilibrium the incentives are undersupplied.

*5.3.9   The Robustness of Contracts

We have seen that the optimal wage schedule depends on the likelihood ratios, which are relatively fine characteristics of the technology. Moreover the sufficient statistic theorem indicates that the optimal wage should depend on all signals that bring information on the action chosen by the Agent. Theory therefore suggests that the optimal incentive contract in moral hazard problems should be a priori a complex nonlinear function of a fairly large number of variables. This prediction does not accord well with experience, however. Real-life contracts usually take a simple form. They are often linear and depend on only a small number of variables.

Holmstrom-Milgrom (1987) tried to break from this deadlock by suggesting that simple (linear) contracts are more robust than complex contracts.[21] They suggest that the complexity of the optimal contract in theoretical models is due to the use of highly restricted production technology by the Agent. If the Agent is given more freedom, the optimal contract is simpler. This is the essence of the argument in this section; the rest of the discussion is mathematically sophisticated and can be skipped.

To illustrate their argument, Holmstrom-Milgrom consider a continuous-time model in which the outcome is produced by a diffusion process whose trend the Agent can control

$$dx_t = a_t\, dt + \sigma\, dW_t$$

---

21. Robustness here refers to the ability to stay (at least approximately) optimal when the environment changes.

where W is a Brownian motion[22] and $t \in [0, 1]$. The choice space of the Agent is therefore rich, and his action at every time t depends on x_t. The utilities of both parties only depend on the final outcome x_1. The utility of the Agent is

$$u\left(x_1 - \int_0^1 a_t dt \right)$$

where u is the CARA[23] function

$$u(x) = -e^{-kx}$$

The Principal is risk-neutral. The authors then show that the optimal contract is linear in x_1.

A way to understand this result is to recognize that the Brownian motion is the continuous-time limit of a discrete-time binomial process, where the outcome can increase or decrease by a fixed amount in each period and the Agent controls the probabilities of these two changes. As the utility function of the Agent is CARA and therefore exhibits no wealth effect, it can be shown that the optimal contract consists in repeating the contract that is optimal in each period. But this contract gives a fixed wage to the Agent, plus a bonus if the outcome increased. The optimal contract for the whole period therefore must give the Agent a bonus that depends linearly on the number of periods in which the outcome increased. The result of Holmstrom-Milgrom clearly obtains by passing to the continuous-time limit.

In its strongest form this result depends on rather special assumptions; however, it does suggest that if the Principal only has imperfect knowledge of the technology, the optimal contract can take a fairly simple form.

---

22. Recall that a Brownian motion is a set of random variables indexed by $t \in [0, 1]$ such that each W_t follows a reduced centered normal $N(0, t)$ and increments are independent: If $t_1 < t_2 < t_3 < t_4$, $W_{t_2} - W_{t_1}$ and $W_{t_4} - W_{t_3}$ are independent. The Brownian motion is the statistical model for a continuous-time random walk.
23. CARA stands for constant absolute risk aversion.

5.3.10   The Multitask Model

Contrary to what we have assumed so far, all decisions taken by the
Agent often cannot be summed up in a single variable. It is more
realistic to consider, for instance, that an employee's work typically
consists of many distinct tasks. Each task requires effort and will
send a signal that is observed by the employer. When the Principal
chooses a wage schedule, he must take into account the multiplicity
of the performed tasks. He must take care, for instance, not to
reward high accomplishment in one task to the point that it induces
the Agent to forgo other tasks. Let us now look at a model that introduces such new trade-offs.

Assume that the Agent controls two effort variables a_1 and a_2. His
utility function is given by

$$-\exp\left(-r(w - C(a_1, a_2))\right)$$

where r is a positive constant (the Agent's absolute risk aversion
index) and C is a convex function. The Principal observes separately
the profits he gets from each task:

$$\begin{cases} x_1 = a_1 + \varepsilon_1 \\ x_2 = a_2 + \varepsilon_2 \end{cases}$$

where the pair of observational noises $(\varepsilon_1, \varepsilon_2)$ follows a centered normal with variance

$$\Sigma = \begin{pmatrix} \sigma_1^2 & \sigma_{12} \\ \sigma_{12} & \sigma_2^2 \end{pmatrix}$$

The global profit of the Principal is the sum $(x_1 + x_2)$.

Since earlier we chose a CARA utility function for the Agent, we
can use the results of Holmstrom-Milgrom (1987) presented in section 5.3.9 to focus on the optimal linear wage contracts:

$$w(x_1, x_2) = \alpha'x + \beta = \alpha_1 x_1 + \alpha_2 x_2 + \beta$$

With a linear contract, a Principal gets expected profits

$$a_1 + a_2 - \alpha_1 a_1 - \alpha_2 a_2 - \beta$$

while the Agent's expected utility has a certainty equivalent[24]

$$\alpha_1 a_1 + \alpha_2 a_2 + \beta - C(a_1, a_2) - \frac{r}{2} \alpha' \Sigma \alpha$$

The parameter β in the formulas above, only represents a transfer between the Principal and the Agent. So the optimal contract has to be found by maximizing the expected total surplus

$$a_1 + a_2 - C(a_1, a_2) - \frac{r}{2} \alpha' \Sigma \alpha$$

under the incentive constraint that states that (a_1, a_2) maximizes

$$\alpha_1 a_1 + \alpha_2 a_2 - C(a_1, a_2)$$

First let us consider the consequences of the incentive constraint. It gives directly

$$\alpha_i = C_i'(a_1, a_2) \qquad (I)$$

By differentiating, we obtain

$$\begin{cases} \dfrac{\partial a_1}{\partial \alpha_1} = \dfrac{C_{22}''}{D''} \\[2ex] \dfrac{\partial a_1}{\partial \alpha_2} = -\dfrac{C_{12}''}{D''} \end{cases}$$

---

24. Recall that for an agent whose von Neumann–Morgenstern utility function is u, the certain equivalent of a random wealth X is the number x such that $u(x) = Eu(X)$. I have used the formula that gives the expectation of an exponential function of a normal random variable X,

$$E \exp(-rX) = \exp\left(-rEX + \frac{r^2}{2} VX\right)$$

applied here to the random variable $\alpha' x$.

where D'' is the determinant of C'' and is positive. This means that the Agent chooses an action a_1 that increases with α_1 and that decreases with α_2 if both tasks are substitutes ($C''_{12} > 0$). This simple insight is the key to the results to come.

Let us now come back to the optimal contract. By differentiating the expression for the expected total surplus with respect to a_i, we obtain

$$1 - C'_i - r\alpha' \Sigma \frac{\partial \alpha}{\partial a_i} = 0$$

whence, after differentiating (I),

$$\alpha = (I + rC'' \Sigma)^{-1} \begin{pmatrix} 1 \\ 1 \end{pmatrix}$$

Next let us study some consequences of the formula above. Suppose that tasks are independent (C'' is diagonal) and that the signals are independent ($\sigma_{12} = 0$). Then we get

$$\alpha_i = \frac{1}{1 + rC''_{ii}\sigma_i^2}$$

which is the same formula as if the Principal had considered the two tasks separately.

Now, in the more interesting case where the matrix C'' is not diagonal, suppose that only the first task generates an observable signal. This can be modeled by letting $\sigma_{12} = 0$ and by making σ_2 go to infinity in the formula that gives α. In the limit one easily obtains $\alpha_2 = 0$ and

$$\alpha_1 = \frac{1 - (C''_{12}/C''_{22})}{1 + r\sigma_1^2 \left[C''_{11} - ((C''_{12})^2/C''_{22}) \right]} \qquad (G)$$

If we take as a benchmark the case of independent tasks, we see that both the numerator and the denominator of the formula have changed. When, for instance, the two tasks are complements ($C''_{12} < 0$: an increase in a_1 makes a_2 less costly), α_1 will be higher if C''_{12} is more negative: The second task is not directly rewarded because it does not generate an observable signal, but the corresponding incentives are carried over to the first task.

Given the same assumption that σ_2 is infinite, now suppose that only total effort reduces the Agent's utility so that $C(a_1, a_2) = c(a_1 + a_2)$. Then not only $\alpha_2 = 0$, but formula (G) also yields $\alpha_1 = 0$ since $C''_{11} = C''_{12} = C''_{22}$. In this limit case where the two tasks are perfect substitutes and one of them is unobservable, inducing the Agent to perform in one task effectively discourages him to perform in the other. This dilemma brings the Principal to the point where he entirely gives up on incentives.

Holmstrom-Milgrom (1991) take this last result to suggest that the multitask model may explain why real-life incentive schedules are less *high-powered*[25] than they are in theoretical models. The fact that many tasks compete for the Agent's effort may induce the Principal to reduce the power of the incentives he can provide to the Agent.

5.4 Examples of Applications

5.4.1 Insurance

The archetypal conflict between risk-sharing and incentives that is at the basis of moral hazard is found in the issuing of insurance. Risk-sharing is the central mission of insurance companies. By pooling risks, they rely on the law of large numbers and can take responsibility for individual risks that (approximately) cancel out through aggregation. However, the magnitude of the risk depends on the behavior of the insurees: A cautious driver has fewer accidents. This creates an incentive problem that limits the risk the insurer is willing to bear and transfers some responsibility to the insurees by letting them bear some of the cost.

We return here to the example in chapter 2 of a driver who buys car insurance from an insurance company. However, we assume now

---

25. As mentioned in section 5.1, a schedule is high-powered when wages depend strongly on performance.

that the driver's characteristics are completely known to the insurer. So using the same notation as in chapter 2 we have the initial wealth of the driver W, an accident that can cost him d, a premium q, and a reimbursement R. The probability of an accident is a decreasing convex function $p(a)$ of the Agent's effort a,[26] and a can be chosen in $[\underline{a}, \bar{a}]$. The cost of an effort a is just a. So the expected utility of the driver is

$$p(a)u(W - d + R - q) + (1 - p(a))u(W - q) - a$$

The expected profit of the (risk-neutral) insurance company is

$$q - p(a)R$$

The driver chooses his effort by maximizing his objective over a; in this simple model in which only two outcomes are possible, it is easy to check that p being decreasing implies MLRC and that its convexity implies CDFC, so we can apply the first-order approach. The Agent's choice thus is given by

$$p'(a)(u(W - d + R - q) - u(W - q)) = 1$$

If the reimbursement R was at least equal to the size of the damage d, the driver will choose the minimum self-protection effort $\underline{a}$, which is usually suboptimal. To induce the driver to be cautious, he must get a reimbursement lower than the size of the damage. This property is called *coinsurance*: In case of an accident, the costs are shared by the insurance company (who pays R) and the driver (who suffers a loss $(d - R)$).

To solve the problem completely, we use the participation constraint

$$p(a)u(W - d + R - q) + (1 - p(a))u(W - q) - a = \underline{U}$$

to obtain a second equation that allows us to write utilities as functions of a:

---

26. The literature sometimes makes a distinction between self-protection efforts, which reduce the probability of an accident, and self-insurance efforts, which reduce the size of the damage. Here we are only concerned with self-protection.

$$\begin{cases} u(W - d + R - q) = \underline{U} + a + \dfrac{1 - p(a)}{p'(a)} \\ u(W - q) = \underline{U} + a - \dfrac{p(a)}{p'(a)} \end{cases}$$

We can therefore write the premium and the reimbursement as functions of a, as $q(a)$ and $R(a)$ in this instance. All that remains to do is to maximize the Principal's objective over a.

$$q(a) - p(a)R(a)$$

5.4.2 Wage Determination

Firms are prominent among economic organizations that worry about providing adequate incentives to their members. The study of how they do it therefore is both a natural application and an empirical test of the theories presented in this chapter. Obviously other sciences such as the sociology of organizations and psychology have much to contribute to this field, but the objective of the economist is still to push economic analysis as far as possible.

Theory tells us that the best way to give incentives to employees is to identify one or more outcomes that constitute objective public signals of their effort and to condition their compensation on these outcomes. A caricatural form of such wage schedules is the piece-rate wage whereby the employee is paid a function of the number of pieces he produces. This type of wage is only applicable in limited cases. Moreover it may be counterproductive if the employee focuses on the quantity he produces (which influences his wage) rather than on the quality of the product (which does not). It also tends to discourage cooperation among employees. In general, the employer must therefore try to identify a vector of outcomes that is as complete as possible. If he cannot do this, he must depend on subjective evaluations of the Agent's work. This method requires a much more delicate touch, since it can have perverse effects by inducing employees to spend much of their time lobbying their supervisors.

If a one-on-one evaluation is not practical, the employer may resort to collective evaluations. The simplest form of this is to use the firm's profit as an "outcome" and to condition wages on it. As for all collective evaluations, it raises the free-rider problem. Also it makes employees bear a risk that they may find difficult to diversify. This solution is a popular one in part for macroeconomic or social reasons. The use of franchises whereby a firm sells dealers the right to carry a certain brand is an extreme example. In that case the Agent pays for the right to keep all profits, as he should in the first-best contract if he is risk-neutral.

Tournaments and the other relative performance evaluation procedures studied in section 5.3.7 can be used, in principle, to determine wages among employees, but the empirical evidence is not convincing on this point. Nevertheless, the formula is widely used (at least implicitly) to decide on promotions within the firm and for corresponding wage increases. Indeed, it is a well-known fact that the dispersion of wages within a firm is channeled toward changes in job levels. Employees at a certain level and with certain seniority in that level have comparable wages,[27] but a change in job level is associated with a substantial wage increase. Thus promotions are the most important incentive in a firm.

The crudest way of inducing employees to work is to threaten them with dismissal. This may be the only incentive available if outcomes from effort are observable but, for whatever reason, are not verifiable and thus do not condition an Agent's wage. However, threatening to fire employees who do not give satisfactory performances is useless when unemployment is low, since an employee who is dismissed will easily find a similar job at an equivalent wage. This idea is the basis of the famous Shapiro-Stiglitz (1984) model of involuntary unemployment. In this model employees choose to shirk if their utility from working does not exceed that of being unemployed. To induce them to put in effort, the wage has to be set

---

27. This is often called "horizontal equity."

higher than the market-clearing wage. This efficiency-wage model is also at the heart of many neo-Keynesian explanations of involuntary unemployment.[28] Lazear (1979) suggests that the reason wages increase with seniority is that this allows the firm to raise the cost of a dismissal for the employees and thus to increase their incentive to work. This explanation is valid if firms want to keep their reputation for being fair employers, so they do not fire older employees whose wages are higher than their marginal productivity.

Managerial compensation raises other problems. Managers speak for shareholders and take in their name decisions that govern the strategy of the firm. Inducing managers to work is generally not thought to be a problem. However, some managers have their own agenda in running a firm (maximizing perks or firm size, launching unprofitable but prestigious investments, etc.). If they are to take decisions that increase the value of a firm, their interests should align with those of the shareholders. There are external measures used to discipline managers, notably their labor market and the threat of hostile takeover.

Let us begin here with internal incentives. The easiest way for a firm to provide incentives to its managers is to link their compensation to the firm's profits by paying them with shares. Neglecting managers' risk-aversion for the moment, this is a good strategy so long as the value of the shares faithfully reflects the value of the firm. A major problem is that unscrupulous managers are in a strategic position to manipulate the value of the shares for their own benefit. Likewise, where managerial wages are indexed on profits, managers may be induced to manipulate the firm's accounts or to take a short-term view. In general, however, managers are compensated by receiving stock options at a strike price that is set higher than the current price of the firm's share. Such options allow the shareholders to reward managers who increase the value of the firm, but all incentive

---

28. On a more technical side, Shapiro-Stiglitz's model is interesting in that it uses labor demand to endogenize the participation constraint.

value gets lost if a negative shock affects the value of the firm. We won't dwell on these issues, since recent corporate scandals in the United States and in Europe suggest that some managerial compensation schemes may owe more to rent-seeking behavior than to the incentive problems considered in this chapter.

Fama (1980) argued that the managerial incentive problem can be solved by the implicit market incentives. In this view managers are disciplined by their concern about their reputation on the labor market. Holmstrom (1982, published 1999) gave a precise form to this argument. It is a dynamic model in which the manager and the market both learn imperfectly his ability over time. The manager's ability η_t is treated as a random walk:

$$\eta_{t+1} = \eta_t + \delta_t$$

where δ_t is a serially uncorrelated shock independent of η_t and the manager and the market have identical priors over η_1.

In each period the manager expends some effort a_t and produces an observable output $y_t = \eta_t + a_t + \varepsilon_t$, where ε_t is independent from the manager's ability and serially uncorrelated. The manager uses effort as a substitute for ability in his attempt to establish a good reputation.

We assume that the labor market for managers is perfectly competitive. Because the market only observes at the beginning of period t the sequence of past outputs $y^{t-1} = (y_1, ..., y_{t-1})$, it pays the manager a wage

$$w_t(y^{t-1}) = E(y_t \mid y^{t-1})$$

The manager is risk-neutral but discounts the future. So his utility from consuming (c_t) and expending effort (a_t) is

$$\sum_{t=1}^{\infty} \beta^{t-1}(c_t - g(a_t))$$

The effort cost function g is increasing and convex, with $g'(0) = 0$ and $g'(\infty) > 1$. Since the manager is risk-neutral, we don't need to worry about his saving and borrowing, and we can let $c_t = w_t$.

The efficient effort is given by $g'(\bar{a}) = 1$, since effort has marginal return one and marginal cost $g'(a)$. Our aim is to study whether this efficient effort can be implemented as time goes to infinity. Therefore we focus on an equilibrium in which the market rationally expects that the manager expends effort $a_t^*(y^{t-1})$. This way it knows that in period t,

$$\eta_t + \varepsilon_t = y_t - a_t^*$$

and we are faced with a signal-extraction problem.

Suppose that $(\eta_1, (\delta_t, \varepsilon_t))$ are jointly normal centered with constant finite variances $(v_1, v_\delta, v_\varepsilon)$. Then standard statistical calculations show that the mean posterior belief on the manager's ability, $m_t = E(\eta_t \mid y^{t-1})$, obeys the adaptive recursion

$$m_{t+1} - m_t = \lambda_t(y_t - a_t^* - m_t)$$

In this equation, λ_t is a parameter in $(0, 1)$ that increases with the ratio v_δ/v_ε. The mean posterior m_t is very important, as it directly determines the manager's wages on the equilibrium path:

$$w_t = m_t + a_t^*$$

Now we return to the manager's effort choice problem. Suppose that it deviates from the equilibrium path in increasing effort by some small da in period t. This has no effect on the manager's in period t, but it changes the sequence of mean posterior beliefs starting in $(t + 1)$ according to the recursion

$$dm_{s+1} - dm_s = -\lambda_s dm_s$$

with $dm_{t+1} = \lambda_t da$. Simple calculations show that in period $s \geq t + 1$, the resulting wage increase is

$$dw_s = \lambda_t \prod_{i=t+1}^{s-1} (1 - \lambda_i) da$$

Thus the discounted utility benefit from increasing effort by da in period t is

$$dU = \lambda_t da \sum_{s=t+1}^{\infty} \prod_{i=t+1}^{s-1} (1 - \lambda_i)$$

While the expression above looks nasty, it can be simplified by noting that λ_t converges to some limit λ^* as time goes to infinity. For t large, dU converges toward

$$dU^* = da \frac{\lambda^* \beta}{1 - \beta(1 - \lambda^*)}$$

Since we deviated from the equilibrium path, the first-order benefit from this deviation must equal the first-order cost, which is just $g'(a)da$. It follows that as time elapses, the equilibrium effort converges towards the a^* given by

$$g'(a^*) = \frac{\lambda^* \beta}{1 - \beta(1 - \lambda^*)}$$

Note that the right-hand side of this equation is positive and smaller than one if $0 < \beta < 1$. It follows that while the implicit incentive of the labor market makes managers expend effort, the equilibrium effort a^* is smaller than the efficient effort $\bar{a}$[29]. Thus there is room for both implicit and explicit incentives provided by a performance-contingent contract[30].

Exercises

Exercise 5.1

Using the two-action, two-outcome model of section 5.1., prove that if $W_1 > W_0$, the Principal's utility is greater when the Agent succeeds than when he fails.

---

29. It is easy to see that given the properties of λ^*, a^* is an increasing function of β and v_δ and a decreasing function of v_ε. In fact, when ability is constant over time ($v_\delta = 0$), $a^* = 0$: as the market learns ability perfectly over time, there is no more incentive for the manager to expend effort so as to acquire a good reputation.
30. Introducing managerial risk-aversion reinforces this conclusion, as expending effort has random returns and thus is a risky activity.

1. Using the definitions of w_S, w_F, and w and Jensen's inequality,[31] show that $pw_S + (1 - p)w_F > w$.

2. Refer to the expression for $W_1 - W_0$ in the text. Show that if $x_S - w_S \leq x_F - w_F$, then $W_1 < W_0$.

3. State your conclusions.

Exercise 5.2

In the standard model, show that first-order stochastic dominance implies MLRC if there are only two possible outcomes.

Exercise 5.3

This exercise shows why the Principal's expected profit may decrease as the Agent becomes more productive—even in the two-by-two model of section 5.1. Start from values of the primitives such that $W_1 > W_0$.

1. Write W_1 as a function of p and P, and show that

$$\frac{\partial W_1}{\partial p} = -\frac{P(1-P)}{(P-p)^2}\left(\frac{1}{u'(w_S)} - \frac{1}{u'(w_F)}\right) < 0$$

2. Conclude that if the Agent gets more productive so that both p and P increase, it may be that W_1 decreases.

Exercise 5.4

Take the continuous-action, two-outcome (success or failure) model. Denote $p(a)$ (increasing, concave) the probability of success.

1. Prove that CDFC and MLRC hold, so that you can use the first-order approach.

---

31. Recall that Jensen's inequality states that if X is a random variable and f is a convex function, then $Ef(X) \geq f(EX)$.

2. Use the incentive and individual rationality constraints to prove that if a is the optimal action, then

$$\begin{cases} u(w_F) & = \underline{U} + a - \dfrac{p(a)}{p'(a)} \\[2mm] u(w_S) = \underline{U} + a + \dfrac{1 - p(a)}{p'(a)} \end{cases}$$

3. Denote $w_S(a)$ and $w_F(a)$ the corresponding levels of wages. Write the Principal's expected utility as a function of a and $\delta x = x_S - x_F$. Show that its cross-derivative is positive and use the implicit function theorem to prove that the optimal a is an increasing function of δx.

Exercise 5.5

Take the same model as in exercise 5.4, but change the information structure. With probability $p(a)$ (increasing, concave) the Principal observes a signal and pays a wage w_1 to the Agent; otherwise, the Agent gets w_0. This signal is positively correlated with success: the conditional probability of success given that the signal is observed is Q, while it is $q < Q$ if the signal is not observed. Note that $q = 0$ and $Q = 1$ in the classical case in which the signal indicates success or failure.

1. Prove that just as above,

$$\begin{cases} u(w_0) = \underline{U} + a - \dfrac{p(a)}{p'(a)} \\[2mm] u(w_1) = \underline{U} + a + \dfrac{1 - p(a)}{p'(a)} \end{cases}$$

2. Denote $w_1(a)$ and $w_0(a)$ these functions. Write the Principal's expected utility as a function of a, x_S and x_F. Show that it is formally analogous to that in exercise 5.4, with x_S and x_F replaced by

$x'_S = Qx_S + (1 - Q)x_F$ and $x'_F = qx_S + (1 - q)x_F$. Use exercise 5.4 to conclude that the optimal a is an increasing function of $Q - q$.

3. Prove that $w_1(a)$ is increasing and $w_0(a)$ is decreasing. Conclude that the power of the incentive scheme $w_1(a) - w_0(a)$ is an increasing function of $Q - q$.

Exercise 5.6

Take the n-action, m-outcome model of Section 5.2. We want to compare MLRC and first-order stochastic dominance (1SD).

1. Show that 1SD means that P_{ij} decreases in i for all j. Also prove that under 1SD, the expected outcome $\sum_{j=1}^{m} p_{ij} x_j$ increases in i: more costly actions generate higher expected outcomes.

2. Take $k < i$. Define $F_0 = 0$ and for $j = 1, \ldots, m$,

$$F_j = P_{kj} - P_{ij}$$

Prove that under MLRC, $(F_j - F_{j-1})$ is positive for low j and negative for high j. Use $F_m = 0$ to conclude that MLRC implies 1SD.

3. Prove that with only two outcomes ($m = 2$), MLRC and 1SD are equivalent.

References

Baker, G. 1992. Incentive contracts and performance measurement. *Journal of Political Economy* 100:598–614.

Bernheim, D., and M. Whinston. 1986. Common agency. *Econometrica* 54:923–42.

Dye, R. 1986. Optimal monitoring policies in agencies. *Rand Journal of Economics* 17:339–50.

Fama, E. 1980. Agency problems and the theory of the firm. *Journal of Political Economy* 88:288–307.

Gjesdal, F. 1982. Information and incentives: The Agency information problem. *Review of Economic Studies* 49:373–90.

Green, J., and N. Stokey. 1983. A comparison of tournaments and contracts. *Journal of Political Economy* 91:349–64.

Grossman, S., and O. Hart. 1983. An analysis of the principal–agent problem. *Econometrica* 51:7–45.

Holmstrom, B. 1979. Moral hazard and observability. *Bell Journal of Economics* 10:74–91.

Holmstrom, B. 1982. Moral hazard in teams. *Bell Journal of Economics* 13:324–40.

Holmstrom, B. 1999. Managerial incentive problems: a dynamic perspective. *Review of Economic Studies* 66:169–182.

Holmstrom, B., and P. Milgrom. 1987. Aggregation and linearity in the provision of intertemporal incentives. *Econometrica* 55:303–28.

Holmstrom, B., and P. Milgrom. 1991. Multitask principal–agent analyses: Incentive contracts, asset ownership and job design. *Journal of Law, Economics and Organization* 7:24–51.

Innes, R. 1990. Limited liability and incentive contracts with ex-ante action choices. *Journal of Economic Theory* 52:45–67.

Itoh, H. 1991. Incentives to help in multi-agent situations. *Econometrica* 59:611–36.

Jewitt, I. 1988. Justifying the first-order approach to principal–agent problems. *Econometrica* 56:1177–90.

Kim, S. K. 1995. Efficiency of an information system in an agency model. *Econometrica* 63:89–102.

Lazear, E. 1979. Why is there mandatory retirement? *Journal of Political Economy* 87:1261–84.

Mirrlees, J. 1999. The theory of moral hazard and unobservable behaviour. Part I. *Review of Economic Studies* 66:3–21.

Mookherjee, D. 1984. Optimal incentive schemes in multi-agent situations. *Review of Economic Studies* 51:433–46.

Page, F. 1987. The existence of optimal contracts in the principal–agent model. *Journal of Mathematical Economics* 16:157-67.

Rogerson, W. 1985. The first-order approach to principal-agent problems. *Econometrica* 53:1357–68.

Shapiro, C., and J. Stiglitz. 1984. Equilibrium unemployment as a worker discipline device. *American Economic Review* 74:433–44.

6   The Dynamics of
         Complete Contracts

We considered so far only very elementary forms of economic relationships: a contract is signed, then all parties take decisions based
on their preferences and on the terms of the contract, and then they
separate. Real-life economic relationships obviously are much more
complex, if only because the actors face each other for more or less
extended time periods. The recognition that contracts have a time
dimension has spawned a very abundant literature since the 1980s.
The aim in this chapter and the next one is to present the general
conclusions.

A contract is properly called *complete* if it takes into account all
variables that are or may become relevant over the time period it is
to be executed. A contract that can be renegotiated is not said to be
complete. Only contracts that bind the parties until the end of their
relationship qualify. The literature, however, calls a contract incomplete if *from the start* the contract does not condition on all relevant
variables. In this book we will adhere to this traditional but inade-
quate distinction: complete contracts will be studied in this chapter
and incomplete contracts in chapter 7.

Note that a complete contract may be contingent on a very large
number of variables. No unforeseen contingency may arise as the
relationship evolves: any change in the economic environment just
activates the ad hoc provisions of the contract.

The dynamics of complete contracts are fairly well understood
today. So in this chapter we will cover reasonably wide theoretical

ground. Where the proofs of the principles are too complex, I will only give the underlying intuition.

6.1   Commitment and Renegotiation

We have seen the importance of institutions in the theory of contracts. Introducing the dynamic of time gives a new weight to two key elements of contracts: commitment and renegotiation.

By commitment we mean that agents pledge in advance to keep their activities in accord with the contract until some predetermined date. The duration of commitment determines how rigid the contract is. The ability to commit depends on a number of factors:

• Institutional setup, in contractual law.

• Credibility of agents, in particular, the value they place on their reputation.

• Existence of "hostages," which are assets or property titles that lose most of their value outside of the relationship under study. For instance, the computer manufacturer Apple launched the Macintosh, it built special factories which helped to signal to Apple's competitors and customers that the firm was firmly behind its new product.

• Penalties to discourage the parties from unilaterally breaking the contract.

Breach of contract and renegotiation are the opposite of commitment. A breach of contract is a unilateral decision. One party chooses to disengage itself from the contract. In most cases the breach of contract will incur the penalties determined by law or in the contract. Where penalties may not exist, the contract can be broken at any time. For example, employees break contracts, sometimes giving advance notice, and the employer is not entitled to any compensation. We speak of renegotiation, on the other hand, when all parties agree to replace the existing contract with a new contract. Renegotiation is multilateral by definition, so no party can claim a penalty.

There are four types of commitment we need to distinguish here:[1]

• We speak of *spot commitment*, or *no commitment*, when the contract only holds for the current period.[2] Once the parties reach the end of this period, they can continue collaborating if they sign a new contract.

• We speak of *full commitment* when the contract that is signed covers the whole duration of the relationship, and it cannot be breached or renegotiated. Such a contract is never reconsidered, and the dynamics of the contractual relationship amount to the execution of the contract.[3]

• We speak of *long-term commitment with renegotiation*, or simply *long-term commitment*, if the contract covers the whole duration of the relationship, but it can be renegotiated multilaterally. The contract can only be reconsidered if all parties agree to do so.

• Last, we speak of *short-term commitment*,[4] or *limited commitment*, in all intermediate cases between spot commitment and long-term commitment. These contracts do not last as long as the relationship and may be renegotiated.

A fundamental result of the theory of individual choices is that no agent, taken in isolation, can gain by limiting his freedom of choice. But this result changes when several agents interact. The Prisoner's Dilemma is a striking example: Two players have two strategies: they can cooperate or defect. The only Nash equilibrium has both players defecting, and it is Pareto-dominated by the outcome in which both players cooperate. If the players can commit to cooperate

---

1. The terminology is not standard in this field, so the terms used here should be treated with caution.
2. The exact definition of a "period" depends on the context.
3. As noted in the discussion at the beginning of this chapter, only contracts with full commitment can be called complete.
4. *Caveat lector*: Some authors do not distinguish between spot commitment and short-term commitment. However, I think this distinction is important.

(thus forbidding themselves to use the "defect" strategy), they both reach a higher utility level.

It is easy to see that full commitment is beneficial if contracts are complete. Suppose that commitment is less than full and that the interaction ends up with some outcome A. If full commitment is available, the agents can then just commit to achieve outcome A. Thus any outcome that is feasible without full commitment can be achieved with full commitment. The agents cannot lose, and may even win, if they choose to cooperate. Therefore the study of the dynamics of complete contracts essentially consists in tracking when and why other forms of commitment involve efficiency losses.

We will see in chapter 7 that commitment has less value when contracts are incomplete. In that case some variables that influence the parameters of the relationship under study are not integrated in the contract in advance. Renegotiation then allows the parties to improve the efficiency of the contractual relationship.

6.2 Strategic Commitment

Before we turn to the dynamics of complete contracts, we will survey briefly here the literature on *strategic commitment*. The central theme of this field is that signing a contract can have *precommitment effects* on a third party by convincing it that the contractants will persist in their plans whatever it does. Thus it offers another illustration of the importance of commitment in contracting.

The idea of strategic commitment goes back to Schelling (1960). Early papers that formalized his intuitions include works by Brander-Spencer (1985), who showed that export subsidies may improve welfare in the home country, and Fershtman-Judd (1987), who studied the strategic use of managerial incentives in a Cournot oligopoly.

We will consider here a study by Aghion-Bolton (1987), who introduced a new way for a firm to prevent entry on its market. Barriers to entry have long been a central theme of industrial organization. Several contractual devices can be used for that purpose. In manufacturer-retailer relationships, for instance, *exclusive dealing*, forbids a retailer for one brand to also sell a competing brand. The legality of such practices depends on prevailing statutes, and even more crucially on the way they are applied. Authors belonging to the Chicago school[5] argue that such contracts are not illegal because buyers will never not agree to sign contracts that are detrimental to their utility. We will see that although this argument is basically right, exclusive contracts can undermine competition and lead to social inefficiencies.

Consider a seller S who can offer a good produced at cost $1/2$. This seller presents the good to a certain buyer B, who can buy none or one unit of the good. The reservation price for this unit is 1. A potential entrant E offers the same good at cost c. Neither B nor S knows the exact value of c. All they have is a prior that we take to be the uniform distribution on $[0, 1]$, so the entrant may or may not be more efficient than the seller.

If E does enter the market, he and S will compete in prices à la Bertrand. The equilibrium price, which is the highest of the two production costs, is written as

$$P = \max\left(\frac{1}{2}, c\right)$$

If there is no contract between S and B, E can enter if, and only if, his cost is smaller than $1/2$, which has probability $\varphi = 1/2$. The price will be 1 if E does not enter and $1/2$ if he does. The buyer has an expected surplus of $1/4$, and so does S.

Now suppose that B and S sign a contract (chosen and offered by S) before E can enter the marketplace. Further suppose that c is not observed by B or S ex post, so the contract cannot be contingent on

---

5. The Chicago school is associated with an indulgent attitude as far as competition policy is concerned.

the value of c. It is easy to show that the optimal contract must be a pair (P, P_0), where P is the price B must pay to S if he buys the good from him and P_0 is the penalty he must pay to S if he decides to buy from E instead.

These circumstances call for B to buy E's good only if the price is set lower than $P - P_0$, and for E to choose a price equal to $P - P_0$ when he enters the market.[6] E will thus enter only if his cost c is lower than $P - P_0$, so the probability of entry becomes

$$\varphi' = \max (0, P - P_0) \qquad (P)$$

which depends on the terms of the contract. Last, the buyer will not sign the contract unless he gets at least as much expected surplus as without the contract,[7] that is, $1/4$. Because the buyer's surplus is $(1 - P)$ if he buys from S, the entrant cannot optimally give him a higher surplus. So we must have

$$1 - P \geq \frac{1}{4} \qquad (IR)$$

Now we compute S's expected surplus. It is $(P - 1/2)$ if E does not enter and P_0 if E enters the market (in which case the buyer buys from him). The optimal contract (P, P_0) therefore must maximize

$$\varphi' P_0 + (1 - \varphi')\left(P - \frac{1}{2}\right)$$

under both constraints (P) and (IR).

We consider two possibilities. If $P < P_0$, we have $\varphi' = 0$, and the objective is $(P - 1/2)$, which, given (IR), is maximal in $P = 3/4$, where it is $1/4$. If $P \geq P_0$, we have $\varphi' = P - P_0$. We then cancel the

---

6. We can assume that if B is indifferent between both sellers, he chooses to buy from E.

7. This is the Chicago school argument mentioned earlier.

derivative of the objective with respect to P_0, get $P_0 = P - 1/4$, and reinject it into the objective to obtain $P - 7/16$. This term, given (IR), is maximal in $P = 3/4$ again, but it equals $5/16$, which is greater than $1/4$. Thus the optimum is given by $(P, P_0) = (3/4, 1/2)$.

At the optimum, B gets the same surplus as without a contract, since $1 - 3/4 = 1/4$. However, the contract allows S to get a higher surplus, which increases from $1/4$ to $5/16$. The probability of entry now is $1/4$. In particular, when $1/4 < c < 1/2$, E does not enter. The less efficient seller produces the good, and there is *market foreclosure*.

Thus signing a contract with B that punishes B when he buys from the entrant allows S to reduce the competitive pressure on his profits. Although this contract does not hurt the buyer, it draws the producers away from the production optimum, which is when B buys from S at $c > 1/2$ and from E at $c < 1/2$. This result suggests that such contractual practice should be forbidden.

In this example, a party (the seller) tries to deter another party (the entrant) from taking a certain decision (here entering the market) by signing a contract with a third party (the buyer) and making it public. This behavior, based on precommitment effects, is the essence of strategic commitment. Katz (1991) has a similar, perfect information model in which a seller who values a good at 1 faces a buyer who values it at 2. If the seller sets the price, he will appropriate all the surplus by pricing the good at 2. However, if the buyer signs a public contract with an intermediary, promising to buy the good only from him and at price 1, then the equilibrium price will be 1 and the buyer will appropriate all the surplus.

The big problem with both the Aghion-Bolton and Katz models is that the public contracts are not robust to renegotiation. In Katz's model, if the seller decides to raise the price of the good to 1.5, the buyer and the intermediary will want to renegotiate their contract. Dewatripont (1988) shows that one must introduce asymmetric information at the renegotiation stage if such contracts are to survive renegotiation. Caillaud-Jullien-Picard (1995) studies two competing Principal–Agent structures that can sign public contracts and then secretly renegotiate them; it shows that more competitive outcomes (which benefit customers and hurt the competing structures) may actually emerge as a result.

6.3 Adverse Selection

We consider in this section an intertemporal price discrimination model that possesses all features of general repeated adverse selection models.[8]

The model has T periods. In each period t the Principal produces at unit cost c a perishable good in quantity q and sells it to a consumer for a price p. The utilities of both parties are

$$\sum_{t=1}^{T} \delta^{t-1}(p_t - cq_t)$$

for the Principal and

$$\sum_{t=1}^{T} \delta^{t-1}(u(q_t)\theta - p_t)$$

for the Agent who is a type θ consumer. The consumer may be of type $\underline{\theta}$ or $\overline{\theta}$, with $\overline{\theta} > \underline{\theta} > 0$. The proportion of types $\underline{\theta}$ in the population is π. The parameter θ, which is only observed by the Agent, therefore represents the consumer's valuation for the good; it is assumed to be constant over time.[9] We will assume that u is increasing and concave, and that

$$u(0) = 0, \quad u'(0) = \infty, \quad \text{and} \quad u'(\infty) = 0$$

8. Laffont-Tirole (1993) study fully a slightly different model but reach similar conclusions.
9. See Baron-Besanko (1984) for a model where θ changes over time.

which implies, inter alia, the Spence-Mirrlees condition.

The first-best optimal consumptions are obtained by solving the program

$$\max_q (u(q)\theta - cq)$$

whence

$$\theta u'(q) = c$$

We denote these two quantities $\underline{q}^*$ and $\overline{q}^*$ in the following. Of course $\underline{q}^* < \overline{q}^*$.

In the one-period model ($T = 1$), we let $(\underline{q}, \underline{p}, \overline{q}, \overline{p})$ be the second-best optimal direct truthful mechanism. The general results we established in chapter 2 apply to this model. The consumption of type $\overline{\theta}$ is $\overline{q} = \overline{q}^*$, and the incentive constraint

$$u(\overline{q})\overline{\theta} - \overline{p} = u(\underline{q})\overline{\theta} - \underline{p}$$

is binding. Type $\underline{\theta}$ gets his reservation utility level

$$u(\underline{q})\underline{\theta} - \underline{p} = 0$$

Therefore $\underline{q}$ is obtained by maximizing the Principal's objective

$$\max_{\underline{q}} \left(\pi(u(\underline{q})\underline{\theta} - c\underline{q}) + (1 - \pi)(u(\overline{q}^*)\overline{\theta} - u(\underline{q})\overline{\theta} + u(\underline{q})\underline{\theta} - c\overline{q}^*) \right)$$

whence

$$u'(\underline{q})(\underline{\theta} - (1 - \pi)\overline{\theta}) = \pi c$$

We can assume[10] that $\underline{\theta} > (1 - \pi)\overline{\theta}$. The low-type consumption $\underline{q}$ then is positive but lower than $\underline{q}^*$: As in chapter 2, the consumption of the lower type is underefficient.

---

10. Otherwise, it would be optimal for the Principal to exclude the low type, as discussed in chapter 2.

6.3.1   Full Commitment

The revelation principle applies when commitment is full: the two parties interact only once because the contract is never reconsidered. The proof of the revelation principle given in chapter 2 holds without change, so the Principal must propose a direct mechanism $(\underline{q}_t, \bar{q}_t, \underline{p}_t, \bar{p}_t)_{t=1}^T$:

- The mechanism must be truthful,

$$
\begin{cases}
\displaystyle\sum_{t=1}^T \delta^{t-1}(u(\underline{q}_t)\underline{\theta} - \underline{p}_t) \geq \sum_{t=1}^T \delta^{t-1}(u(\bar{q}_t)\underline{\theta} - \bar{p}_t) \\[2em]
\displaystyle\sum_{t=1}^T \delta^{t-1}(u(\bar{q}_t)\bar{\theta} - \bar{p}_t) \geq \sum_{t=1}^T \delta^{t-1}(u(\underline{q}_t)\bar{\theta} - \underline{p}_t)
\end{cases}
$$

- The mechanism must satisfy both intertemporal individual rationality constraints,

$$
\begin{cases}
\displaystyle\sum_{t=1}^T \delta^{t-1}(u(\underline{q}_t)\underline{\theta} - \underline{p}_t) \geq 0 \\[2em]
\displaystyle\sum_{t=1}^T \delta^{t-1}(u(\bar{q}_t)\bar{\theta} - \bar{p}_t) \geq 0
\end{cases}
$$

We let $M_1^T = (\underline{q}_t, \bar{q}_t, \underline{p}_t, \bar{p}_t)_{t=1}^T$ be the optimal mechanism. Consider, in the one-period model, the stochastic mechanism M that consists in giving the Agent the following lottery:

$$
\begin{cases}
(\underline{q}_1, \bar{q}_1, \underline{p}_1, \bar{p}_1) & \text{with probability} & \dfrac{1}{1 + \delta + \ldots + \delta^{T-1}} \\[1.5em]
\ldots & \ldots & \ldots \\[1em]
(\underline{q}_T, \bar{q}_T, \underline{p}_T, \bar{p}_T) & \text{with probability} & \dfrac{\delta^{T-1}}{1 + \delta + \ldots + \delta^{T-1}}
\end{cases}
$$

It can be checked that just as mechanism M_1^T in the T-period model, the stochastic mechanism M is truthful and satisfies the individual rationality constraints in the one-period model. Thus it cannot give the Principal more utility than the optimal mechanism in the one-period model, so

$$\frac{1}{1 + \delta + \ldots + \delta^{T-1}} \sum_{t=1}^{T} \delta^{t-1}\left(\pi(\underline{p}_t - c\underline{q}_t) + (1 - \pi)(\bar{p}_t - c\bar{q}_t)\right)$$

$$\leq \pi(\underline{p} - c\underline{q}) + (1 - \pi)(\bar{p} - c\bar{q})$$

In the T-period model we thus obtain

$$\sum_{t=1}^{T} \delta^{t-1}\left(\pi(\underline{p}_t - c\underline{q}_t) + (1 - \pi)(\bar{p}_t - c\bar{q}_t)\right)$$

$$\leq \sum_{t=1}^{T} \delta^{t-1}\left(\pi(\underline{p} - c\underline{q}) + (1 - \pi)(\bar{p} - c\bar{q})\right)$$

This argument proves that when commitment is full, the optimal mechanism consists in proposing for each period the so-called static optimum of the one-period model.

This result is intuitive: with full commitment the Principal must propose a contract that binds the parties for the T periods. In such a stationary model there is no reason to give an allocation that is not itself stationary.

The properties of the full commitment optimum are summed up in figure 6.1, which illustrates the sequence of consumptions q that each type of Agent gets in each period in a two-period model. The Agent of type $\bar{\theta}$ takes the upper branch in figure 6.1, and the Agent of type $\underline{\theta}$ takes the lower branch. The two types thus separate in the first period.

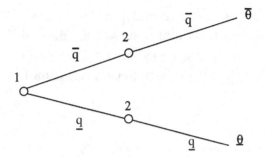

Figure 6.1
The full commitment optimum

6.3.2 Long-Term Commitment

Suppose that the Principal and the Agent can renegotiate the full commitment optimal contract $(\underline{q}, \bar{q}, \underline{p}, \bar{p})_{t=1}^{T}$. Consider, for instance, the beginning of the second period. Since the contract is separating in the first period, the Principal knows the Agent's type. For the Agent of type $\underline{\theta}$, the full commitment optimum has him consume the underefficient quantity $\underline{q}$ until the end of the relationship. To reach the highest level of efficiency ex ante (before the relationship starts and in expectation over types), we have to accept that contractual allocations will be inefficient ex post (once the execution of the contract has started). This property is often summed up by saying that the parties commit ex ante to ex post inefficient allocations.

The Principal and the type $\underline{\theta}$ Agent will be better off by signing at the beginning of the second period a new contract under which the Agent can consume the efficient quantity q^* in each period $t = 2$, ..., T. The full commitment optimal contract therefore cannot be an equilibrium in a long-term commitment situation: we say that the contract then is not robust to renegotiation. This property means that such a contract may not be a very useful descriptive tool. It is indeed difficult to imagine a mechanism that would allow the parties to commit ex ante never to renegotiate the contract. There is nothing in contractual law to prevent the parties from renegotiating a contract by common agreement. To ensure compliance overall, they could stipulate in the contract that either party would pay a penalty to a third party if he chooses to renegotiate. Then there is the possibility that the party aiming to renegotiate could gain ex post by bribing the third party so that it does not enact the proposed penalty. This can increase both the utility of this party and that of the third party, since the latter does not get any penalty in equilibrium anyway. Thus full commitment is a relevant concept only if the costs of renegotiating are high enough or if the parties must adhere to rigid policy, but both circumstances are beyond the scope of our model.[11]

When full commitment is not available, the Principal cannot commit to the mechanism he announced at the start of the game and thus the proof of the usual revelation principle fails. Bester-Strausz (2001) in fact prove that a weaker revelation principle holds:

• The Principal still only needs to use direct mechanisms, in which the Agent announces his type.

• Announcing the truth still is an optimal strategy for the Agent under the optimal mechanism.

• The Agent sometimes is indifferent between truth and lying.

Thus, when commitment is less than full, some types of the Agent will randomize between announcing their true type (which they always do with positive probability) and lying: the Agent only gradually reveals his type. We will see several examples of this below.

The long-term commitment contract was first analyzed by Dewatripont (1989). At the optimum, although renegotiation is allowed, there is actually no renegotiation, since any future renegotiation *can be anticipated and built* into the long-term contract. This is sometimes called the *renegotiation-proofness principle*. The long-term commitment

---

11. But see, for instance, Maskin-Tirole (1999, sec. 8) for an argument that while renegotiation indeed is pervasive, we lack a theory explaining why it is so.

optimal contract covers periods 1 to T. At no point in time can its continuation be replaced by a renegotiation-proof contract that gives more utility to the Principal and at least as much utility to the Agent on the remaining periods. To the usual incentive and individual rationality constraints, one can therefore add nonrenegotiation constraints at each period. These three constraints can be considered together as *sequential efficiency* constraints, since they ensure that the contract is ex post efficient. However, they make the computation of the optimum very difficult. Therefore we will consider only its properties here. The interested reader should turn to Hart-Tirole (1988) or Laffont-Tirole (1990) for the proofs.

While renegotiation eliminates ex post inefficiencies due to the sequential efficiency constraints, it encourages ex ante inefficiencies. The optimal mechanism must satisfy the new constraints and provide for a more progressive revelation of information than under the full commitment optimum, as was discussed earlier.

To describe the long-term commitment optimum, we will concentrate on the consumption paths followed by the different types of the Agent. In each period t, two consumption levels are possible: the efficient consumption for $\bar{\theta}$, which is $\bar{q}^*$, and a lower consumption q_t. The consumption level $\bar{q}^*$ is only chosen by type $\bar{\theta}$. In fact an Agent who chooses $\bar{q}^*$ in period t reveals that his type is $\bar{\theta}$ and so must consume $\bar{q}^*$ until the end of the relationship. On the other hand, consumption q_t is chosen by the $\underline{\theta}$ type and, with some probability, by the $\bar{\theta}$ type. In each period of the long-term optimum contract,

- Agent $\underline{\theta}$ consumes q_t;
- Agent $\bar{\theta}$, if he has not chosen $\bar{q}^*$ yet, plays a mixed strategy in that he consumes q_t or $\bar{q}^*$, with probabilities fixed by the optimality conditions;
- Agent $\bar{\theta}$, if he has already consumed $\bar{q}^*$ in the past, keeps doing so.

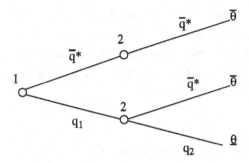

Figure 6.2
The long-term optimum

The long-term optimum therefore has a much more complex structure than the full commitment optimum: Agent $\bar{\theta}$ reveals his type in the first period with some probability; if he does not, then he will reveal it in the second period, and so on. The Principal only learns the type of the Agent once the latter has consumed $\bar{q}^*$, which he can do in any period.

Figure 6.2 shows the long-term optimum in a two-period model.[12] Agent $\bar{\theta}$ follows the two upper branches, and Agent $\underline{\theta}$ only follows the lowest branch. To compute q_2, we assume that in the first period the honest type takes the upper branch with probability x. Then at the beginning of the second period, and if the Agent consumed q_1 in the first period, the Principal can use Bayes's rule to revise his prior π to

$$\pi_2 = \frac{\pi}{\pi + (1 - \pi)(1 - x)}$$

He then faces an Agent who is a low type with probability π_2 and a high type with probability $(1 - \pi_2)$. Since this is the last period

---

12. The shape of the optimal contract can vary, depending on the parameters of the model and especially on the prior probabilities. The configuration in figure 6.2 is the most typical case.

of the game, the solution is exactly the same as in the one-period problem, with the only difference that π is replaced with π_2: The Principal will give the Agent the choice between $\bar{q}^*$ and an undereficient consumption level q_2 designed for the low type and given by the by now familiar equation

$$u'(q_2)(\underline{\theta} - (1 - \pi_2)\bar{\theta}) = \pi_2 c$$

This characterizes the solution in the second period. The determination of x and q_1 is more involved.

6.3.3   No Commitment

In the long-term commitment optimum, the Agent of type $\bar{\theta}$ gets a positive informational rent in each period, even after he has revealed his type. The Principal may be tempted, once he sees the Agent consuming $\bar{q}^*$, to break the contract. He then has perfect information. Because he faces an Agent whom he knows is of type $\bar{\theta}$, he can extract all his surplus[13] by pricing the good at $p = u(\bar{q}^*)\bar{\theta}$ in each remaining period.

In the absence of commitment, any party can effectively end the contract in any period. In particular, the Principal can immediately exploit any information that is revealed by the Agent. The Agent will therefore be reluctant to reveal more information on his type. This is the well-known *ratchet effect*: it tells us that it is extremely costly for the Principal to get the Agent to reveal information on his type because the Agent knows that then he will allow the Principal to reap all the surplus. To get the Agent $\bar{\theta}$ to reveal his type in the first period, the Principal must bribe him by giving him all his expected discounted informational rent in the first period. In doing so, he risks inducing Agent $\underline{\theta}$ to pretend he is $\bar{\theta}$ so as to take the bribe.[14] To avoid

---

13. This then leaves the Agent with zero utility.
14. This stands in contrast to the one-period model where a binding incentive constraint prevents $\bar{\theta}$ from mimicking $\underline{\theta}$.

this dilemma, the Principal must adopt revelation schemes that are even more progressive than under long-term commitment.[15]

Solving the Principal's problem with no commitment requires computing the perfect Bayesian equilibrium of the game with two possible revelation schemes:

• In the first period the Principal proposes a nonlinear tariff $p_1(q_1)$ and the Agent chooses a consumption q_1.

• The Principal uses the observed consumption q_1 in the first period to update his prior π, which becomes $\pi_2(q_1)$; then he offers in the second period a new nonlinear tariff $p_2(q_1, q_2)$, and so on.

The complete solution of this game is very complex.[16] All we need to know here is that the ratchet effect depends on the patience of both parties (summed as δ) and the duration T of the relationship. If δ and T are both small, then the Agent will face much discounting of his informational rent by revealing his type early; informational revelation will be gradual but reasonably fast. If δ and T are large, then the Agent chooses to reveal his type very slowly (see Laffont-Tirole 1987).

6.3.4   Short-Term Commitment

Categorized here as "short-term commitment" are all levels of commitment that are intermediate between no commitment and long-term commitment. Short-term contracts can be renegotiated, though their duration period is shorter than that of the relationship.

Rey-Salanié (1996) study two-period contracts that are renegotiable in each period but cannot be broken unilaterally before they

---

15. This conclusion is not so clear-cut where the types are observed with noise. In a related model Jeitschko-Mirman-Salgueiro (2002) show that such noise can alleviate the ratchet effect: if the variance is large enough, the types will separate in the first period under the optimal contract.

16. Freixas-Guesnerie-Tirole (1985) solve the game under the restriction that contracts are linear (the payment p is linear in q). The use of a linear contract considerably simplifies the analysis, so their paper is a good place to start.

expire. They show that if price and quantity transfers are not limited, the long-term optimum is implementable. To see this, consider a contract $C_1 = (p_1(q_1), \tilde{p}_2(q_1, q_2))$ offered by the Principal at the start of the first period; the contract specifies the transfers that the Agent will make to the Principal in the first two *periods as functions of his consumptions*. Because the contract can be renegotiated (and will be in equilibrium) at the beginning of the second period, the only part of the "promise" $\tilde{p}_2(q_1, q_2)$ is set up as a condition for the second-period renegotiation. The problem is to choose $\tilde{p}_2$ so that it gives every Agent type the right continuation utility. It can be shown that the renegotiation brings both parties to replicate the equilibrium path that leads to the long-term optimum. We will eschew the details because they are messy. The key element of the proof is that for every q_1 there are as many unknowns as there are possible values of q_2, and there are as many equations as values of θ. In any reasonable model there is at least as many possible quantities as types, and thus it is possible to solve the system of equations.

6.3.5   Conclusion

To sum up, we have identified four kinds of contractual commitments in this section. The main points we need to remember about them are as follows:

• Full commitment leads to the most efficient kind of contracts, and it brings immediate revelation of information. However, it is often not realistic to take this direction because the parties must commit to ex post allocations that inefficient may turn out to be vulnerable to renegotiation.

• Long-term commitment allows a gradual revelation of information but implies an ex ante efficiency loss.

• Short-term commitment can, under certain conditions, permit the same allocations as long-term commitment.

• No commitment induces a ratchet effect, whereby the information revelation is very gradual, and the allocations that obtain are less efficient than under all other forms of commitment.

6.4 Moral Hazard

The study of intertemporal moral hazard is considerably more complex than that of adverse selection models. There are two reasons for this:

• The wage that the Agent receives at period t depends on his effort and on a shock that he does not control; it is therefore a stochastic income for him. Like any consumer who has a concave utility function and receives a random income stream, he will want to smooth his consumption by saving, borrowing, or by running down his savings. The study of intertemporal moral hazard therefore cannot abstract from the conditions under which the Agent can access credit markets.

• With repetition, a moral hazard problem can create endogenously private information for the Agent. As we will see later, this is what happens when the technology or preferences of the Agent in any given period depend on his actions in earlier periods. The dynamic moral hazard problem further is complicated by an intertemporal adverse selection problem similar to that which we analyzed in section 6.3.

Before we turn to the characteristics of the repeated moral hazard problem, we will study a model due to Fudenberg-Tirole (1990) that shows that even one-period moral hazard problems have dynamic aspects.

6.4.1 Renegotiation after Effort

Suppose that the technology in the one-period model we studied in chapter 5 is $x = a + \varepsilon$, where ε is an observational noise with mean zero. At the optimum the Principal announces a wage schedule

$w^*(x)$, the Agent makes an effort a^*, and the Agent expects a random wage $w^*(a^* + \varepsilon)$, whereby the Principal gets a surplus $(a^* + \varepsilon - w^*(a^* + \varepsilon))$. As in chapter 5, the shape taken by the function w^* results from a trade-off between incentives and risk-sharing.

We now consider a point in time when the Agent has made effort a^* but the outcome x has not yet been observed. The function w^* has played its part in providing incentives to the Agent, so only risk-sharing matters at this point in time. If as usual we assume that the Principal is risk-neutral and the Agent is risk-averse, the risk-sharing properties of the function w^* cannot be optimal, however. The optimum must be a constant wage (independent of ε) so that the Principal can insure the Agent perfectly against the risk represented by the shock ε.

This argument shows that once the Agent has made effort a^*, the parties would gain by renegotiating toward a perfect insurance contract that gives all risk to the Principal. The optimal contract therefore is not robust to renegotiation. Obviously, if the Agent anticipates that his wage schedule will be renegotiated to a constant wage after he chooses his level of effort, he will obviously choose the least costly action. So the contractual w^* no longer serves as an incentive because the Agent knows that it will ultimately be replaced by a constant wage.

The idea that the parties will renegotiate after the Agent has chosen his action is more or less natural according to the situation under study. It is, of course, not unreasonable in an employer–employee relationship. In other situations renegotiation may carry more weight as the time interval between the choice of action and the observation of the outcome becomes longer. Think, for instance, of the construction of a bridge or a weapons system for the government.

Where renegotiation is possible, it must be taken into account in the design of the optimal contract. Suppose that the contractual action can take only two values, $a = 0$ and $a = 1$. By the argument above, $a = 1$ cannot be implemented with probability 1. The optimal contract must let the Agent choose $a = 0$ with some nonzero probability. As it usually is not optimal to implement $a = 0$ with probability 1, the Agent has a completely mixed strategy. At the renegotiation date the Principal faces two possible types of Agent: one who chooses $a = 1$, and one who chooses $a = 0$. The Principal therefore must solve an adverse selection problem similar to that of the monopoly insurance model studied in section 3.1.3. Suppose he offers two different wage schedules, one for each type of Agent. By analogy with the insurance model, the wage schedule designed for the Agent who chooses action $a = 0$ is that which insures him perfectly.

The essential lesson of this model is that if two parties can renegotiate after the effort level is chosen, then the Principal can no longer get the Agent to choose the optimal effort with probability 1. As in the repeated adverse selection model, the ability to renegotiate brings an efficiency loss.

*6.4.2 Convergence to the First-Best

In chapter 5 we saw how the incentive problem the Principal faces can be related to the classical problem of statistical inference. The Principal can infer an action a from observing an outcome x. It therefore is not surprising that the law of large numbers applies in the incentive problem. As the interaction between the Principal and the Agent is repeated indefinitely, the Principal will observe a large number of outcomes. From these outcomes he will be able to infer the Agent's action with great precision and punish the Agent accordingly if the action chosen is not optimal. In the limit the Principal can then implement the first-best optimal action.

Rubinstein-Yaari (1983) show that this intuition is right when neither the Principal nor the Agent has a preference for the present. To see this, suppose that the technology is given by

$$x_t = a + \varepsilon_t$$

within each period t, where the ε_t are independent and identically distributed noises with mean zero and a finite variance σ^2. Let a^* be the first-best optimal action. If the Agent chooses a^* in each period, then by the law of large numbers, the average

$$A_t = \frac{1}{t} \sum_{\tau=1}^{t} (x_\tau - a^*)$$

will go to zero almost surely as t goes to infinitely. To induce the Agent to choose action a^* in each period, the Principal can then punish the Agent if the absolute value of the average A_t is greater than some positive threshold, indicating that the Agent has deviated relatively often. The difficult point is how to choose this threshold: it should go to zero as t goes to infinity in order to take advantage of the law of large numbers, but it should not vanish too fast. Otherwise the Agent will be punished too often when he chooses a^*, which is not good for risk-sharing.

The appropriate tool for this problem is the law of the iterated logarithm, whereby it is possible to set boundaries to the large deviations from the law of large numbers. Let λ be any real number greater than 1, and let

$$\delta_t = \frac{\left(\sum_{\tau=1}^{t} \varepsilon_\tau\right)/t}{\sqrt{2\lambda\sigma^2 \ln \ln t / t}}$$

Then the law of the iterated logarithm states that

$$\Pr\left(\lim_{t\to\infty} \sup \delta_t < 1\right) = 1$$

The policy consisting in choosing a $\lambda > 1$ and punishing the Agent at date t if

$$|A_t| > \sqrt{\frac{2\lambda\sigma^2 \ln \ln t}{t}}$$

thus implements the first-best action if the punishment is rough enough and the interaction is repeated indefinitely. Note that if the Agent does choose a^* in each period, then he will be punished with vanishing probability.

The problem with this result is that it rests on two critical assumptions:

• That the interaction be infinitely repeated.
• That both agents be extremely patient.

The rest of this section is devoted to models in which the interaction is repeated over a finite horizon. Then the argument developed above fails, and the optimum is clearly second-best.

6.4.3   Finitely Repeated Moral Hazard

Assume that the interaction between the Principal and the Agent lasts for T periods. The Principal's utility function is

$$\sum_{t=1}^{T} (x_t - w_t)$$

while that of the Agent is

$$\sum_{t=1}^{T} (u(c_t) - a_t)$$

where u is increasing and concave and c_t is the consumption of the Agent at time t. The common discount parameter is assumed to be zero for simplicity. (It is important to distinguish between wages and consumption if the Agent has access to a credit market.)

Suppose that the outcome in period t only depends on the action chosen in the same period. If, for instance, the outcome in period t also depends on the action a_{t-1}, which is only observed by the

Agent, then the latter will have an informational advantage over the Principal at the beginning of period t because he will have a better knowledge of the period-t technology. Elements of adverse selection that we won't deal with now will then complicate the moral hazard problem.[17]

The following discussion is adapted from Chiappori-Macho-Rey-Salanié (1994).

No Access to Credit

First assume that the Agent cannot save or borrow, so his consumption equals his wage within any period.[18] An immediate application of the dynamic programming principle shows that full commitment coincides with long-term commitment in this model: The Agent's characteristics are fully known to the Principal when the contract is signed, and the Principal therefore can choose the optimal sequence of wage schedules without ever feeling the need to adapt it to the arrival of new information.

Because this Agent has a concave utility function, he wants to smooth his consumption over time. However, the outcome x_t can rise high as a result of a favorable shock. Suppose that such a shock took place in period t, and the Principal wants to spread this positive shock over several periods so as to help the Agent maintain a smooth consumption stream.[19] He can do this by increasing the wage he gives to the Agent in all future periods. Thus the wage given in any period t will depend not only on the current outcome x_t but also on the sequence of past outcomes. This property is called by Rogerson (1985) the *memory effect*. It is a simple consequence of

---

17. Adverse selection turns up to complicate the analysis when an Agent has free access to credit markets.
18. This is an extreme assumption, but the analysis is the same if the Agent is liquidity constrained and this constraint is active at the optimum.
19. Note that the Principal only cares about total discounted wages, not about their timing.

the need for the Principal to smooth the Agent's consumption at the full commitment optimum.

In the absence of commitment the Principal cannot spread the effect of a shock on x_t over several periods: He cannot indeed commit to anything in period $t + 1$, and not in particular to giving the Agent a wage in period $t + 1$ that depends on x_t. Therefore the period t wage can only depend on the current outcome x_t, and the optimal sequence of spot contracts is memoryless. Spot contracts clearly involve efficiency losses.

Alternatively, as Rey-Salanié (1990) show, through short-term commitment the Principal can smooth the Agent's consumption optimally and also implement the full commitment optimum. Again, "promises" in each period must be designed so as to set up a reservation utility for the Agent that makes it optimal for both parties to renegotiate toward the next-period component of the full commitment optimum. The only difficulty is to find a solution to the corresponding system of equations, but this has exactly as many equations as unknowns (the number of possible outcomes), and thus has a solution under some technical conditions.

The full commitment optimum has further a counterfactual property: it constrains the Agent to saving less than he would like. To see this, suppose that $T = 2$, and denote the following:

- w_i the first-period wage when the first-period outcome is x_i.

- w_{ij} the second-period wage when the first-period outcome is x_i and that for the second period is x_j.

- a_i the action the Agent chooses in the second period when the first-period outcome is x_i.

- $p_j(a)$ the probability of outcome x_j in any period when the chosen action in that period is a.

The solution of the incentive problem determines the gross utility U_{ij} the Agent must receive in each state of the world,

$$u(w_i) + u(w_{ij}) = U_{ij} \qquad (C_{ij})$$

On the other hand, the Principal must provide incentives at least cost, that is, by minimizing for all i the wage bill

$$w_i + \sum_{j=1}^{m} p_j(a_i)w_{ij}$$

under the m constraints $(C_{ij})_{j=1,...,m}$ when the first-period outcome is x_i. To solve this problem, we let λ_j be the multiplier associated to C_{ij} in this program. Maximizing the Lagrangian gives

$$\begin{cases} 1 = \sum_{j=1}^{m} \lambda_j u'(w_j) \\ p_j(a_i) = \lambda_j u'(w_{ij}) \end{cases}$$

The first-order condition[20] for this problem is then

$$\frac{1}{u'(w_i)} = \sum_{j=1}^{m} \frac{p_j(a_i)}{u'(w_{ij})}$$

By Jensen's inequality[21] applied to the convex function $x \to 1/x$,

$$\sum_{j=1}^{m} \frac{p_j(a_i)}{u'(w_{ij})} \geq \frac{1}{\sum_{j=1}^{m} p_j(a_i)u'(w_{ij})}$$

---

20. Note, in passing, that this equality proves the memory effect. Consider i and k such that for all j, $w_{ij} = w_{kj}$. Then it must be that $a_i = a_k$, so

$$\frac{1}{u'(w_i)} = \sum_{j=1}^{m} \frac{p_j(a_i)}{u'(w_{ij})} = \sum_{j=1}^{m} \frac{p_j(a_k)}{u'(w_{kj})} = \frac{1}{u'(w_k)}$$

which implies that $w_i = w_k$. The second-period wages can therefore only be independent of the first-period outcome if the first-period wages are constant. This means that the Principal will give up trying to get the Agent to put in effort.

21. Recall that Jensen's inequality states that if X is a random variable and f is a convex function, then

$$Ef(X) \geq f(EX)$$

Therefore

$$u'(w_i) \leq \sum_{j=1}^{m} p_j(a_i)u'(w_{ij})$$

which implies as announced that the Agent would want to save if he could.[22]

This result makes it somewhat difficult to interpret the model as a situation where the Agent has no access to credit markets. Indeed, while it is clear that many economic agents cannot borrow as they would like, it is not easy to see what prevents them from saving to their heart's content. This leads us to examine the case where the Principal dictates his savings to the Agent so that both wages and consumptions are determined by the contract. This in fact links different periods exactly as short-term commitment does when the Agent cannot save or borrow. Thus we should expect that the no commitment optimum coincides with the full commitment optimum. Malcolmson-Spinnewyn (1988) prove this result.

Unfortunately, not many real-world situations can fit this model. The first to consider is sharecropping in developing countries. Sharecropping is an agreement between a landlord and a tenant that lets the tenant cultivate the landlord's fields in exchange for a share of the proceeds from the crops. Although this arrangement has nearly disappeared from the developed world, it is still very common in the third world. Since credit markets are underdeveloped in third world countries, the tenant can often only get credit through a landlord. A second case to consider is corporate shareholding

---

22. Let $F(s)$ be the utility the Agent gets by saving s. Then

$$F(s) = u(w_i - s) + \sum_{j=1}^{m} p_j(a_i)u(w_{ij} + s)$$

and the inequality on marginal utilities in the text is simply $F'(0) \geq 0$.

whereby the Agent is the firm and the Principal is the main share-
holder or banker. This relationship can, however, engender other
features that do not make it a very convincing example.

Free Access to Credit
The polar case is when the Agent can save and borrow as he wishes.
We will suppose that the Principal cannot observe the Agent's savings. We let s_{T-1} denote the savings of the Agent in period $T-1$
(savings depend, of course, on the whole past history) and let the
market interest rate be zero, again for simplicity. Then the utility
function of the Agent in period T, expressed as a function of the
wage he gets from the Principal, is $u(w_T + s_{T-1})$ which depends on
his past savings s_{T-1}.

Since the Principal does not observe s_{T-1}, he faces at the beginning of period T an Agent whose utility function he does not know.[23]
An adverse selection problem thus emerges on top of the moral hazard problem.[24] This has several important consequences. The first
one is that as in all adverse selection models, full commitment and
long-term commitment lead to different solutions: The full commitment optimum is not renegotiation proof. As argued in section 6.3,
we should therefore concentrate on the long-term optimum.

Unfortunately, the existing results on the long-term optimum
with free savings are disturbing. Chiappori-Macho-Rey-Salanié
(1994) prove the following striking result: if the long-term optimum
only involves pure strategies, it can only implement the cost-
minimizing action from the second period onward. To see this, let
$T = 2$, and use the same notation as above, with in addition s_i as the

---

23. The only exception is when the Agent's utility function is CARA, which excludes wealth effects and therefore the emergence of adverse selection. This case is
dealt with by Fudenberg-Holmstrom-Milgrom (1990).
24. Note that uncertainty as to the Agent's characteristics is created endogenously
by his past actions, whereas it is exogenous in the standard adverse selection model.

savings when the first-period outcome is i and a_0 the optimal action in the first period. Now suppose that the optimal contract implements a_i in the second period after a first-period outcome of i. If a_i is not the cost-minimizing action, then at least one second-period incentive constraint must be binding. So there should exist an a' such that

$$\sum_j p_j(a_i)u(w_{ij} + s_i) - a_i = \sum_j p_j(a')u(w_{ij} + s_i) - a'$$

Let s' be the optimal savings when the Agent chooses a'; namely s' maximizes over s

$$u(w_i - s) + \left(\sum_j p_j(a')u(w_{ij} + s) - a' \right)$$

Now suppose that instead of responding to the optimal contract (w_i, w_{ij}) with (a_0, s_i, a_i), the Agent responds with (a_0, s'_i, a'_i), which coincides with (a_0, s_i, a_i) except that $a'_i = a'$ and $s'_i = s'$. We will show that this improves the Agent's expected utility. Indeed we have

$$\sum_j p_j(a_0)\left(u(w_j - s_j) - a_0 + \left(\sum_k p_k(a_j)u(w_{jk} + s_j) - a_j \right) \right)$$

$$= \sum_j p_j(a'_0)\left(u(w_j - s_j) - a'_0 + \left(\sum_k p_k(a'_j)u(w_{jk} + s_j) - a'_j \right) \right)$$

$$< \sum_j p_j(a'_0)\left(u(w_j - s'_j) - a'_0 + \left(\sum_k p_k(a'_j)u(w_{jk} + s'_j) - a'_j \right) \right)$$

where the first equality follows from the definition of a' and the inequality holds (generically) because s' is a better choice of savings than s_i given a'.

Because this inequality violates the first-period incentive constraint, our premise that a_i was not the cost-minimizing action must be wrong. The conclusion follows immediately. Park (2004) shows that the same conclusion can be made in the general case where the

agent may use mixed strategies, except of course when his utility
function is CARA.[25]

Conclusion
As this rapid survey of finitely repeated moral hazard models
shows, there is still much work to be done in this area. Both polar
assumptions of no access to credit or free access to credit lead to dis-
appointing conclusions. In the first case, the Agent is prevented
from saving at the optimum. In the second case, the optimum must
involve mixed strategies if it is to have good incentive properties.

There are nevertheless two general conclusions to be drawn, and
both result from the importance of consumption smoothing. The
first one concerns the memory effect: consumption in any given
period will depend on the whole history of past outcomes. The second is that the relative efficiency of different degrees of commitment
is determined by their ability to smooth the Agent's consumption.

References

Aghion, P., and P. Bolton. 1987. Contracts as a barrier to entry. *American Economic Review* 77:388–401.

Baron, D., and D. Besanko. 1984. Regulation and information in a continuing relationship. *Information Economics and Policy* 1:267–302.

Bester, H., and R. Strausz. 2001. Contracting with imperfect commitment and the
revelation principle: the single-agent case. *Econometrica* 69:1077–98.

Brander, J., and B. Spencer. 1985. Export subsidies and international market share
rivalry. *Journal of International Economics* 18:83–100.

Caillaud, B., B. Jullien, and P. Picard. 1995. Competing vertical structures: Precommitment and renegotiation. *Econometrica* 63:621–46.

---

25. Note that this result is not unlike that by Fudenberg-Tirole (1990) presented in
section 6.5.1, in which effort cannot be implemented with probability one. In both
cases the renegotiation constraints are to blame.

Chiappori, P.-A., I. Macho, P. Rey, and B. Salanié. 1994. Repeated moral hazard: The role of memory, commitment, and the access to credit markets. *European Economic Review* 38:1527–53.

Dewatripont, M. 1988. Commitment through renegotiation-proof contracts with third parties. *Review of Economic Studies* 55:377–90.

Dewatripont, M. 1989. Renegotiation and information revelation over time: The case of optimal labor contracts. *Quarterly Journal of Economics* 104:589–619.

Fershtman, C., and K. Judd. 1987. Equilibrium incentives in oligopoly. *American Economic Review* 77:927–40.

Freixas, X., R. Guesnerie, and J. Tirole. 1985. Planning under incomplete information and the ratchet effect. *Review of Economic Studies* 52:173–92.

Fudenberg, D., B. Holmstrom, and P. Milgrom. 1990. Short-term contracts and long-term agency relationships. *Journal of Economic Theory* 51:1–31.

Fudenberg, D., and J. Tirole. 1990. Moral hazard and renegotiation in agency contracts. *Econometrica* 58:1279–1320.

Hart, O., and J. Tirole. 1988. Contract renegotiation and coasian dynamics. *Review of Economic Studies* 55:509–40.

Jeitschko, T., L. Mirman, and E. Salgueiro. 2002. The simple analytics of information and experimentation in dynamic agency. *Economic Theory* 19:549–70.

Katz, M. 1986. Game-playing agents: Unobservable contracts as precommitment. *Rand Journal of Economics* 22:307–28.

Laffont, J.-J., and J. Tirole. 1987. Comparative statics of the optimal dynamic incentives contract. *European Economic Review* 31:901–26.

Laffont, J.-J., and J. Tirole. 1990. Adverse selection and renegotiation in procurement. *Review of Economic Studies* 75:597–626.

Laffont, J.-J., and J. Tirole. 1993. *A Theory of Incentives in Procurement and Regulation.* Cambridge: MIT Press.

Malcolmson, J., and F. Spinnewyn. 1988. The multiperiod Principal–Agent problem. *Review of Economic Studies* 55:391–408.

Maskin, E., and J. Tirole. 1999. Unforeseen contingencies and incomplete contracts. *Review of Economic Studies* 66:83–114.

Park, I.-U. 2004. Moral hazard contracting and private credit markets. *Econometrica* 72:701–46.

Rey, P., and B. Salanié. 1990. Long-term, short-term and renegotiation: On the value of commitment in contracting. *Econometrica* 58:597–619.

Rey, P., and B. Salanié. 1996. On the value of commitment in contracting with asymmetric information. *Econometrica* 64:1395–1414.

Rogerson, W. 1985. Repeated moral hazard. *Econometrica* 53:69–76.

Rubinstein, A., and M. Yaari. 1983. Insurance and moral hazard. *Journal of Economic Theory* 14:441–52.

Schelling, T. 1960. *The Strategy of Conflict*. Cambridge: Harvard University Press.

Incomplete Contracts

Thus far in this book contracts were assumed to be complete, at least at the beginning of the relationship. This is obviously a very strong assumption. It implies that all contingencies that may affect the contractual relationship are taken into account in the contract. In the real world, negotiating a contract is a costly business that mobilizes managers and lawyers. It must therefore be that at some point the cost of writing a specific clause to cover an unlikely contingency outweighs the benefit. The inability, or unwillingness, of courts and third parties to verify ex post the value of certain variables observed by contractants is another reason why contracts are often incomplete. It is useless to condition a contract on a variable if no one can settle its value in a dispute. Even if we abstract from the costs associated with negotiating and writing the contract and from the constraints due to the legal system, bounded rationality may force the parties to neglect some variables whose effect on the relationship they find difficult to evaluate. Further it is sometimes difficult, and even impossible, to assign probability to relevant events and to condition the clauses of the contract on these events. For our purposes, opening a window on to bounded rationality considerations would not be very productive at this stage, as also the profession has made very little progress in modeling these considerations.

For all the reasons above, contracts typically take into account a limited number of variables that are believed to be the most relevant ones, or simply those most verifiable by a court of law. If during the relationship some unforeseen contingencies arise that have an impact on the conditions of the relationship and the contract gives no clue as to how the parties should react, the logical remedy will be to renegotiate the contract.

Renegotiation therefore has different implications when contracts are incomplete than when contracts are complete. We saw in chapter 6 that when contracts are complete, the ability to renegotiate serves as an ex ante constraint on the Principal's program, and it will therefore often bring an efficiency loss. The renegotiation-proofness principle demonstrates further that long-term contracts need never to be renegotiated in equilibrium. However, when contracts are incomplete, renegotiation allows the parties to react to unforeseen contingencies. Renegotiation can therefore be socially useful, and occur in equilibrium.

The theory of incomplete contracts in many ways builds on and formalizes the intuitions of transaction cost economics due to Coase and Williamson.[1] Transaction cost economics accepts that agents are opportunistic but claims that they are boundedly rational, so contracts will be incomplete. It also claims that many assets are relationship specific in that they have little value outside the relationship under study. Since many investments (especially investments in human capital) in relationship-specific assets are nonverifiable, parties do try to avoid being expropriated of the surplus created by these specific investments, and as a result they tend to underinvest. This is the famous *holdup* problem, to which we turn in section 7.1.

As in most of the literature, we will concentrate here on examining some very simple cases where information is symmetric: all variables are observed by all parties, but some of them may not be included in

---

1. The 1937 paper by Coase on *The Nature of the Firm*, is reprinted in Coase (1988). Williamson (1989) gives a useful survey of transaction cost economics.

a contract. We will say that such variables are *observable but nonverifiable*, meaning that no court or other third party will accept to arbitrate a claim based on the value taken by these variables. The symmetric information assumption[2] allows us to isolate phenomena that are due to contract incompleteness and greatly simplifies the analysis of renegotiation. As we saw in section 6.4, the analysis can become quite complex when information is asymmetric.

The modern theory of incomplete contracts originated in Grossman-Hart (1986) and Hart-Moore (1988). It focused on the effect of property rights on relationship-specific investments (which we examine in section 7.1) and on other issues in corporate finance. The foundations of the theory were much debated in the 1990s. The "irrelevance theorem" of Maskin-Tirole (1999a) was the high point of this literature; we study it in section 7.2. It has split contract theorists between the skeptics and the enthusiasts; we review their arguments in section 7.3.

7.1 Property Rights, Holdup, and Underinvestment

Specific investments and holdups are often illustrated by the relationship between Fisher Body, an American maker of car parts, and General Motors.[3] In the 1920s Fisher Body started producing car doors for General Motors. It invested in some rather specialized machine tools and organized its production so as to respond best to the needs of General Motors. Clearly, Fisher Body would have lost a considerable part of the value of its investments if it had left General Motors for another carmaker. Therefore a clause in the contract signed in 1919 gave Fisher Body a ten-year exclusive deal to protect

---

2. At a theoretical level, the nonverifiability assumption often implies asymmetric information between two parties and a third party. This is because the third party cannot check the value of a variable that it cannot observe.

3. This case study comes from the classic paper by Klein-Crawford-Alchian (1978); see, however, Casadesus-Masanell and Spulber (2000) for a rather different account.

it from being held up by General Motors. To prevent Fisher Body from possibly raising prices outrageously, the contract also contained a cost-plus clause. It turned out, however, that Fisher Body manipulated the price-protection clause by choosing a very low capital intensity and locating its plants far from those of General Motors. General Motors thus was effectively held up by Fisher Body and eventually bought it in 1926.

7.1.1 The Buyer–Seller Model

Such stories can be made more formal by an archetypical model of the incomplete contracts literature: the buyer–seller relationship. The seller S and the buyer B jointly operate a physical asset that is used to produce at cost c to the seller a good that has value v for the buyer. Either party can make a *specific investment*, that is, an investment that

- increases the productivity of the relationship under study,
- has a lower value outside of this relationship,
- is costly for the party that makes it.

To be more precise, the seller can reduce his production cost by investing i_S in human capital, and the buyer can increase the value of the good by investing i_B. Thus c is a decreasing convex function $c(i_S)$ and v is an increasing convex function $v(i_B)$. We assume that $\underline{v} = v(0) \geq \overline{c} = c(0)$, so it is always efficient to produce and trade—and the problems that we examined in section 3.2.7 do not arise here. The parties are risk-neutral and do not discount the future. If trade occurs at price p, their utilities are $p - c(i_S) - i_S$ and $v(i_B) - i_B - p$. If they don't agree, then what happens depends on who owns the right to control the asset. If only one of them does, then he can use it to trade on a competitive market where the equilibrium price of the good is p^C. Since the specific investments have no value on this market, the value of the good is $v(0)$, and it is produced at cost $c(0)$. Note that this implies that $c(0) \leq p^c \leq v(0)$.

The first-best outcome is easily described in this model: the buyer
and the seller always trade. Since the total surplus is

$$v(i_B) - i_B - c(i_S) - i_S$$

their investments i_B^* and i_S^* are given by $c'(i_S^*) = -1$ and $v'(i_B^*) = 1$.

7.1.2 The Complete Contract

In what follows, we assume that the specific investments i_S and i_B are
observed by all parties. There is therefore no asymmetric information
in this model, not even uncertainty.[4] Under these conditions a simple
contract achieves the first-best: it prescribes trade at some price
$\bar{c} \le p \le \underline{v}$. Faced with this contract, both parties choose the efficient
investment level, and they accept the contract as by definition,

$$c(i_S^*) + i_S^* \le \bar{c} \le p \le \underline{v} \le v(i_B^*) - i_B^*$$

Note that it is not necessary to write the values of the specific
investments in the contract, so they needn't be verifiable by a court.
Conceptually the fixed-price contract is enough to ensure that buyer
and seller choose first-best investment levels.

In a world of complete contracts, the allocation of property rights
also has no effect on efficiency: if the good initially belongs to the
buyer (resp. the seller), then it is likely that the price p will end up
closer to $\bar{c}$ (resp. $\underline{v}$). This changes the income streams and matters, of
course, to the parties, but the efficiency of the fixed-price contract
does not hinge on it. This is one of the biggest shortcomings in the
theory of complete contracts: it has little to say on the efficient allocation of property rights, and in particular, on what determines the
boundaries of firms.

---

4. The functions c and v could be made random anything in what follows provided
that their values are observed by both parties ex post.

7.1.3   Incomplete Contracts and Property Rights

The theory of incomplete contracts allows the question of property rights to be connected to legal tradition. Roman law defined property rights as the combination of *usus* (the right to use the good), *fructus* (the right to what it produces), and *abusus* (the right to sell or give away the good). Closer to us, Grossman-Hart (1986) argue that property rights should be seen as *residual control rights:* when an unforeseen contingency occurs, the owner of an asset has the right to decide how it should be used. The owner also gets exclusive rights on all income streams that have not been shared in advance by a contractual agreement. These rights clearly have no value if contracts are complete because, by definition, no unforeseen contingency can arise. Property rights only matter if contracts are incomplete.[5]

In the preceding subsection we glossed over an essential difficulty: in practice, every delivery contract specifies the characteristics of the good. If these characteristics can be described by few parameters, then it is not hard to condition the price p on them, and a court can verify the relevant characteristics upon delivery. But both of these assumptions become much stronger for a complex good.

Let us now make the polar assumption that the characteristics of the good, like the specific investments i_S and i_B, cannot be verified by a court, though they are observable by both parties. Then ex ante there can be no contract even though ex post trade is always efficient. After the values of the specific investments are observed, the buyer and the seller will get together in order to decide on a price for the delivery of the good. This can be imagined in many ways, but most of the literature assumes that when renegotiating, B and S decide to

---

5. For a legal perspective, especially on Anglo-Saxon law, the reader is referred to the interesting paper by Schwartz (1992).

share the increase in total surplus equally (e.g., this is the Nash bargaining solution). The final price will depend on points of threat to both parties. Because these in turn are determined by property rights, the incentives to invest of buyer and seller this time will depend on the initial allocation of property rights, as will efficiency.

To see this, first assume that the seller owns the asset. Then, if he does not agree on a price with the buyer, he can produce and sell the good on the competitive market. The buyer has just spent i_B in vain. Thus, if the parties renegotiate toward a trade at price p, the seller registers a utility gain $(p - p^C)$ and the buyer gains $(v(i_B) - p)$. At the Nash solution these gains are equal, so the final price is

$$p = \frac{v(i_B) + p^C}{2}$$

The buyer's ex post utility is

$$v(i_B) - i_B - p = \frac{v(i_B) - p^C}{2} - i_B$$

while the seller's ex post utility is

$$p - c(i_S) - i_S = \frac{v(i_B) + p^C}{2} - c(i_S) - i_S$$

These formulas show that while the seller has the incentive to choose the efficient level of investment i_S^*, the buyer underinvests:

$$v'(i_B) = 2$$

The case of buyer-ownership is similar. As the buyer owns the asset, he can ask another seller to operate it for price p^C; on the other hand, the original seller has spent i_S in vain. Trading increases the buyer's utility by $p^C - p$ and the seller's utility by $p - c(i_S)$. Simple calculations show that the buyer invests at the efficient level and the seller underinvests:

$$c'(i_S) = -2$$

Last we take the case of joint ownership. Neither party can operate the asset without the consent of the other. If the parties do not trade, they both lose the value of their investments. It follows that trade yields them utility gains of $p - c(i_S)$ and $v(i_B) - p$. As a result the equilibrium price is

$$p = \frac{v(i_B) + c(i_S)}{2}$$

and final utilities are

$$\frac{v(i_B) - c(i_S)}{2} - i_B \text{ and } \frac{v(i_B) - c(i_S)}{2} - i_S$$

In this case both parties underinvest, since $v'(i_B) = 2$ and $c'(i_S) = -2$.

In this simple model, a buyer ownership or seller ownership can be optimal, depending on the precise shapes of the functions c and v. Joint ownership presents, however, the worst of possible worlds. These conclusions are special: this particular model implies that the owner always invests efficiently. The important lesson of this section is that when contracts are incomplete, property rights protect their holders against a holdup of their specific investments. The optimal allocation of property rights then depends on the respective social costs of underinvestment by the parties to the contract. More generally, Hart (1995) shows that the efficient allocation of property rights over multiple assets depends on their complementarity: for instance, complementary assets should be owned jointly.

7.2   The Irrelevance Theorems

7.2.1   Restoring Efficient Investment Incentives

While the above story offers convincing basic results, some authors have shown that more complex, but feasible contracts can yield the first-best outcome. Maskin-Tirole (1999b) consider, for instance, an option-to-sell contract. The contractual arrangement is as follows:

• The parties start from a situation of joint ownership, in which neither can operate the asset without the consent of the other party.

• After they invest in human capital and the realized values of $c(i_S)$ and $v(i_B)$ are observed, a fair coin is tossed. If the seller wins the toss, he may sell his share to the buyer at price

$$p_S = \frac{v(i_B^*) - \bar{c}}{2}$$

and the buyer must make some payment t to a charity. If the buyer wins the toss, he may sell his share to the seller at price

$$p_B = \frac{\underline{v} - c(i_S^*)}{2}$$

and the seller must pay t to a charity.

The contract only requires three things: investments must be observed by the two parties, a third party can be used to guarantee that the toss is fair, and the charity can observe whether a party exercises his option to sell, and then claim its payment t. Thus, while this type of contract is unusual, it is not infeasible given our assumptions. We will proceed to prove that it deters both parties from underinvesting. The intuition is simple: if the buyer underinvests, then the seller will know it, and given the strike price of the option to sell, he will choose to sell if given the opportunity. If we make the payment t large enough, then the possibility (probability 0.5) that the buyer has to pay t will deter him from underinvesting.

More formally, assume the buyer underinvests $i_B < i_B^*$, while the seller chooses any i_S. If the seller is given the opportunity to sell, he must compare his utilities:

• His utility if he does not exercise the option to sell. Then there is still joint ownership, and we know from section 7.1.3 that the seller's final utility is

$$\frac{v(i_B) - c(i_S)}{2} - i_S$$

• His utility if he does. Then he gets p_S, and the buyer turns to him again to operate the asset, since the total surplus to be shared is higher than by turning to the competitive market, by $(\bar{c} - c(i_S))/2$. Finally the seller gets

$$p_S + \frac{\bar{c} - c(i_S)}{2} - i_S = \frac{v(i_B^*) - c(i_S)}{2} - i_S.$$

Thus the seller always exercises his option to sell if he can when the buyer has underinvested. The buyer therefore has to pay t if he underinvests and the seller wins the toss. If t is large enough, this is larger than any gain he may obtain from underinvesting, whether or not he is lucky enough to win the toss. The option-to-sell contract can therefore deter the buyer from underinvesting, and a symmetric argument applies to the seller. So clearly the option-to-sell contract can achieve a first-best outcome.

The perspicacious reader may wonder what went wrong in the reasoning behind the underinvestment results of section 7.1.3. Those arguments were indeed correct under the assumption that the ownership structure cannot change as the relationship evolves. The option-to-sell contract shows that allowing for such changes in ownership can induce efficient investments.

There exist other feasible contracts that can restore the first-best outcome in the model of section 7.1. We can enrich the buyer–seller relationship a little by assuming that besides price, the parties must also agree on a quantity q to be delivered. Now the buyer's valuation is $v(q, i_B)$ and the seller's cost is $c(q, i_S)$. We will assume that for any i_B and i_S, the surplus from trade $v(q, i_B) - c(q, i_S)$ is maximal in some unique $q^*(i_B, i_S)$. Thus the first-best outcome is given by the investments (i_B^*, i_S^*) that maximize

$$v(q^*(i_B, i_S), i_B) - c(q^*(i_B, i_S), i_S) - i_B - i_S$$

and the corresponding quantity is $q^*(i_B^*, i_S^*)$.

Consider the case of seller-ownership. Suppose that B and S sign a contract, according to which

- if they don't agree at the renegotiation stage, they will trade some quantity q_0 at some price p_0;
- the seller gets all the surplus at the renegotiation stage.

Again, this is a feasible contract. If renegotiation breaks down, either party can go to a court of law with the contract and ask that q_0 be traded at price p_0. We must also assure that the court can check that the renegotiation process had the form of a take-it-or-leave-it offer by the seller; this may be more problematic. (See Aghion-Dewatripont-Rey 1994 for a discussion of this assumption.)

The threat points in the renegotiation game now are $p_0 - c(q_0, i_S) - i_S$ for the seller and $v(q_0, i_B) - i_B - p_0$ for the buyer. Since renegotiation is efficient, they will end up trading the quantity $q^*(i_B, i_S)$, for a gain in total surplus[6] of

$$G = (v(q^*(i_B, i_S), i_B) - c(q^*(i_B, i_S), i_S)) - (v(q_0, i_B) - c(q_0, i_S))$$

By contract, all the surplus goes to the seller, who ends up with final utility

$$\begin{aligned} p_0 - c(q_0, i_S) - i_S + G &= v(q^*(i_B, i_S), i_B) \\ &\quad - c(q^*(i_B, i_S), i_S) - v(q_0, i_B) - i_S + p_0 \end{aligned}$$

As for the buyer, he is stuck at his threat point $v(q_0, i_B) - i_B - p_0$, and therefore chooses to invest at a level $i_B(q_0)$ given by

$$v_i'(q_0, i_B(q_0)) = 1$$

However, under reasonable conditions—for instance, if $v_i'(0, i_B^*)$ is continuous and satisfies the Inada conditions $v_i'(0, i_B^*) = \infty$

---

6. If the quantity is fixed at one unit, as in the previous section, then $G = 0$ of course.

and $v_i'(\infty, i_B^*) = 0$—there exists a q_0^* such that $i_B(q_0^*) = i_B^*$. Then by specifying a disagreement option of trading this q_0^* at any price p_0, the buyer can invest efficiently. But for $i_B = i_B^*$, the seller's utility is clearly maximal in i_S^*. Thus both parties can invest efficiently and later renegotiate to the efficient quantity.

Thus choosing an appropriate disagreement option and assigning all bargaining power in the renegotiation game to either party again is feasible and yields the first-best outcome. The same result was obtained in various guises by Chung (1991), Aghion-Dewatripont-Rey (1994), and Nöldeke-Schmidt (1995).

7.2.2 Using Mechanism Design

We saw in the simple model of section 7.1 that relatively straightforward (or at least feasible) contracts can achieve the first-best. Can we extend this conclusion to a general class of models? It turns out that the answer is a qualified yes. For the intuition behind the results we go back to the mechanism design problem briefly sketched in section 2.1. After specific investments are made, both parties become completely informed about their values. Because these values are not verifiable ex ante, they cannot be set in a contract. On the other hand, a court of law or some other third party can play the role of a so-called Center, as in section 2.1, and try to set up a revelation mechanism that will implement the first-best outcome.

As each party knows the other's type (here its investment), we face an implementation problem under complete information. The first important result for our purpose was given by Moore-Repullo (1988); they proved that a very large class of allocation rules can be implemented if the Center can use a multiple-stage mechanism. Rogerson (1992) built on this result to show that where both parties are risk-neutral, and renegotiation can be prevented, the Center will always elicit the true value of the investments and thus implement the first-best outcome.

Maskin-Tirole (1999a) went two steps further. First, they showed that Rogerson's result extends to parties with risk-averse preferences. Second, they studied the more realistic case where the parties cannot commit not to renegotiate. The relevant implementation result here is due to Maskin-Moore (1987, published 1999). While we cannot study the details of the argument here,[7] Maskin and Tirole proved that when agents are risk-averse, the first-best outcome can still be implemented very generally even if renegotiation cannot be prevented.

From the examples of this section and the implementation results above it is evident that even if parties are unable to specify completely the characteristics of the good to be traded ex ante, they can be made to play sophisticated revelation games after investing. The tension here is that all papers in this field make use of the principle of dynamic programming, which presumes a strong dose of rationality. Then there is no more reason to expect that incomplete contracts should lead to a different outcome than complete contracts: the incompleteness of contracts, when it is due to the parties' unability to specify all relevant contingencies, is simply irrelevant.

7.3 Concluding Remarks

While these negative results have dampened the enthusiasm for research on incomplete contracts, it is clear that the ideas sprung in the literature on incomplete contracts can shed some useful light on property rights, and also on political economy.[8] This suggests several directions for research.

First, the results of Maskin-Tirole (1999a) are more convincing when renegotiation is banned. If renegotiation is allowed, then an

---

7. Maskin (2002) gives a nontechnical summary of the mechanism used in Maskin-Tirole (1999a).
8. Politicians are given loose mandates but are constrained by rules of decision-making processes. These are central issues in the incomplete contracts literature.

implementation result is only obtained when both parties are risk-averse. To see why, let us look a little more closely at the mechanism used to elicit the truth when renegotiation is forbidden. In the first stage, both parties announce their types (truthfully or not). Then a party (e.g., the seller) can challenge the announcement of the other party; this challenge in fact is a choice of two allocations that are designed to prove that the buyer lied. If the challenge is successful, then the buyer must pay a fine to the seller. Otherwise, the seller must pay a fine for having raised an unsuccessful challenge. This fine cannot be paid to the buyer, as this would distort incentives for truthful revelation. Rather, it is paid to the Center, though any fine F paid to a third party cannot be renegotiation-proof. The parties can still get together and decide that the seller must pay say $F/2$ to the buyer instead. Only fines paid by one party to the other can be renegotiation-proof.

It follows that the mechanism used by Maskin-Tirole must be modified to include the case where the parties cannot commit not to renegotiate. They do this by having the proposer of an unsuccessful challenge (here the seller) pay a stochastic fine to the buyer. If the buyer is risk-averse, then this fine can be designed so that it hurts both the seller and the buyer.[9] The suboptimal outcome that results is then used for the implementation.

This construction does not work for risk-neutral parties. This is, of course, a nongeneric exception; still, if parties are close to risk-neutral, the stochastic fine that is required needs to have a very large variance, which is not very credible as it will violate the wealth constraints. Thus the applicability of the irrelevance theorem is doubtful in this case.

Another problem with the Maskin-Tirole mechanism is that it only works to elicit payoff-relevant information. If, for instance, the

9. For a risk-neutral seller, it suffices to take an $\tilde{F}$ with positive expectation and a large enough variance, so that it also has a negative expected equivalent for the buyer.

parties have CARA preferences, then there are no wealth effects and income cannot be elicited.

These objections have a rather abstract character (which does not mean that they should not be taken seriously). Other, more pragmatic arguments suggest a more sanguine view of the literature.[10]

The irrelevance theorems are driven by the ability of the agents to reason backward and to play complicated message games. Thus a first avenue of progress calls for building an explicit theory of bounded rationality and studying its implications for contracting. Unfortunately, while many authors have insisted on the need for such an approach, little progress has been made, and we still have no useful criterion to decide whether a contract is "too complicated." The study of environments where the optimal complete contract is very simple and looks very much like what the promoters of incomplete contracts had in mind has shown more promise. This has taken three interesting directions. The intuition behind the first is that as the contracting environment becomes more complex, renegotiation will constrain the exchange of messages so much that the standard incomplete contracts will be achieved in the limit (see Segal 1999 for a good example). A second consists in challenging the received wisdom that complete contracts cannot explain authority and property rights. Tirole (1999) indeed presents a model in which, with renegotiation allowed, the optimal complete contract can be implemented by an allocation of property rights as is typical of simple incomplete contracts.

More recently the Maskin-Tirole assumption that the Center's can verify the actions taken after the message game is played was relaxed by Aghion-Dewatripont-Rey (2004). They consider the case of a banker who extends a line of credit to a borrower. The borrower is unknown to the banker, and his type may be good or bad. The credit line is worth keeping open only if the borrower is good.

---

10. Tirole (1999) provides a highly readable discussion of this topic.

With complete contracts, the banker can set up a message game, elicit information about the borrower's type, and decide according to the contract whether to close the credit line or keep it open. The inference is that the Center will verify that the contract has been executed fairly. However, we see little of this in reality. What we do see is that bankers extend "test" credit lines in order to obtain information on the borrowers' types. Then they can decide whether to close them or offer more generous loans. Aghion-Dewatripont-Rey show examples where this actually is the optimal contract.[11]

Last we should consider a more practical approach to incomplete contracting that focuses on simple contracts, and disregards the debate on their foundations. Simple contracts, in this view, are robust because they allow agents to learn how to behave.[12] The book by Hart (1995) gives many interesting insights on the theory of firms obtained in this way. The study of venture capital contracts by Kaplan-Stromberg (2003) also gives support to the view of financial contracting in Aghion-Bolton (1992). The difficulty remains, however, that we have no good definition of what constitutes a "simple" contract. The option-to-sell may not qualify because it is based on a public randomization device. But what of contracts that merely constrain the renegotiation game? In any case, proponents of this approach should eventually study the consequences of incomplete contracting when information is asymmetric[13]. Because renegotiation then may not be efficient, this raises a host of other problems.

---

11. This is close to the analysis of Aghion-Tirole (1997), which we examined in section 4.4. Here the borrower is sometimes given real authority, though the banker keeps formal authority.
12. This was already the idea behind the argument for linear contracts by Holmstrom-Milgrom (1987); see section 5.3.9.
13. Unforeseen contingencies and symmetric information do not go well together. When events are hard to describe, it is inevitable that the parties will have different views.

References

Aghion, P., and P. Bolton. 1992. An incomplete contracts approach to financial contracting. *Review of Economic Studies* 59:473–94.

Aghion, P., M. Dewatripont, and P. Rey. 1994. Renegotiation design with unverifiable information. *Econometrica* 62:257–82.

Aghion, P., M. Dewatripont, and P. Rey. 2004. Transferable control. *Journal of the European Economic Association* 2:115–38.

Aghion, P., and J. Tirole. 1997. Formal and real authority in organizations. *Journal of Political Economy* 105:1–29.

Casadesus-Masanell, R., and D. Spulber. 2000. The fable of Fisher Body. *Journal of Law and Economics* 43:67–104.

Chung, T. Y. 1991. Incomplete contracts, specific investments, and risk-sharing. *Review of Economic Studies* 58:1031–42.

Coase, R. 1988. *The Firm, the Market, and the Law.* Chicago: University of Chicago Press.

Grossman, S., and O. Hart. 1986. The costs and benefits of ownership: A theory of vertical and lateral integration. *Journal of Political Economy* 94:691–719.

Hart, O. 1995. *Firms, Contracts, and Financial Structure.* Oxford: Oxford University Press.

Holmstrom, B., and P. Milgrom. 1987. Aggregation and linearity in the provision of intertemporal incentives. *Econometrica* 55:303–28.

Hart, O., and J. Moore. 1988. Incomplete contracts and renegotiation. *Econometrica* 56:755–85.

Kaplan, S., and P. Stromberg. 2003. Financial contracting theory meets the real world: An empirical analysis of venture capital contracts. *Review of Economic Studies* 70:281–315.

Klein, B., R. Crawford, and A. Alchian. 1978. Vertical integration, appropriable rents and the competitive contracting process. *Journal of Law and Economics* 21:297–326.

Maskin, E. 2002. On indescribable contingencies and incomplete contracts. *European Economic Review* 46:725–33.

Maskin, E., and J. Moore. 1999. Implementation and renegotiation. *Review of Economic Studies* 66:57–82.

Maskin, E., and J. Tirole. 1999a. Unforeseen contingencies and incomplete contracts. *Review of Economic Studies* 66:83–114.

Maskin, E., and J. Tirole. 1999b. Two remarks on the property rights literature. *Review of Economic Studies* 66:139–49.

Moore, J., and R. Repullo. 1999. Subgame perfect implementation. *Econometrica* 56:1191–1220.

Nöldeke, G., and K. Schmidt. 1995. Option contracts and renegotiation: A solution to the hold-up problem. *Rand Journal of Economics* 26:163–79.

Rogerson, W. 1992. Contractual solutions to the hold-up problem. *Review of Economic Studies* 59:777–94.

Schwartz, A. 1992. Legal contract theories and incomplete contracts. In *Contract Economics* L. Werin and H. Wijkander, eds. Oxford: Basil Blackwell.

Segal, I. 1999. Complexity and renegotiation: A foundation for incomplete contracts. *Review of Economic Studies* 66:57–82.

Tirole, J. 1999. Incomplete contracts: Where do we stand? *Econometrica* 67:741–81.

Williamson, O. 1989. Transaction cost economics. In *Handbook of Industrial Organization*, vol. 1. Amsterdam: North-Holland.

8

Some Empirical Work

It is a capital mistake to theorise before one has data.
—**Arthur Conan Doyle,** *A Scandal in Bohemia*

The reader should be aware by now of the explosive development of the theory of contracts since the early 1970s. The theoretical models have become increasingly more realistic and shed light on many fields of economic activity. For a long time, however, the empirical validation of the models lagged despite the increasing sophistication of the theory. Many papers consisted of theoretical analyses with little attention to the facts. Others stated so-called stylized facts often based on anecdotal evidence and went on to study a model from which these stylized facts could be derived. A rather small number of authors derived qualitative predictions from the theory and went on to test them on actual data. But contrary to most other fields of economic theory, econometrics was very rarely used to check the predictions of the theory of contracts.

In the 1990s, a growing number of scholars came to deplore this state of affairs. After all, even if the philosophy of science held by Sherlock Holmes is somewhat outdated, it does seem that economists can do more to draw inferences from whatever data they can lay their hands on. Fortunately, a good number of empirical researchers have turned their attention to the theory of contracts in recent years. There is not the space here to give a survey of this burgeoning and exciting line of work. We will attempt to cover a few important themes. The reader can turn to the recent survey of Chiappori-Salanié (2003),[1] complemented by Prendergast (1999) on incentives within firms and Laffont (1997) on auctions. We just note here that two broad conclusions that emerge from this literature.

• There is accumulating evidence that incentives do matter: contracts influence behavior in the ways predicted by theory.

• On the other hand, it is much harder to account for the specific form that contracts take; much progress remains to be done in this direction.

In the first section of this chapter, we will study one of the main difficulties of the empirical contracts literature, which is to measure the effect of contracts on agents' behavior when they self-select by choosing a particular contract. In the next two sections we will consider briefly the work in two important fields: auctions in section 8.2 and insurance in section 8.3. These presentations are kept as simple as possible, but the reader should be warned that this chapter presupposes a little familiarity with standard econometric concepts and methods.

8.1   Dealing with Unobserved Heterogeneity

The basic objective in empirical work on contracts is to measure what influences behavior, or, to put it more bluntly: Do incentives matter? Unfortunately, empirical observation can only provide evidence on *correlations* between contracts and human behavior. Theoretical predictions, on the other hand, are concerned with *causality* relationships. Assessing causality from correlations is an old problem in economics, as it is in all science, and the question of causality is important in the study of contracts. Typically, although different

---

1. Parts of this chapter draw heavily on this survey.

contracts can be associated with different behaviors, as is documented by a large literature, the interpretation of observed correlations is not straightforward. One explanation is that contracts *induce* the corresponding behavior through their underlying incentive structure; this is the so-called incentive effect of contracts. Another offers a priori a convincing argument that differences in behavior reflect an unobserved heterogeneity across agents, and that this heterogeneity is responsible for the variations in contract choices.

Interestingly, this distinction is familiar to both theorists and econometricians, although the vocabulary differs. Econometricians have for a long time stressed the importance of endogenous selection. In the presence of unobserved heterogeneity, the matching of agents to contracts must be studied with care. If the outcome of the matching process is related to the unobserved heterogeneity variable (as can be expected), then the choice of the contract is endogenous. In effect, any empirical analysis taking contracts as given will be biased.

Contract theory, on the other hand, systematically emphasizes the distinction between adverse selection (whereby unobserved heterogeneity preexists and constrains the form of contract) and moral hazard (whereby behavior directly responds to the incentive structure created by the contract). As an illustration, consider the literature on automobile insurance contracts. The idea here is to test a standard prediction of the theory: everything equal, people who face contracts entailing more comprehensive coverage should exhibit a higher accident probability. Such a pattern, if observed, can be given two interpretations. One is the classical adverse selection effect à la Rothschild-Stiglitz: high risk agents, knowing they are more likely to have an accident, self-select by choosing contracts entailing a more comprehensive coverage. Alternatively, one can evoke moral hazard: if some agents, for *exogenous* reasons (e.g., picking the insurance company located down the corner), end up facing a contract with only partial coverage, they will be motivated to adopt a more cautious behavior, which will result in lower accident rates. In practice, the distinction between adverse selection and moral hazard is crucial, especially from a normative viewpoint. But it is also very difficult to implement empirically, especially with cross-sectional data.

A recent contribution by Ackerberg and Botticini (2002) gives a striking illustration of this selection problem. They consider the choice between sharecropping and fixed rent contracts in a tenant–landlord relationship. As we saw in chapter 5, the standard moral hazard models stress the trade-off between incentives and risk-sharing in the determination of contractual forms. Fixed rent contracts are efficient because the tenant is both the main decision maker and the residual claimant. However, fixed rent contracts can generate an inefficient allocation of risk, whereby all the risk is borne by one agent, the tenant, who is presumably more risk averse. When uncertainty is small, risk-sharing matters less, and fixed rent contracts are more likely to be adopted. In contrast, in a very uncertain environment, risk-sharing is paramount, and sharecropping is the natural contractual form. This prediction can readily be tested from data on existing contracts, provided that a proxy for the level of risk is available. For instance, if some crops are known to be more risky than others, the theory predicts that these crops are more likely to be associated with sharecropping contracts.

A number of papers have tested this prediction by regressing contract choice on crop riskiness. The underlying argument, however, has an obvious weakness: it takes contracts as exogenously given, and disregards any possible endogeneity in the matching of agents to contracts. In other words, the theoretical prediction described above only holds for *given* characteristics of the landlord and the agents. It can be taken to the data only to the extent that this "everything equal" assumption is satisfied so that agents facing different contracts do not differ by some otherwise relevant characteristic. To see this, suppose, on the contrary, that agents exhibit ex ante heterogeneous degrees of risk aversion. To keep things simple, we can assume that a fraction of the agents are risk neutral, while the rest are risk averse. Different agents will be drawn to different crops; efficiency suggests that risk-neutral agents should specialize in the riskier crops. But note that risk-neutral agents should also be offered fixed rent contracts, since risk-sharing is not an issue for them. Thus given heterogeneous risk aversions, fixed rent contracts are associated with the riskier crops, and the standard prediction is reversed.

Clearly, the core of the difficulty lies in the fact that although risk aversion has a crucial role in this example, it is not directly observable. *Conditional on risk aversion*, the initial theoretical argument remains valid: more risk makes fixed rent contracts look less attractive. This prediction can in principle be tested, but it requires that differences in risk aversion be controlled for in the estimation or that the resulting endogeneity bias be corrected in some way.

Most empirical studies relating contracts and behavior involve, at least implicitly, a selection problem of this kind. Various strategies can be adopted to address it. Some writers explicitly recognize the problem, and merely test for the presence of asymmetric information without trying to be specific about its nature (see section 8.3 on models of insurance markets). Others, however, use available data to disentangle selection and incentives. Such is the case, in particular, when the allocation of agents to contracts is exogenous, either because it results from explicit randomization or because some "natural experiment" has modified the incentive structure without changing the composition of the population. The guiding example here is the celebrated Rand Health Insurance Experiment (HIE).[2]

Families participating in the HIE were randomly assigned to one of 14 different insurance plans, with different coinsurance rates and different upper limits on annual out-of-pocket expenses. In addition

---

2. See Manning et al. (1987).

lump-sum payments were introduced in order to guarantee that no family would lose by participating in the experiment. The HIE has provided extremely valuable information about the sensitivity of the demand for health services to out-of-pocket expenditures, but it was a very costly experiment that is not likely to be imitated often.

Some studies rely on simultaneous estimation of selection and incentives effects in their modelization of the economic and/or econometric structure at stake. Paarsch-Shearer (1999) and Cardon-Hendel (2001) are leading papers in labor economics and in health insurance respectively. Finally there is a promising direction on the use of panel data, the underlying intuition being that the dynamics of behavior exhibit specific features under moral hazard.

8.2 Auctions

Much empirical study has been devoted since the 1980s to the actual behavior of bidders in auctions. There are two strands in this literature. The first aims at testing the standard model of bidding developed in section 3.2.3 (or more elaborate extensions) by producing qualitative predictions of the theory and testing them using descriptive statistics or reduced-form econometrics; Porter (1995) is a well-known example. The second, which we will consider here, adopts a fully structural approach to recover estimates of the parameters of the theoretical model.

The pioneering paper in this area is Laffont-Ossard-Vuong (1995).[3] We will adopt their approach in the context of an independent private values model using the first-price sealed-bid auction studied in section 3.2.3. Recall that there are n bidders in this model, each of whom has a valuation θ_i with cumulative distribution function F on $[\underline{\theta}, \overline{\theta}]$, and these valuations are independently distributed

---

3. But see also Paarsch (1992).

across individuals. For estimation purposes, we will assume that F is lognormal, so that

$$\log \theta \xrightarrow{D} N(X\beta, \sigma^2)$$

where X is a vector of exogenous variables and β and σ are the parameters we want to estimate. In each auction we observe both the exogenous variables X and the value of the winning bid b_w.

We saw in section 3.2.3 that the equilibrium bidding strategies are given by

$$B(\theta_i) = \theta_i - \frac{\int_{\underline{\theta}}^{\theta_i} F(\theta)^{n-1} d\theta}{F(\theta_i)^{n-1}}$$

Then the winning bid is $b_w = B(\theta_{(1)})$, where

$$(\theta_{(1)}, \ldots, \theta_{(n)})$$

is the vector of valuations arranged in decreasing order. In theory, we could use this formula and the fact that we observe b_w to derive a maximum-likelihood estimator of the parameters of the distribution F. However, this is a very cumbersome way to proceed. A better idea is to rely on the expected revenue of the seller, which is

$$Eb_w = E\theta_{(2)}$$

While it is hard to compute $E\theta_{(2)}$ analytically, it is easy to approximate it using simulations. To do this, we draw S n-vectors $(u_1^s, \ldots, u_n^s)$ independently from the centered reduced normal distribution $N(0, 1)$. For each of these draws s, we pick the second highest u_i^s and denote it $u_{(2)}^s$. Then $\exp (X\beta + \sigma u_{(2)}^s)$ is an unbiased simulator of $E\theta_{(2)}$ and a more accurate one is

$$E_S b_w(X, \beta, \sigma) = \frac{1}{S} \sum_{s=1}^{S} \exp \left(X\beta + \sigma u_{(2)}^s \right)$$

Now suppose that we have data $(b_w^l, X^l)_{l=1}^L$ on L auctions and that these auctions can be considered to be independent.[4] The natural idea is, following Laroque-Salanié (1989), to minimize the squared distance between the observed winning bids b_w^l and the (simulated) expected theoretical bids $E_S b_w(X, \beta, \sigma)$. A simulated nonlinear least-squares estimator of β and σ thus obtains after we minimize

$$\sum_{l=1}^L (b_w^l - E_S b_w(X^l, \beta, \sigma))^2$$

We get a consistent estimator as both L and S go to infinity. Moreover Laffont-Ossard-Vuong exhibit a simple bias correction that allows the estimator to be consistent and asymptotically normal when L goes to infinity, even when the number of simulations S is fixed.[5] A remarkable feature of this estimation procedure is that it does not require the introduction of statistical errors; in fact the valuations θ_i play that role because they are randomly drawn from the distribution F.

This method has been extended in recent years to more realistic models of auctions and to nonparametric estimators. Its proponents have further uncovered fundamental nonidentification issues in the affiliated private values model of Milgrom-Weber (1982) that can only be remedied by creative use of more complete datasets. For all of this, the interested reader is referred to Laffont (1997).

8.3 Tests of Asymmetric Information in Insurance Markets

In the contracting literature a vexing problem is to find convincing evidence for the importance of asymmetric information in the various fields to which the theory have been applied. Insurance was an

---

4. Auctions are independent in the sense that bidders draw new private values before each auction.

5. The simulations entail an efficiency loss that is of order $1/S$, and thus the efficiency loss can be made very small by increasing the number of simulated draws.

early application of the theory of contracts, and it also represents a respectable share of GDP in all developed countries. Moreover it is relatively easy to get plentiful and high-quality data from insurance companies. Therefore several papers have recently used data on insurance markets in order to test for the presence of asymmetric information.

The starting point for this literature has already been presented in section 8.1: both the Rothschild-Stiglitz model of adverse selection and the pure moral hazard model predict that coverage and risk must be positively correlated across contracts. In simpler terms, consider the basic 0–1 model in which insurees either file no claim or file a claim of a fixed size. Then these two models predict that the proportion of insurees who file a claim must be larger for contracts that offer more generous coverage.

This outcome was tested originally by Chiappori-Salanié (1997, 2000) in an automobile insurance context where insurees choose between two types of coverage (e.g., comprehensive versus liability only). They then did or did not have an accident in the subsequent year. The simplest representation of this framework uses two probit equations. One describes the choice of a contract, and takes the form

$$y_i = I[X_i\beta + \varepsilon_i > 0]$$

where $y_i = 1$ when the insuree chose the comprehensive coverage contract at the beginning of the year, and 0 otherwise; here the X_i are exogenous covariates that control for all the information available to the insurer, and β is a vector of parameters to be estimated. The second equation relates to the occurrence of an accident:

$$z_i = I[X_i\gamma + \eta_i > 0]$$

where $z_i = 1$ when the insuree had an accident during the year, and 0 otherwise, and γ is a vector of parameters to be estimated. In this context asymmetric information should result in a positive correlation between y_i and z_i conditional on X_i, which is equivalent to a positive correlation between ε_i and η_i. This can be tested in a number of ways; for instance, Chiappori and Salanié (2000) propose two parametric tests and a nonparametric test.[6] Interestingly none of the tests can reject the null hypothesis of zero correlation (corresponding to the absence of asymmetric information).

These results are confirmed by most studies on automobile insurance; similarly Cawley and Philipson (1999) find no evidence of asymmetric information in life insurance. However, evidence of adverse selection has been repeatedly found in annuity markets. Recently Finkelstein and Poterba (2004) have studied the annuity policies sold by a large UK insurance company. Again, the systematic and significant relationships they find between ex post mortality and some relevant characteristics of the policies suggest that adverse selection plays an important role in that market. For instance, individuals who buy more backloaded annuities are found to be longer-lived, whereas policies involving payment to the estate in the event of an early death are preferred by customers with shorter life expectancy.

How can the negative tests on the presence of asymmetric information in many insurance markets be reconciled with the common feeling that both moral hazard and adverse selection play an important role in this field? Chiappori-Jullien-Salanié-Salanié (2004) examine this question. They first prove that the theoretical prediction of a positive correlation of coverage and risk holds (in a generalized form) in two cases:

• A general class of competitive models with adverse selection on risk and/or preferences and possibly moral hazard, and a general distribution of claim sizes.

---

6. One parametric test is based on a computation of generalized residuals from independent estimations of the two probits, while the other requires a simultaneous estimation of the two probits using a general covariance matrix for the residuals. The nonparametric approach relies on the construction of "cells" of identical profiles, followed by a series of χ^2 tests.

• Imperfectly competitive models, provided that insurers observe the risk-aversion of the insurees.

They then argue that since the data reject this prediction, theoretical models must be found that allow for imperfect competition and privately known risk-aversions. Jullien-Salanié-Salanié (2003) study such a model and show that it can generate both positive and negative correlations of risk and coverage. Finkelstein-McGarry (2004) exhibit some corroborating evidence for this model.

The recent literature on insurance markets is characterized by the constant interaction between theory and empirical studies that is the hallmark of scientific research but was largely neglected in the contracting literature until recently. It is the hope of this author that we will see more such work in the future.

References

Ackerberg, D., and M. Botticini. 2002. Endogenous matching and the empirical determinants of contract form. *Journal of Political Economy* 110:564–91.

Cardon, J., and I. Hendel. 2001. Asymmetric information in health insurance: Evidence from the National Health Expenditure Survey. *Rand Journal of Economics* 32:408–27.

Cawley, J., and T. Philipson. 1999. An empirical examination of information barriers to trade in insurance. *American Economic Review* 89:827–46.

Chiappori, P.-A., B. Jullien, B. Salanié, and F. Salanié. 2004. Asymmetric information in insurance: General testable implications. Forthcoming in the *Rand Journal of Economics*.

Chiappori, P.-A., and B. Salanié. 1997. Empirical contract theory: The case of insurance data. *European Economic Review* 41:943–950.

Chiappori, P.-A., and B. Salanié. 2000. Testing for asymmetric information in insurance markets. *Journal of Political Economy* 108:56–78.

Chiappori, P.-A., and B. Salanié. 2003. Testing contract theory: A survey of some recent work. In *Advances in Economics and Econometrics*, vol. 1, M. Dewatripont, L. Hansen, and S. Turnovsky, eds., Cambridge: Cambridge University Press.

Finkelstein, A., and K. McGarry. 2004. Multiple dimensions of private information: Evidence from the long-term care insurance market. Mimeo. Harvard University.

Finkelstein, A., and J. Poterba. 2004. Adverse selection in insurance markets: Policy-holder evidence from the U.K. annuity market. *Journal of Political Economy* 112:183–208.

Jullien, B., B. Salanié, and F. Salanié. 2003. Screening risk-averse agents under moral hazard. Mimeo. CREST, Paris.

Laffont, J.-J. 1995. Game theory and empirical economics: The case of auction data. *European Economic Review* 41:1–35.

Laffont, J.-J., H. Ossard, and Q. Vuong. 1995. Econometrics of first-price auctions. *Econometrica* 63:953–80.

Laroque, G., and B. Salanié. 1989. Estimation of multimarket fix-price models: An application of pseudo-maximum likelihood methods. *Econometrica* 57:831–60.

Manning, W., J. Newhouse, N. Duan, E. Keeler and A. Leibowitz. 1987. Health insurance and the demand for medical care: Evidence from a randomized experiment. *American Economic Review* 77:251–77.

Milgrom, P., and R. Weber. 1982. A theory of auctions and competitive bidding. *Econometrica* 50:1089–1122.

Paarsch, H. 1992. Deciding between the common and private value paradigms in empirical models of auctions. *Journal of Econometrics* 51:192–215.

Paarsch, H., and B. Shearer. 1999. The response of worker effort to piece rates: Evidence from the British Columbia tree-planting industry. *Journal of Human Resources* 34:643–67.

Porter, R. 1995. The role of information in U.S. offshore oil and gas lease auctions. *Econometrica* 63:1–27.

Prendergast, C. 1999. The provision of incentives within firms. *Journal of Economic Literature* 37:7–63.

Appendix

Some Noncooperative Game Theory

In solving a problem of this sort, the grand thing is to be able to reason backwards.

—**Arthur Conan Doyle,** *A Study in Scarlet*

This appendix presents some equilibrium concepts for noncooperative games that are used mostly in chapters 4 and 6. Readers interested in a more detailed study of these concepts can turn to chapter 11 of Tirole (1988), to chapter 12 of Kreps (1990a), or to Fudenberg-Tirole (1991). It is presumed that the reader already knows what a game is and how it is modeled.

Consider an n-player game. Player i has strategies $s_i \in S_i$ and a utility function denoted by $u_i(s_1, \ldots, s_n)$. Denote mixed strategies by σ_i. If $\sigma = (\sigma_1, \ldots, \sigma_n)$ is a vector of strategies, σ_{-i} represents the vector $(\sigma_1, \ldots, \sigma_{i-1}, \sigma_{i+1}, \ldots, \sigma_n)$. Recall that a mixed strategy σ_i is called *totally mixed* if it has full support on the set of pure strategies S_i. By a slight abuse of notation we can denote $u_i(\sigma)$ the expected utility of player i when players adopt mixed strategies $\sigma = (\sigma_1, \ldots, \sigma_n)$. We can assume that the strategy spaces are finite, and let $\sigma_i(s_i)$ be the weight of pure strategy s_i in the mixed strategy σ_i. Then

$$u_i(\sigma) = \sum_{s_1 \in S_1} \cdots \sum_{s_n \in S_n} \left(\prod_{j=1}^{n} \sigma_j(s_j) \right) u_i(s)$$

A.1   Games of Perfect Information

A.1.1   Nash Equilibrium

A Nash equilibrium is a strategy profile $(\sigma_1^*, \ldots, \sigma_n^*)$ such that each σ_i^* is a best response to the equilibrium strategies σ_{-i}^* of the other players:

$$\forall i, \quad \sigma_i^* \in \arg \max_{\sigma_i} u_i(\sigma_i, \sigma_{-i}^*)$$

A.1.2   Subgame-Perfect Equilibrium

Dynamic games are usually described by their extensive form. The sequential unrolling of the game is represented through a *game tree,* as shown in figure A.1 in which player 1 chooses between strategies T and B and player 2 then chooses between strategies t and b. The utilities achieved by the two players are indicated on the right terminal nodes of the tree.

The extensive form makes it easy to define subgames because they correspond to various branches of the game tree. Thus there are three subgames in the previous example: the game itself, and the two subgames starting with the nodes marked by a 2. Each strategy

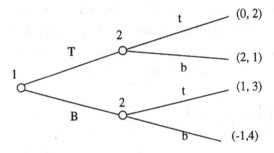

Figure A.1
An extensive-form game

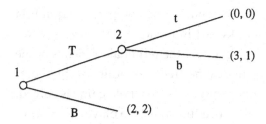

Figure A.2
Subgame-perfect equilibria

conceived for the whole game engenders strategies in each sub-game. When global strategies form a Nash equilibrium, the strategies induced in each subgame must form a Nash equilibrium in each subgame that is effectively reached at equilibrium. On the other hand, Nash equilibrium may prescribe strategies that are not a Nash equilibrium in a subgame that is not reached in equilibrium. Some Nash equilibria may thus rest on the fact that player 1 threatens player 2 with a punishment if player 2 deviates from equilibrium, even though this punishment may hurt player 1 himself. If player 2 should deviate from equilibrium, then it would not be in player 1's interest to carry out his threat: this type of threat therefore is not credible.

The concept of subgame-perfect equilibrium was designed to eliminate such noncredible threats. It is defined as a strategy profile that is a Nash equilibrium in all subgames, *including those that are not reached in equilibrium.*

Consider now the game depicted in figure A.2. There are two Nash equilibria in this game. In the first equilibrium, denoted by (T, b), player 1 plays T and player 2 plays b; in the second equilibrium, denoted by B, player 1 plays B and the game stops. However, B is a Nash equilibrium only because player 1 anticipates that 2 will play t if 1 plays T. Since t is a dominated strategy for 2, this cannot be a subgame-perfect equilibrium. The only subgame-perfect equilibrium of this game is (T, b).

In finite-horizon games the search for subgame-perfect equilibria uses Kuhn's algorithm of backward induction.[1] That is to say, we start by looking for Nash equilibria on the terminal branches of the game. Then we apply to the nodes the "reduced utilities" thus computed. Last we iterate the algorithm until the whole game is solved. In the preceding example this procedure affects to player 1's T strategy the utility vector (3, 1), since b is player 2's preferred strategy. Player 1 then chooses T, which gives him a higher utility than B.

A.2 Games of Incomplete Information

Some authors make a subtle distinction between games of incomplete information and games of imperfect information. In games of imperfect information, the player is not perfectly informed as to what other players have done before him; in games of incomplete information, players do not know all characteristics (or types) of their opponents.

In fact every game of incomplete information can be transformed into a game of imperfect information by adding an $(n + 1)$th player, called Nature. Nature randomly picks the types of the other n players before the game starts. This distinction therefore is not essential, and for that reason we only need to study here games of incomplete information.

A.2.1 Bayesian Equilibrium

Each player i now has a type θ_i, which we can take in a finite set to simplify the exposition. The player's utility is $u_i(s_1, \ldots, s_n, \theta_i)$, and the strategy he chooses of course depends on his type. Types are

---

1. This was indeed the modus operandi of Sherlock Holmes, as noted by the quotation at the head of this appendix.

drawn from a joint distribution $\pi(\theta_1, \ldots, \theta_n)$. We can assume that the prior beliefs of the players are consistent with this joint distribution:[2] the prior of player i is the conditional distribution $\pi_i(\theta_{-i} \mid \theta_i)$, where $\theta_{-i} = (\theta_1, \ldots, \theta_{i-1}, \theta_{i+1}, \ldots, \theta_n)$.

The analogous concept to the Nash equilibrium in this setup is the Bayesian equilibrium. A type-dependent strategy profile

$$(\sigma_1^*(\theta_1), \ldots, \sigma_n^*(\theta_n))$$

is a Bayesian equilibrium if every player chooses his "expected best response":

$$\forall \theta, \forall i, \quad \sigma_i^*(\theta_i) \in \arg\max_{\sigma_i} \sum_{\theta_{-i}} \pi_i(\theta_{-i} \mid \theta_i) \, u_i(\sigma_i, \sigma_{-i}^*(\theta_{-i}), \theta_i)$$

We can also define a subgame-perfect Bayesian equilibrium concept by imposing that strategies form a Bayesian equilibrium in each subgame. This notion is only used in practice as a building block for perfect Bayesian equilibrium or its refinements, to which we now turn.

A.2.2   Perfect Bayesian Equilibrium

Bayesian equilibrium does not take into account the fact that players can learn their opponents' types by observing their play, since every move by a player can reveal information on his type. Suppose, for instance, that the first player, who has two possible types, can play L or R. Suppose also that the first type of player 1 has a higher utility in branch L, while its second type has a higher utility in branch R. Then the first type will tend to choose L and the second type will tend to choose R. When the second player observes that the first player chose to play L, he logically will revise his prior belief on

---

2. The presence of *common priors* is an assumption that is nearly universal in the literature.

player 1 and increase his prior that player 1 is of the first type. The concept of perfect Bayesian equilibrium aims at formalizing this process of updating beliefs, by modeling the mutual links between equilibrium strategies and beliefs.

At each node of the game, the player whose turn it is to play has an information set that describes his uncertainty as to what types the other players are, and beliefs π that are a probability distribution on this information set; accordingly these beliefs evolve as the game unfolds. These beliefs thus specify, at each node of the game, a probability distribution on the types of each other player.

Perfect Bayesian equilibria integrate two requirements:

• *Sequential rationality.* The strategies σ played at equilibrium must form a subgame-perfect Bayesian equilibrium, given the beliefs π at every node.

• *Bayesian consistency.* The beliefs π at every node must obtain through Bayesian updating of prior beliefs, given the equilibrium strategies σ.

"Bayesian updating" means that players use Bayes's rule whenever it is possible. Suppose, for instance, that player 1 has only two possible types θ_1 and θ_2 that are a priori equiprobable and two possible strategies T and B. Let p_i be the probability that type θ_i of player 1 plays T in equilibrium. Then the probability that player 1 plays T in equilibrium is

$$\frac{p_1 + p_2}{2}$$

If $p_1 + p_2 \neq 0$, Bayes's rule allows us to compute the beliefs of player 2 after player 1 has played T: Player 2 then assigns probability $p_1/(p_1 + p_2)$ to type θ_1. On the other hand, if $p_1 = p_2 = 0$, that is, if T is never played in equilibrium, then Bayes's rule does not apply and player 2's beliefs are unrestricted after T.

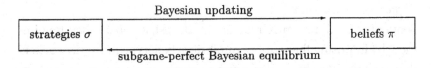

Figure A.3
The perfect Bayesian equilibrium

A perfect Bayesian equilibrium thus is a n-tuple of strategies σ and a n-tuple of beliefs π at every node such that

• the strategies σ form a subgame-perfect Bayesian equilibrium, given the beliefs π,

• the beliefs π are obtained from the prior beliefs by applying Bayes's rule at every node that is reached with nonzero probability in equilibrium when players follow the strategies σ.

Figure A.3 sums up the mutual determination of beliefs and strategies in a perfect Bayesian equilibrium.

A.2.3 Refinements of Perfect Bayesian Equilibrium

Perfect Bayesian equilibrium does not restrict out-of-equilibrium beliefs at all. If a node of the game is never reached in equilibrium, then Bayes's rule has no bite there. In many games it will therefore be possible to support a large number and sometimes a continuum of perfect Bayesian equilibria by choosing particular out-of-equilibrium beliefs.[3]

Several more restrictive equilibrium concepts have been proposed to remedy this. They all aim at limiting possible beliefs when an out-of-equilibrium move takes place. We will only consider two of these refinements; they are the only ones used in this book.

---

3. Chapter 4 presents a good example of out-of-equilibrium beliefs.

Sequential Equilibrium.
Sequential equilibrium reinforces the Bayesian consistency requirement by imposing that out-of-equilibrium beliefs be the limit of beliefs that are generated by totally mixed strategies that are close to equilibrium strategies. This definition exploits the fact that Bayes's rule uniquely determines beliefs when strategies are totally mixed, since every node of the game then is reached with nonzero probability.

More formally, (σ, π) is a sequential equilibrium if the strategies σ are a subgame-perfect equilibrium given the beliefs π and if there exists a sequence of totally mixed strategies σ^n and a sequence of beliefs π^n such that

- π^n is obtained from σ^n by applying Bayes's rule in every node of the game,

- $\lim_{n \to \infty}(\sigma^n, \pi^n) = (\sigma, \pi)$.

Note that we *do not* require that the strategies σ^n form a subgame-perfect Bayesian equilibrium given the corresponding beliefs π^n, only that this is true at the limit. Figure A.4 shows how a sequential equilibrium is computed.

Selten (1975) introduced the idea of trembling-hand perfect equilibrium that relies on a robustness property when equilibrium strategies are slightly perturbed.[4] Kreps-Wilson (1982) showed that a set of trembling-hand perfect equilibria coincides with that of sequential equilibria in almost all finite games.

Intuitive Equilibrium.
Signaling models are typical of games involving a very large number of perfect Bayesian equilibria. As chapter 4 shows, sequential equilibrium does not solve this difficulty. To solve these games, Cho-Kreps (1987) proposed what they call the "intuitive criterion." The procedure is to give zero probability to the type θ of any player who has just played an out-of-equilibrium strategy s when that strategy

---

4. The underlying idea is that the equilibrium should not change much when players are allowed to make mistakes with a small probability.

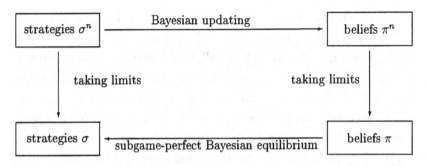

Figure A.4
The sequential equilibrium

is dominated for type θ. By "dominated," we mean here that whatever beliefs the other players adopt after observing s, their best responses can only give type θ a lower utility than what he gets in equilibrium. An intuitive equilibrium then is a perfect Bayesian equilibrium that passes the intuitive criterion.

Giving a precise definition of the intuitive criterion involves a lot of notation, so we will only study here a rough outline. Start from a perfect Bayesian equilibrium. Suppose that at some stage in the game, type θ's equilibrium strategy is some s_0 and that the other players' equilibrium response is s_0' so that in the end θ's expected payoff is $U(s_0, s_0', \theta)$. Now let s be a possible deviation by θ. If the other players revise their beliefs to μ when they observe s, they will then play their best response $s'(\mu, s)$, and θ will eventually obtain $U(s, s'(\mu, s), \theta)$. The intuitive criterion rejects perfect Bayesian equilibria which are supported by out-of-equilibrium beliefs such that

$$\max_{\mu} U(s, s'(\mu, s), \theta) < U(s_0, s_0', \theta)$$

and yet μ gives some weight to type θ.[5]

This equilibrium concept thus formalizes the idea according to which some deviations from equilibrium strategies can only be

---

5. There is a slight technicality here. It might be that the inequality in the text holds for all types θ, in which case μ would have total weight zero. Then the intuitive criterion should not be applied.

reasonable for some types: Type θ will only deviate if he has some indication that the other players will react in ways that increase his utility. Any other deviation by θ will be counterproductive, and the intuitive criterion therefore excludes it. As chapter 4 shows, the intuitive criterion is successful at selecting an equilibrium in signaling games, at least with only two types.[6] The trouble with the intuitive criterion is that as with all *forward induction* arguments,[7] it relies on counterfactual "speeches" by deviating players that should (ideally!) be modeled in a communication game.

Much work was aimed at refining perfect Bayesian equilibrium in the early 1980s,[8] but the activity has quieted now. The consensus among game theorists seems to be that more attention needs to be given issues of robustness and learning that do not presume the players to be hyperrational. (Kreps 1990b gives some good reasons to turn to such an approach.)

References

Cho, I. K., and D. Kreps. 1987. Signaling games and stable equilibria. *Quarterly Journal of Economics* 102:179–221.

Fudenberg, D., and J. Tirole. 1991. *Game Theory.* Cambridge: MIT Press.

Kreps, D. 1990a. *A Course in Microeconomic Theory.* Princeton: Princeton University Press.

Kreps, D. 1990b. *Game Theory and Economic Modeling.* Oxford: Oxford University Press.

Kreps, D., and R. Wilson. 1982. Sequential equilibria. *Econometrica* 50:863–94.

Selten, R. 1975. Reexamination of the perfectness concept for equilibrium points in extensive games. *International Journal of Game Theory* 4:25–55.

Tirole, J. 1988. *Industrial Organization.* Cambridge: MIT Press.

Van Damme, E. 1991. *Stability and Perfection of Nash Equilibria.* New York: Springer-Verlag.

---

6. With three types, one needs stronger refinements to select a unique equilibrium.
7. The idea of forward induction is that when an opponent deviates from equilibrium behavior, one should not presume that this is due to an unintended error (as in trembling-hand heuristics). Instead one should keep assuming that the player is fully rational and then draw whatever conclusions are possible from his deviation.
8. Van Damme (1991) gives a very thorough survey of this literature.

Name Index

Ackerberg, D., 214
Aghion, P., 115, 164, 203, 204, 207, 208, 208n.11
Akerlof, G., 97, 98
Alchian, A., 195n.3
Armstrong, M., 78, 79
Arrow, K., 1, 2
Aumann, R. J., 1
Ausubel, L., 5

Baker, G., 140
Baron, D., 44, 168n.8
Benabou, R., 115n.15
Bernheim, D., 142
Besanko, D., 168n.8
Bester, J., 173
Bolton, P., 90n19, 164, 208
Botticini, M., 214
Bulow, J., 71

Caillaud, B., 44, 168
Cardon, J., 216
Casadesus-Masanell, R., 195n.3
Cawley, J., 220
Champsaur, P., 58n.7, 61
Chiappori, P.-A., 184, 188, 212, 219, 220
Cho, I. K., 105
Choné, P., 78
Chung, T. Y., 204
Coase, R., 1, 194n.1
Cramton, P., 5

Crawford, R., 97, 107, 195n.3
Cremer, J., 71

Debreu, G., 1, 2
Deneckere, R., 5
Dewatripont, M., 167, 173, 203, 204, 207

Fagart, M.-C., 59
Fama, E., 154
Fershtman, C., 164
Finkelstein, A., 220, 221
Freixas, X., 77n.15
Fudenberg, D., 179, 188n.23, 190n.25, 223

Gale, D., 90
Green, J., 99n.2, 141
Grossman, S., 128, 129, 135, 196, 198
Guesnerie, R., 33n.19, 44, 177n.15

Hart, O., 128, 129, 135, 174, 195, 198, 208
Hellwig, M., 90
Hendel, I., 216
Hildenbrand, W., 1
Holmstrom, B., 119n.1, 139, 140, 141, 144, 146, 149, 154, 188n.23, 208n.12

Innes, R., 137n.18
Itoh, H., 141

Jeitschko, T., 177n.15
Judd, K., 164
Jullien, B., 168, 220, 221

Kamien, M., 38
Kaplan, S., 208
Katz, M., 167
Khalil, F., 91
Klein, B., 195n.3
Klemperer, P., 65n.9
Kreps, D., 105, 223, 232
Krishna, V., 65n.9

Laffont, J.-J., 13n.4, 33n.19, 38, 44, 45, 46, 47, 75, 77n.16, 78, 168n.8, 174, 177, 212, 216, 218
Laroque, G., 115n.15, 218
Lazear, E., 153
Leland, H., 114

Macho, I., 184, 188
Malcolmson, J., 187
Manning, W., 215n.2
Martimort, D., 61, 63, 75
Mas-Colell, A., 99n.2
Maskin, E., 27n.12, 78, 86, 87, 116, 173n.11, 195, 200, 205, 205n.7

McGarry, K., 221
McLean, R., 71
Milgrom, P., 33n.18, 65n.9, 66, 119n.1, 144, 146, 149, 188n.23, 208n.12, 218
Mirman, L., 177n.15
Mirrlees, J., 124n.8, 136
Mookherjee, D., 75, 140
Moore, J., 13n.4, 33n.18, 195, 204, 205
Mussa, M., 19n.8, 61
Myerson, R., 4, 71, 82

Nöldeke, G., 204

Ossard, H., 216

Paarsch, H., 216, 216n.3
Page, F., 139
Park, I.-U., 89
Philipson, T., 220
Picard, P., 168
Porter, R., 216
Poterba, J., 220
Prendergast, C., 212
Pyle, D., 114

Repullo, R., 204
Rey, P., 44, 177, 184, 185, 188, 203, 204, 207
Riley, J., 27n.12, 66n.10, 70

Riordan, M., 71
Roberts, J., 71
Rochet, J.-C., 58n.7, 61, 77n.16, 78, 79
Rogerson, W., 27n.12, 46, 136, 184, 204
Rosen, S., 19n.8, 61
Ross, S., 6
Rothschild, M., 58, 59, 60, 91, 92
Rubinstein, A., 181

Salanié, B., 51, 76, 177, 184, 185, 188, 212, 218, 219, 220, 221
Salanié, F., 220, 221
Salgueiro, E., 177n.15
Samuelson, W., 66n.10, 70
Sappington, D., 71
Satterthwait, M., 82
Scharfstein, D., 90n.19
Schelling, T., 164
Schmidt, K., 204
Schwartz, N., 38, 198n.5
Segal, I., 207
Shannon, C., 33n.18
Shapiro, C., 152
Shearer, B., 216
Sobel, J., 97, 107
Spencer, B., 164
Spinnewyn, F., 187
Spulber, D., 195n.3

Stiglitz, J., 12n.3, 51n.2, 55, 58, 59, 60, 91, 92, 152
Stokey, N., 141
Stole, L., 61, 63
Strausz, R., 173
Stromberg, P., 208

Tirole, J., 44, 45, 46, 47, 73, 75, 86, 87, 115, 116, 168n.8, 173n.11, 174, 177, 177n.15, 179, 190n.25, 195, 200, 205, 205n.7, 207, 207n.10, 208n.11, 223
Townsend, R., 90
Tsumagari, M., 75

Van Damme, E., 232n.8
Vickrey, W., 69
Vuong, Q., 215

Weber, R., 66, 218
Weiss, A., 12n.3
Whinston, M., 99n.2, 142
Williamson, O., 194n.1
Wilson, C., 78, 91

Yaari, M., 181

Subject Index

Adverse selection, 4, 11–13, 52, 97
in annuity market, 220
and auction theory, 65–73
and auditing of agent, 89–91
and bilateral private information, 82–88
and collusion among organization members, 73–75
and equilibria, 98
exercises on, 40–42, 91–93
and informed Principal, 86–88
in insurance market, 213, 220
and insurer as monopolist (example), 51–56
in intertemporal price discrimination, 168–78
and least-cost separating equilibrium, 107
and mechanism design, 13–18
and moral hazard problem, 184, 188, 213–14
with multidimensional characteristics of Agent, 26n.11, 78–82
and multiple Principals, 61–65
and optimal taxation (example), 47–51
and perfect competition in contracts, 57–60
and price discrimination, 18–27
and regulation of firm (example), 43–47
and renegotiation, 181
and risk-averse agents, 76–77
Rothschild-Stiglitz model of, 219

standard model of, 27–39, 71–72, 89
and type-dependent reservation utilities, 88–89
underproduction from, 107n.10
Agency problem, 6, 120n.2. *See also* Moral hazard
Agent, auditing of, 89–91, 140
Annuity markets, 220
Asymmetric information. *See also* Moral hazard
and adverse selection, 21–27
and adverse selection (exercise), 92–93
and general equilibrium models, 1–2
in insurance markets, 218–21
and secondhand-car market, 98–99
study of bargaining under, 5
Auctions, theory of, 65–73
and correlation of bidders' valuations, 71–73
and empirical contracts literature, 216–18
and optimal auction, 70, 70n.13, 71
and revenue equivalence theorem, 69
shading bid in, 68
Auditing, of Agent, 89–91, 140
Authority, formal and real, 115–16
Automobile insurance, and adverse selection vs. moral hazard, 213–14

Babbling equilibrium, 107, 109, 113
Backward induction, Kuhn's algorithm of, 226

Banking
and adverse selection, 12
example of, 207–208
Barriers to entry, 164–67
Bayesian consistency, 228, 230
Bayesian equilibrium, 226–27
and contract models, 3
perfect, 3, 5n.2, 104, 105, 110–11,
227–29, 231
refinements on, 229–32
Bayesian updating, 228
Behavioral norms, contract expressed
in, 3
Bilateral private information, 82–88
Borch's rule, 129n.11
Bounded rationality, 193, 194, 207
Breach of contract, 162
Bribe, for supervisors, 73, 73n.14, 74–75
Brownian motion, 145, 145n.22
Bunching, 51, 77, 78, 81–82
Bunching equilibria, 107
Bunching optimum, 38–39
exercise on, 40–41
Buyer–seller relationship. *See also*
Signaling models
and incomplete contracts, 196–97
in secondhand car market, 98–99

CARA (constant absolute risk
aversion), 145, 146, 188n.23, 189,
206–207
Causality, problem of, 212
CDFC (convexity of the distribution
function condition), 131–32, 132n.14,
133, 136, 140, 150
exercises on, 157
Center, 15–16, 204–205, 206, 207
Cheap talk, 97, 114
and Crawford-Sobel model, 107
in worker-and-manager example, 115
Chicago school, 165, 166n.5
Cho-Kreps intuitive equilibrium, 105, 114
Coase theorem, and bilateral private
information, 86
Coinsurance, 150

Collusion
exercise on, 92–93
among multiple Principals, 62
and optimal contract, 74
among organization members, 73–75
Collusion-proofness principle, 74
Commitment, 162–64
absence of, 163, 176–77, 185
full, 163, 164, 170–72, 178, 188
long-term, 163, 172–76, 178, 188
short-term, 163, 177–78, 178–79
spot, 163
strategic, 164–68
Common agency model, 61, 142
Common priors, 227n.2
Common value auctions, 65
Common values model, 53
Communication game, 232
Comparative statics
and continuous-action model, 136
and unique equilibrium, 104–105
Compensation. *See* Incentives(s); Wage
determination
Competitive equilibrium, Wilson,
91–92
Complete contracts, 161–62, 197. *See also*
Commitment
assumption of, 193
and property rights, 197, 207
and renegotiation, 162, 207
simple, 207
Complex goods, and contracts, 198
Concavity of the distribution function
condition, 131n.13
Consumer surplus, in regulation of
natural monopoly, 44
Consumption paths, 174
Consumption smoothing, 184–85, 190
Contracting literature, and interaction
between theory and empirical
studies, 221
Contracts, 3
accounting for specific form of, 212
adverse selection and moral hazard
distinguished in, 213

breach of, 162
and commitment, 162–68
complete, 161–62, 193, 197, 207 (*see also*
  Complete contracts)
exclusive, 165
fixed-price, 197
fixed-rent, 214
implicit, 3
incentive effect of, 212, 213
incomplete, 161, 193–208 (*see also*
  Incomplete contracts)
insurance, 180
long-term, 194
optimal, 74, 90, 129, 141, 144
option-to-sell, 200–204, 208
perfect competition in, 57–60
and renegotiation, 162 (*see also*
  Renegotiation)
robustness of, 144–45
short-term, 177
side-contracts, 74, 75
simple, 207, 208
spot, 185, 190
Contract theory(ies), 2–3, 211–13
adverse selection models, 4 (*see also*
  Adverse selection)
classification of, 3–4
and empirical observation on
  asymmetric information in insurance
  markets, 218–21
and empirical observation on auctions,
  216–18
and empirical observation on
  unobserved heterogeneity, 212–16
explosive development of, 211
factual data lacking in, 211
institutions in, 162
moral hazard models, 4 (*see also* Moral
  hazard)
and private information, 82
signaling models, 4 (*see also* Signaling
  models)
spot, 185
Control rights, property rights as, 198
Convergence, to first-best, 181–83

Convexity of the distribution function
  condition (CDFC), 131–32, 132n.14,
  133, 136, 140, 150
exercise on, 157
Cooperation, and piece-rate wage, 151.
  See also Teamwork
Coordination problem, in stag-hunt
  example, 108
Corporate shareholding, 187–88
Corporate scandals, and managerial
  compensation, 154
Costless signals, 107–108
general model of, 109–14
in stag-hunt example, 108–109, 118
Costly signals, 99–107
Cost-plus contract, in regulation of
  firm, 47
Crawford-Sobel model, 97, 107, 109–14
and equilibria, 98
exercise on, 117–18
and treacherous-journalist example,
  115
Credit market, and finitely repeated
  moral hazard, 183, 184n.17, 187, 188–89
Cutoff rule, 108

Direct truthful mechanism, 17–18, 87
and competition among Principals, 61
and full commitment, 170
and informed Principal, 87
and optimal auction, 70
and optimal taxation, 48
"Dominated," 231
Doyle, Arthur Conan
quoted (*A Scandal in Bohemia*), 211
quoted (*A Study in Scarlet*), 223, 226n.1
Dutch auction, 66
Dynamic programming, 205

Econometricians, and endogenous
  selection, 213
Economics of information, 2
and theory of contracts, 6
Education, and productivity (signaling
  models), 100–101, 102, 104, 105

Efficiency-wage model, 153
Efficient investment incentives,
  restoring of, 200–204
"Effort," 120
  and managerial incentives, 154, 155
Empirical contracts literature
  on asymmetric information in
    insurance markets, 218–21
  on auctions, 216–18
  and unobserved heterogeneity across
    agents, 212–16
Empirical observation, correlations not
  causation as object of, 212
English auction, 66
Entry, barriers to, 164–67
Equilibrium(a)
  babbling, 107, 109, 113
  Bayesian, 3, 226–27
  Bayesian (perfect), 3, 5n.2, 104, 105,
    110–111, 227–29, 231
  Bayesian (refinements on), 229–32
  bunching, 107
  Cho-Kreps intuitive, 105, 114
  intuitive, 230–32
  least-cost separating, 106–107, 116
  multiple, 104–105
  Nash, 224, 225
  partial, 2
  partition, 111
  pooling, 60, 102, 103, 104
  selection of, 103–107
  semiseparating, 107, 117
  separating, 60, 102, 106–107, 116
  sequential, 117, 230
  subgame-perfect, 224–26
  trembling-hand perfect, 230
  Walrasian, 14, 16
Exclusion phenomenon, 26n.11
Exclusive dealing, 165
Extensive form of game, 224–25
  observation of difficult, 97

Federal Communications Commission,
  spectrum auction by (1994), 66
Fines, and renegotiation, 206

First-best, convergence to, 181–83
First-order stochastic dominance (1SD)
  in exercise, 159
First-price sealed bid auction, 66–73
Fisher Body–GM relationship, 195–96
Fixed-price contract, 197
Fixed-rent contracts, 214
Forward induction arguments, 232,
  232n.7
Franchises, 152
Freedom of choice, limitation of, 163–64
Free riders, 140, 152
Fubini's theorem, 36, 36n.25, 49, 50
Full commitment, 163, 164, 170–72, 178,
  188
Functional analysis, and moral-hazard
  outcomes, 138

Games
  extensive form of, 97, 224–25
  of incomplete information, 226–32
  of perfect information, 224–26
  preplay communication, 114
Game theory
  and limitations of general equilibrium
    models, 2
  Prisoner's Dilemma, 163–64
Game tree, 224
General equilibrium theory and
  models, 1, 2
  and contract theory, 2
  limitations of, 1–2
GM–Fisher Body relationship, 195–96
Government-regulated firms, and
  adverse selection, 13
Grossman-Hart approach, to moral
  hazard, 128–29

Hazard rate, 35, 35n
Health Insurance Experiment (HIE),
  Rand, 215–16
Heterogeneity across agents,
  unobserved, 212–16
Holdup problem, 194
  GM–Fisher Body as example of, 195–96

"Hostages," 162
Huckleberry Finn (Twain), quoted, 119, 121n.5
Hunting (stag hunt) story, 108–109
exercise on, 110n.13, 118

IC constraints. *See* Incentive compatibility constraints
Imperfect information. *See* Asymmetric information
Incentive(s). *See also* Wage determination
contracts as providing, 212, 213
investment, 200–204
and law of large numbers, 181
managerial, 154, 155
provided by two Principals, 144
Incentive compatibility (IC) constraints, 22, 28, 29–33, 174
and auditing of agent, 89
and informed Principal, 87
and insurance market, 60
and moral hazard, 122, 123, 125, 127, 135, 137, 147, 189
and moral hazard (exercise), 158
and multidimensional characteristics of Agent, 79–80, 81–82
and relaxed program, 80
and revelation principle, 90
Incentive-compatible contract, exercise on, 93
Incentive-compatible functions, 83
Incentive-compatible mechanisms, 84
Incentive problem, in mechanism design, 15
Incentive schedules, real-life vs. theoretical, 149
Incomplete contracts, 161, 193–95, 205–208
and buyer–seller model, 196–97
and holdup problem, 194
irrelevance theorems on, 200–205, 206–207
and political economy, 205
and property rights, 198–200, 205

Independent private values auctions, 65
Individually rational functions, 83
Individual rationality (IR) constraints, 22, 28, 34, 174
and informed Principal, 87
and moral hazard, 122, 123, 126, 137
and moral hazard (exercise), 158
and multidimensional characteristics of Agent, 79–80
and optimal taxation, 48
and relaxed program, 80
and trading mechanisms inefficiency, 86
and type-dependent reservation utilities, 88
Induction
backward, 226
forward, 232, 232n.7
Informational asymmetries. *See* Asymmetric information
Informational rent, in adverse selection models, 26, 34, 36, 55n.4
Informed Principal, 86–88, 116
Institutions, in theory of contracts, 162
Insurance contract, 180
Insurance markets
and adverse selection vs. moral hazard, 213–14
asymmetric information in, 218–221
moral hazard in, 120, 149–51, 220
and types of Agent, 60n.8
Insurance model, vs. standard adverse selection model, 60
Insurer as monopolist, as adverse-selection example, 51–56
Intertemporal moral hazard, 179–90
Intertemporal price discrimination, adverse selection in, 168–78
Intuitive criterion, 230–31
Intuitive equilibrium, 230–32
Investment, lack of. *See* Underinvestment
Investment, specific, 196
Investment incentives, restoring as efficient, 200–204

IR constraints. *See* Individual
rationality constraints
Irrelevance result, 59–60
Irrelevance theorems, 195, 200–205,
206–207
Iterated logarithm, law of, 182

Jensen's inequality, 186, 186n.21
Joint ownership, 200
and option-to-sell contract, 201

Labor markets, and adverse selection,
12–13
Labor supply in autarky, elasticity of,
50–51
and correlation of bidders' valuations,
71–73
Laffont-Tirole model of regulation, 45,
46, 47
exercise on, 93
Law of iterated logarithm, 182
Law of large numbers, in incentive
problem, 181
Least-cost separating equilibrium,
106–107, 116
"Lemons." *See* Secondhand cars,
market for
Lender-borrower relationship, and
auditing, 90, 90n.19
Life insurance, and adverse selection,
12. *See also* Insurance markets
Limited commitment, 163
Limited liability model, and moral
hazard, 136, 138
Long-term commitment, 163, 172–76,
178, 188
Long-term contracts, renegotiation of,
194

Managerial compensation, 153–56
Market foreclosure, 167
Maskin-Tirole mechanism, 205,
206–207, 207
Mechanism, 15
optimal, 26–27, 41

Mechanism design
and adverse selection, 13–18
for incomplete contracts, 204–205
Memory effect, 184–85, 190
Message game,15–16, 207, 208
Mixed strategies, 190, 223
MLRC (monotone likelihood ratio
condition), 130–31, 136, 140, 150
exercises on, 157, 159
Monopolies. *See* Natural monopolies
Monopolist insurer, as adverse-
selection example, 51–56
Monotone likelihood ratio condition
(MLRC), 130–31, 136, 140, 150
exercises on, 157, 159
Moral hazard, 4, 119–21
and adverse selection, 184, 188, 213–14
and agency problem, 6
and continuum of actions, 135–36
and "effort," 120
example in, 122–24
exercises on, 156–59
finitely repeated, 183–90
and imperfect performance
measurement, 140, 158
and infinity of outcomes, 138–39
informativeness of value for, 134–35
in insurance, 120, 149–51, 220
intertemporal, 179–90
intuition untrustworthy on, 133
and limited liability model, 136–38
multisignal case for, 139–40
and multitask model, 146–49
and robustness of contracts, 144–45
and several Agents, 140–41
and several Principals, 142–44
standard model in, 124–33
and "technology," 124
and wage determination, 123–25,
125n.9, 151–56
Multidimensional characteristics, and
Principal–Agent model, 26n.11, 78–82
Multiple equilibria, undesirability of,
104–105
Multiple (several) Principals, 142–44

competition among, 61–65
Multiprincipals model, 61
exercise on, 92–93
"Multiprincipals with symmetric
information," 142
Multisignal case, for moral hazard,
139–40
Multitask model, 146–49

Nash bargaining solution, 199
Nash equilibrium, 224, 225
Natural monopolies, 43n.1
and adverse selection, 43–47
Noncooperative game theory, 223
and contract models, 3
games of incomplete information,
226–32
games of perfect information, 224–26
Nonverifiability assumption, 195n.2

Optimal auction, 70, 70n.13, 71
Optimal contract, 74, 90
and Agents helping each other, 141
and long-term commitment, 175n.12
and moral hazard, 129–33, 144
and renegotiation, 180–81
Optimal control theory, 38
Optimal mechanism, 26–27
exercises on, 41
Optimal reserve price, exercise on, 92
Optimal taxation
as adverse-selection example, 47–51
exercise on, 91
Optimal wage schedule, 144
Option-to-sell contract, 200–205, 208
Organizational behavior, and collusion,
75

Pareto optima
and equilibria, 1
and Principal–Agent paradigm, 5
Partial equilibrium models, in contract
theory, 2
Participation constraints, 22, 76
Partition equilibria, 111

Perfect Bayesian equilibria, 3, 5n.2, 104,
105, 110–11, 227–29, 231
Perfect competition, in contracts, 57–60
Performance measurement
imperfect, 140, 158
for teamwork, 140
Piece-rate wage, 151
Political economy, and incomplete
contracts, 205
Politicians, and incomplete contracts,
205n.8
Pontryagin minimum principle, 76n.15
Pooling equilibria, 60, 102, 103, 104
Precommitment effects on third party,
164
Predation, and auditing, 90n.19
Preplay communication game, 114
Price-cap contracts, in regulation of
firm, 46–47
Price discrimination
discrete model of, 18–27
first-degree, 11n.2, 20
Price system, and strategic interactions,
1
Principal–Agent model, 3, 5–6
and adverse selection, 11–12, 16–17
(see also Adverse selection)
and auditing of Agent, 89–91, 140
and informed Principal, 86–88, 116
and moral hazard, 119–21 (see also
Moral hazard)
with multiple Principals, 61–65,
142–44
and unobserved heterogeneity across
agents, 212–16
Prior beliefs, 227, 227n.2
Prisoner's Dilemma, 163–64
Private information, 2
bilateral, 82–88
in classification of contracts, 4
Private values model, 53
Privileged information, in signaling-
models example, 115
Productivity, and education (signaling
models), 100–101, 102, 104, 105

"Profitable entrant," 58
Promotions, 152
Property insurance, moral hazard in, 120. *See also* Insurance markets
Property rights
and Anglo-Saxon law, 198n.5
and complete contracts, 197, 207
and incomplete contracts, 198–200, 205
Roman law on, 198
Public goods
and incentives provided by two Principals, 144
and mechanism design (bridge example), 14, 16, 17
Pure strategies, 190

Rand Health Insurance Experiment (HIE), 215–16
Ratchet effect, 176, 177n.15, 179
Rational expectations equilibria, 2
Rationality, individual. *See* individual rationality constraints
Rationality, sequential, 228
Regulation of firm, as adverse-selection example, 43–47
Renegotiation, 162
and complete contracts, 207
after effort, 179–81
and incomplete contracts, 164, 194, 205, 205–206, 207, 208
long-term commitment with, 163, 172–73
for option-to-sell contract, 203
and public contracts, 167–68
secret, 168
of short-term contracts, 177
Renegotiation-proofness principle, 173–74, 194
Reservation utilities, type-dependent, 88–89
Residual control rights, property rights as, 198
Revelation, and adverse selection problems, 12
Revelation principle, 17–18, 90, 91

and full commitment, 170
and long-term commitment, 173
in multidimensional settings, 79
and multiple Principals, 62
and no commitment, 177
Revenue equivalence theorem, 69
Risk
and adverse selection, 51–56, 60
and fixed-rent contracts vs. sharecropping, 214–15
and incomplete contracts, 205
and insurance, 51–56, 60, 149, 220, 221
and moral hazard, 121, 125, 129, 136–37
and renegotiation after effort, 180
Risk-averse agents, 76–77
Robustness of contracts, 144–45
Rothschild-Stiglitz equilibrium, 58–59, 59–60
exercises on, 91, 92
Rothschild-Stiglitz model of adverse selection, 219
Rousseau, Jean-Jacques, 108n.12

Scarcity constraint, 48, 49
Sealed-bid auction, 66–73
Secondhand cars, market for, 98–99
Second-price sealed bid auction, 66
Self-fulfilling prophecies, 104
Self-protection efforts, vs. self-insurance efforts, 150n.26
Self-revelation, and adverse selection problems, 12
Semiseparating equilibria, 107, 117
Separating equilibria, 60, 102
least-cost, 106–107, 116
Separating optimum, 37–38
Sequential efficiency constraints, 174
Sequential equilibria, 117, 230
Sequential rationality, 228
Service activities, moral hazard in, 120
Shapiro-Stiglitz model of unemployment, 152–53, 153n.28
Sharecropping
vs. fixed rent contracts, 214

and moral hazard, 120, 187
Shareholding, corporate, 187–88
Shares in firm, as managerial
 compensation, 153–54
Short-term commitment, 163, 177–78,
 178–79
Short-term contracts, renegotiation of,
 177
Side-contract, and collusion, 74, 75
Signal(s)
 Apple's Macintosh factories as, 162
 outcomes as (moral hazard), 130
Signal-extraction problem, in
 managerial incentives, 155
Signaling models, 4, 97–98
 and costless signals, 107–14
 and costly signals, 99–107
 and informed Principal model, 116
 and risk-averse-entrepreneur model,
 114–15
 and secondhand-car market, 98–99
 and treacherous-journalist example,
 115
 and warranty, 114
 and worker-and-manager example,
 115–16
Simple contracts, 207, 208
Single-crossing condition, 31
Social choice problem, and mechanism
 design, 13–14
Social surplus, 25, 25n.10
 in regulation of natural monopoly, 44
 and socially efficient auction, 70
 and virtual surplus, 25–26, 36
Social welfare, in regulation of natural
 monopoly, 46
Sorting condition, 31
Specific investment, 196
Spence-Mirrlees condition, 19, 31
 and adverse selection, 169
 and education as signal for
 productivity, 100
 and incentive constraints, 31, 32–33,
 33n.18
 and insurer example, 53, 54

and multiple Principals, 63
and optimal taxation, 48
and pure strategies, 190
Spence's signaling model, 100–102
 exercises on, 117
 and informed Principal model, 116
 overproduction in, 107n.10
 and risk-averse-entrepreneur model,
 114
 and warranty, 114
Spot commitment, 163
Spot contracts, 185, 190
Stackelberg game, Principal–Agent
 game as, 5, 6
Stag hunt story, 108–109
 exercise on, 110n.13, 118
Statistical inference, and moral hazard
 problem, 135
Stochastic matrix, 134, 134n.16
Stock options, as managerial
 compensation, 153–54
Strategic commitment, 164–68
Strategic interactions, and general
 equilibrium model, 1
Strategies
 mixed, 190, 223
 pure, 190
Stylized facts, 211
Subgame-perfect equilibrium, 224–26
Sufficient statistic theorem, 139, 140,
 141, 144
Symmetric information
 for multiple Principals, 62
 and unforeseen contingencies, 208n.13
Symmetric information assumption,
 195

Taxation, optimal, 47–51, 91
Taxation principle, 18, 27
Teamwork. See also Cooperation
 creating conditions for, 141
 and performance measurement, 140
"Technology," 124, 144
Theory of contracts. See Contract
 theory(ies)

Theory of games. *See* Games; Game
  theory
Third party, 3. *See also* Center
Tournaments, 141, 152
Trading mechanisms, inefficiency of,
  82–86
Transaction cost economics, 194
Trembling-hand perfect equilibrium,
  230
Truthful mechanism, direct. *See* Direct
  truthful mechanism
Twain, Mark (*Huckleberry Finn*), quoted,
  119, 121n.5
Type-dependent reservation utilities,
  88–89

UMTS auctions (2000), 66
Uncertainty, about quality of good, 98
Underinvestment, 194, 199, 200, 202
  deterrence of, 201

Unemployment, Shapiro-Stiglitz model
  of, 152–53, 153n.28
Unobserved heterogeneity across
  agents, 212–16
Updating, Bayesian, 228

Vickrey-Clark-Groves mechanisms, 83
Virtual surplus, 36, 85, 89
Virtual valuation, 71

Wage determination
  and moral hazard, 123–25, 125n.9,
    151–56
  and moral hazard (finitely repeated),
    184
Wage schedule, optimal, 144
Walrasian equilibrium, 14, 16
Warranty, 114
"Weighted utilitarian" criterion, 47–48
Wilson competitive equilibrium, 91–92

Printed in the United States
by Baker & Taylor Publisher Services